TEACHING SUSTAINABILITY

TEACHING SUSTAINABILITY:

PERSPECTIVES FROM THE HUMANITIES AND SOCIAL SCIENCES

WENDY PETERSEN BORING,
WILLAMETTE UNIVERSITY

WILLIAM FORBES,
STEPHEN F. AUSTIN STATE UNIVERSITY, EDITORS

FOREWORD BY DAVID W. ORR

STEPHEN F. AUSTIN STATE UNIVERSITY PRESS
NACOGDOCHES, TEXAS

For information address:
Stephen F. Austin State University Press,
1936 North Street, LAN 203
Nacogdoches, TX 75962

sfapress@sfasu.edu

Book Design: Laura Davis and Troy Varvel

LIBRARY OF CONGRESS CATALOG-IN-PUBLICATION DATA

Boring, Wendy Petersen and Forbes, William
Teaching Sustainability/Wendy Petersen Boring and William Forbes—1st ed.
p.cm.
ISBN 978-1-62288-061-4

I. Title

First Edition: 2014

TABLE OF CONTENTS

II. In the Classroom: Case Studies and Innovative Pedagogies

III. The Campus as Site for Place-Based Learning

Appendices

FOREWORD

Shallow versus Deep Environmental Education

David W. Orr, Oberlin College

The facts are straightforward, but the implications for educators are not. Fossil fuel combustion, deforestation, and industrialized agriculture have raised the temperature of the Earth by .9°C and have locked us in to another .5 to ~.8°C of warming—no matter what we do. In fact, we will be very lucky to cap the warming at 2° (3.6°F). Given present trends, the increase will likely be 4°C or higher. But the word "warming" is misleading. We have unleashed a long-term destabilization of Earth that, in time, will threaten civilization itself. As temperatures rise, so does the likelihood of "carbon-cycle feedbacks," including large methane releases that would amplify the warming. Twenty percent of the CO_2 emitted today will still be in the atmosphere 1,000 years from now, continuing to affect climate. There is no quick fix, no magic bullet, and no technological miracle that will rescue us from the remorseless working of the large numbers that govern the biosphere. To head off the worst that could happen will very soon require a global effort to radically increase energy efficiency and rapidly deploy renewable energy. But it is already too late to avoid massive, long-term disruptions and suffering that will result from the warming to which we are already committed.

There are climate science deniers but, in time, their numbers will diminish like the vanishing membership in the Flat Earth Society. There are others who accept the science but choose to be silent about the implications of planetary destabilization, in the belief that the truth would demoralize or paralyze the public. Like Plato's guardians, only self-appointed elites can handle the truth. But educators can neither deny nor evade. They are obliged to tell the truth as clearly as they can see it. And the truth is that we have evicted ourselves from the only paradise humans have ever known—what geologists call the Holocene. We now live in the "Anthropocene," or what Bill McKibben calls "Eaarth," a progressively hotter and more capricious world for a very long time to come.

For environmental educators, the implications are many. The first is to highlight a distinction once drawn by philosopher Arne Naess between "deep" and "shallow" ecology. Deep environmental educators know, for example, that climate destabilization is not an anomaly, but a symptom of fault-lines embedded in our paradigms, institutions, and manner of thinking. They know that it is necessary to understand why we have been so slow to see and to act in the face of a planetary emergency. They know that we must reckon with the darker side of human psychology and its manifestations in economics, politics, and governance, relative to our place in the ecosphere. We are not so much rational creatures as we are very clever rationalizers. Further, these "deep" environmental educators know that we must develop antidotes to the pathologies inherent in a culture that, ironically, has taken "shallowness" to an unprecedented depth. Americans, in particular, are addicted to commercialized fun and consumption and marinated in a theology of progress defined as the accumulation of gadgetry, not genuine human improvement. We seem to be oblivious to the reality that most of our economic and "life-style" gains have come at the expense of others somewhere else or at some later time. But we must now reckon with what Spanish philosopher Miguel Unamuno once called "the tragic sense of life." The practice of deep environmental education must be part of a process of sobering down that is midwife to a maturing phase of human evolution. We must come to understand that not everything works out as we would like, that we cannot have it all, and that technologically driven fantasy undermines moral imagination. We live now in "the age of consequences" that gives us no leeway for evasion, denial, or procrastination.

For the young people we purport to educate, the truth of the situation can be overwhelming. In conventional environmental education, the goal is to connect them to nature and particular places (i.e. shallow EE). And it is important that we do so. But deep environmental educators know that virtually every place and every ecosystem on Earth is under a death sentence of sorts and will be mutilated by rising heat, drought, storms, and changing ecological conditions. Deep environmental educators must therefore equip students with the stamina to witness ecological losses and collateral societal damages without being immobilized by despair. They will need our help to transform their grief into a stronger and deeper attachment to life and a more authentic hope that lies on a farther horizon. It will help a great deal if they can read human history as a chapter in the larger universe story, as Thomas Berry once proposed.

So, what do deep environmental educators actually do? A good starting point is Amory Lovins' rewording of Corinthians 1:13: "there is faith, hope, and clarity, but the greatest of these is clarity." Clarity requires that we:

discard wishful thinking, but deepen our ecological imagination;
face hard realities without losing the awareness of possibilities;
expand our horizons yet be grounded in the present; and
cherish nature and enlarge compassion for our neighbors.

We must enable our students, in other words, to think clearly and deeply about the proper role of humankind on Earth over the long-haul and what that implies for economies, technologies, political systems, and, not the least, their own lives.

But much of the dialogue about sustainability is shallow and badly muddled. The word "sustainability" relative to the environment was born in confusion, between those who saw it as a radical redirection of the human enterprise and those who regarded it as no more than a smarter way to do what we were already doing - which was to grow the economy as fast as possible and to "effect all things possible," as Francis Bacon once put it. A deeper understanding of sustainability requires going beyond asking what and why. What is our proper role in the web of life and in the larger ecosphere? Beyond our will to live, why do humans deserve to be sustained? If we knew better why we deserve to be sustained, we might know better how to go about it.

Second, by engaging our students in the processes of redemption and ecological restoration we might redirect the anxiety that comes from an understanding of the precariousness of the human situation. The green campus movement has helped to harness their intelligence, creativity, idealism, and energy to the challenges of making colleges and universities models and laboratories for a world that is more resilient and durable. But changes in the curriculum must follow. The rising generation must have the capacity to think in systems and patterns. To comprehend causes of our plight and to craft better alternatives, they will need ecologically grounded courses in the humanities and social sciences. They must know how the world works as a physical system. In an educational system built to extend human mastery over nature we must somehow equip them for lives and careers as designers of a better and more resilient civilization.

In various ways, the authors here describe a curriculum of applied hope. No discipline is exempt from the effort to extend awareness of our implicatedness in the world, and from the effort to create a better future than that in prospect. As scholars and teachers, they are responding to the intellectual and moral imperatives of "the long emergency." I do not presume to know what a life-centered education would be, but I know that the questions explicit and implicit here should be asked at all levels, from boards of trustees to every academic department. The overwhelming fact of our time is that life on Earth is in peril, humans are the cause, and that no amount of tinkering at the margin of the *status quo* will do. We have every reason to reexamine our beliefs, worldviews, institutions, cultural foundations, and manner of living - and get down to work.

David W. Orr is the Paul Sears Distinguished Professor of Environmental Studies and Politics and Senior Adviser to the President, Oberlin College. He is the author of seven books, including *Down to the Wire: Confronting Climate Collapse* (Oxford, 2009) and co-editor of three others. He has authored nearly 200 articles, reviews, book chapters, and professional publications. In the past twenty-five years he has served on the boards of many organizations, including the Rocky Mountain Institute and the Aldo Leopold Foundation. He has been awarded seven honorary degrees, a Lyndhurst Prize, a National Achievement Award from the National Wildlife Federation, and a "Visionary Leadership Award" from Second Nature. He has lectured at hundreds of colleges and universities throughout the U.S., Europe, and Asia. He headed the effort to design, fund, and build the Adam Joseph Lewis Center, which was named by an AIA panel in 2010 as "the most important green building of the past thirty years," and as "one of thirty milestone buildings of the twentieth century" by the U.S. Department of Energy. He is executive director of the Oberlin project and a founding editor of the journal *Solutions*.

PREFACE

Dr. William Forbes, Stephen F. Austin State University

This book is the second in our series on sustainability, as seen through the humanities and social sciences. Our first edited volume, *Toward a More Livable World: Social Dimensions of Sustainability*, was published by SFA Press in 2012. The anthology coincided with the start-up of our new research initiative, the Center for a Livable World. The Center's mission is to address sustainable community development and livability through the humanities and social sciences and the "triple bottom line" of economics, environment, and society. Both our anthology and a pilot community project drew from expertise across our College of Liberal and Applied Arts and our campus, as well as outside experts. Academic disciplines included economics, education, geography, health sciences, history, philosophy, public administration, social work, and sociology.

This volume on teaching sustainability offers the next logical step in the series. The heart of sustainability is not only its interdisciplinary nature, but its concern for future generations. What could be more relevant than engaging students in critical thinking about future economic, environmental, and social quality? This anthology offers expertise from many disciplines and case studies. Those looking to teach sustainability can hopefully draw from these essays to enhance courses in their respective disciplines. The enthusiasm and prompt responses from authors and my co-editor clearly indicate a growing interest in sustainability in the humanities and social sciences.

These subjects can complement more typical efforts to address sustainability through engineering and technology. At a recent "Sustainability Summit" in Dallas, an industrial engineer agreed with the need for interdisciplinary education on sustainability. He related the lack of critical thinking skills among recent graduates in his field. Many engineers had difficulty realizing the broader economic, environmental, and social context of their work, which was imperative. Many of us are taking small steps along the long road to sustainability. We hope this collection acts as a longer stride, the authors cheering us all on to collectively include the humanities and social sciences to help affect change—not change for the sake of change—but change to increase the livability and resilience of humans and nature for years to come.

INTRODUCTION

Dr. Wendy Petersen Boring, Willamette University

"The dialogue about sustainability is about a change in the human trajectory that will require us to rethink old assumptions and engage the large questions of the human condition that some presume to have been answered once and for all."
- David Orr, "The Four Challenges of Sustainability"

"We have many sophisticated scientific and policy analyses of climate change, species loss, and other environmental issues...but our situation also requires the knowledge and wisdom of psychologists and philosophers, poets and preachers, historians and humanists to help us see and communicate hard truths and inspire individual and social change."
- Leiserowitz and Fernandez,
Toward a New Consciousness: Values to Sustain Human and Natural Communities

"Restoration work is wild nature, abstract thought, and human desire engaged in creative negotiation... Negotiation requires constant intuition and constant adjustment of our own narratives, not just data-based policies poured down from on high."
- David James Duncan, "Being Cool in the Face of Global Warming"

The essays in this volume represent grassroots restoration work in higher education for sustainability. Over the last five years, faculty in the humanities and social sciences at a wide range of institutions across North America have individually and together begun to do what David Orr called for in the 1990s in *Earth in Mind*. They have gone back to their respective disciplines and, with intellectual agility, courage, and a sense of adventure and responsibility, begun to rethink old assumptions, ask the big questions, and readjust their own narratives about what it means to educate, to learn, and to know - with the challenges of sustainability in mind.

Sustainability educators have had to engage entirely new disciplines, work closely with non-academic institutional and community partners, take pedagogical risks, invent new courses and entirely reconfigure old ones, and learn anew how to draw on cultural wisdom from their own experience and disciplinary training. They have inspired, cajoled, and tended individual change, institutional change, and social change. They have come together in conferences, working groups, and networks to reflect on pedagogical theory, learning outcomes, and assessment for sustainability. The curricular innovation these essays describe, then, is restoration - not as refurbishing an older reality - but as restitution and renewal of teaching that requires creativity, intuition, constant negotiation, and thoughtful, sustained cooperation between diverse partners.

The main purpose of this volume is to provide a snapshot of this curricular restoration for sustainability within U.S. higher education. The impetus behind this collection of essays was the sense, gathered from regional and national conferences and networks, that descriptions of "brown" curriculum lagging behind "green" building and infrastructure miss out on the range of innovations and the institutional significance of sustainability curricular change currently underway.

Sustainability education is, in fact, increasingly taking a lead role in transforming the landscape of higher education, serving as a catalyst for the integration of cutting edge pedagogical practices, including project and problem-based learning, multi-disciplinary learning, and transformative and collaborative education. If, as Arjen Wals and John Blewit have suggested, we are in what could be called a "third wave" of sustainability in higher education, curricular innovation is key to the movement of this wave.

As institutions reorient teaching, learning, research, and university-community relationships to make sustainability "an emergent property" of their "core activities," sustainability's place in higher education curricula is "shifting from one of campus greening and curriculum integration to one of innovation and systemic change across the whole university" (56, 70). As these essays make clear, curriculum, rather than lagging behind, is often driving these "third wave" efforts.

A second major impetus behind this collection was the desire to capture the distinctive flavor of sustainability education in the humanities and social sciences. Our answers to the challenges of sustainability cannot be primarily data-driven, technological, or resolved from within current perceptions or paradigms. To sustain what is worth sustaining we must re-examine values, draw on cultural wisdom, and re-energize spiritual and philosophical traditions.

The essays in this volume represent creative answers to these calls for non-technological solutions. They attest to the enormous fruit borne from intersection of problem-based, project-based interdisciplinary learning and liberal arts reflective practices. As Neil Weissman has suggested, sustainability and the liberal arts are natural partners. The breadth of the concept of sustainability requires input from virtually all disciplines. The holistic, critical thinking, learning to learn, intellectual flexibility, and ability to translate across disciplinary boundaries that mark sustainability education have long been the central aims of a liberal arts education. The origin and ultimate worth of sustainability centers on "citizenship"—something that the humanities and social sciences study and seek to cultivate ("Sustainability and Liberal Education: Partners by Nature").

The final impetus behind this project was to provide a resource for those wanting to infuse sustainability into traditional humanities and social science curricula. This resource can act as a space for theoretical reflection on the kind of dialogue that happens between sustainability education and disciplinary frameworks. As these essays make clear, integrating sustainability pushes back at traditional disciplinary approaches, re-energizing and re-orienting old frameworks, questions, and patterns of thinking. At the same time, the humanities and social sciences bring much-needed skills and dispositions to contemporary challenges: historical and theoretical depth, complexity and sophistication in analysis, and perspective and creativity in response.

Our contributors speak about the dialogue from the perspective of a wide range of disciplines, including art and design, education, English, environmental studies, geography, history, Latin American studies, philosophy, political science, psychology, religious studies, womens' studies, and sustainability studies, and they have formed curricular partnerships with a wide range of professional schools, including Engineering, Law, Business, and Nursing.

Our authors also represent a range of institutions, from small liberal arts colleges to major research institutions, with a range of commitment to sustainability, from strategic, institution-wide investment to sustainability education primarily driven by the energy and vision of a few individuals. Our hope is that this volume adds to the recent excellent collections on sustainability and higher education (e.g., Bartlett and Chase, Johnston, and Jones et al.) by providing additional examples of pedagogical innovation that focus on the humanities and social sciences.

Third Wave Curricular Creativity

An overarching theme amongst these essays is permeability. Just as efforts to green the campus break down the notion of a university as a hermeneutically sealed entity, creating porous boundaries that lead to new and creative relationships, so, too, does sustainability curriculum create permeability: a) across boundaries of traditional academic disciplines; b) between the curriculum and business, government, and community partners; and c) between the curriculum and the co-curriculum, including service learning, vocational discernment, and campus life.

The essays utilize a wide range of approaches to "sustainability." Indeed, another overarching theme of these essays is the fruitfulness of theoretical and practical interrogation of what we mean by "sustainability." As several essays suggest, sustainability education is not as much about delivering content as it is about cultivating the skills, dispositions, and values that equip students to move towards sustainability.

As John Jensen puts it, the right question as we design our courses is not, "How can I teach *about* sustainability," but rather, "How can I encourage students to move *towards* sustainability?" or even more directly, "How can we nurture students to be leaders in a sustainability revolution?" The pedagogical strategies for encouraging lifelong movement towards sustainability go several steps beyond "making it relevant." The essays describe inviting students into a different relationship with their education, one that focuses on reflection, values clarification, and supports personal discernment, drawing students into a shared vision, institutionally and culturally, for our collective future, and giving them the tools to move towards it. On the whole, what emerges is the picture of sustainability education as cultivating a stance towards knowledge from a particular context and for a particular purpose.

The essays in Part I, "Conceptual Frameworks: Sustainability's Challenges to Traditional Curriculum, Disciplinary Frameworks and Educational Paradigms," engage in a more theoretical interrogation of sustainability in order to reflect on the "big" questions, such as what constitutes justice, knowledge, right action, or historical identity. They also urge the development of a critical awareness of the political and historical contexts from which the term "sustainability" emerged.

Developing this critical awareness, and along with it a healthy suspicion of the term's current popularity, prompts questions that are crucial for students in developing their own ethical frameworks. As the essays in this section suggest, engaging with sustainability shifts how we perceive the relationship between environmental conservation, ethics, and justice (Vanderheiden, University of Colorado, Boulder) and challenges how we think about ideas central to the social sciences, such as efficiency, class, citizenship, and democracy (Paehlke, Trent University). It also pushes us to rethink how we conceive our curriculum nationally and (Gould, Drexel University) across the university (Meagher, University of Scranton), and how we set our learning outcomes (Jensen, Luther College).

Engaging sustainability calls on us to tell new stories about our past and cultivate a new historical consciousness (Petersen Boring, Willamette University) and urges us to shift our culture's relationship to time and consumption (Cladis, Brown University). Theoretical reflection also drives practical change. As Mark Cladis suggests, we can see sustainability as a cultural journey towards a set of virtues, an evolving cluster of nurtured dispositions or capacities, that dispose us to see, think, and feel in ways that sustain the beauty, integrity, and resiliency of the earth.

The essays in Part II, "In the Classroom: Case Studies and Innovative Pedagogies," reflect on sustainability pedagogy in intentionally trans-disciplinary settings. Students engage in a multi-disciplinary, trans-historical seminar for a sustainability minor, drawing on undergraduate and graduate school collaboration (Galgano and Rosier, Villanova University). The also pair ecocritical readings of literature with contemplative pedagogy (Grewal, University of South Florida), apply psychological research to real-world environmental problems and explore what it means to develop an ecological sense of place (Morfei, Wells College), utilize the multi-disciplinary perspective of geography to understand concepts of sustainability for teacher training (Forbes, Williams, and Ingram, Stephen F. Austin University), and experience trans-disciplinary, sustainability-focused study abroad field classes in which they work collaboratively with international partners (Walther, Intolubbe-Chmil, and Swap, Utah Valley University, University of Virginia).

Those in Part III, "The Campus as a Site for Place-Based Learning," interrogate sustainability on a more pragmatic level. As Lisa Barlow points out, in project-based and "campus as learning laboratory" courses, the aim is not a deeper understanding of a theoretical definition or the wider cultural implications of sustainability, but instead a deeper understanding of what it takes to move specific individuals and institutions towards more sustainable living.

These courses emphasize practical systems thinking, the importance of understanding human behavior, institutional structure, and culture, and how to change perceptions and paradigms. Working on concrete projects with the triple bottom line in view often entails recognizing the provisional, changing nature of sustainability solutions, institutional roadblocks, the importance of planting seeds, and the fact that change often happens in ripple effects, spill-overs, or delayed release.

The breadth and diversity of the project and problem-based learning described in these essays is impressive. Students create pedagogical landscapes that serve as demonstration-scale models of sustainable energy and ecological design (SEED, El-Mogazi, Bucknell University), and pair theoretical reflection with semester-long team-based campus projects (LEEP, Stephens, Clark University). A local agricultural wikki simultaneously connects students to their landscape and allows them to explore temporal and spatial complexity of sustainability, adding sense of connection and perception of value while also providing a community resource (Chambers, Schlegel, Giombolini, and Dunne, Willamette University). Students create sustainable design solutions in a multi-disciplinary design course ("reDesign") that integrates the curriculum with the community (Avila, Cooley, and Smith, Pacific Lutheran University). Students also serve as on-campus consultants for institutionally supported sustainability projects (Barlow, University of Colorado, Boulder).

Learning laboratories and project-based courses wrestle with practical and pedagogical implications of extending learning beyond the four-walled classroom. Real projects give students experience with "messy" data and force them to make decisions based on imperfect information (Hansen, Carleton College, Macalester College); even "failed" projects often hold "success" when viewed over a longer timeline or from a wider perspective (Johnson and Long, Rice University); often the problems encountered are, in fact, part of the process (Roberts, Earlham College). Courses that integrate practical projects with multi-disciplinary expertise and reflection, or mix ethical development with community partnership, help shape a curriculum with increased relevance, coherence, and practicability (Stephens, Clark University).

Perhaps most importantly, as campus-based courses become the main driver for significant institutional change, students get to experience themselves as change agents in real time. Elizabeth Long and Richard Johnson trace the following university initiatives to their campus-based sustainability course, cross listed in Environmental Studies and Sociology: adoption of LEED standards for new construction; adoption of trayless dining; green purchasing; recycling of construction materials; composting of food waste; motion sensored lighting; purchase of a plastic recycling baler; provision of reusable water bottle filling stations, and a stormwater runoff city partnership. They conclude: never underestimate the ability of a student project to effect real change. The essays in this volume reiterate that message, pointing to the transformative and restorative energy provided through curricular innovation for sustainability.

Notes

1.   The co-editors wish to thank Willamette University student Colleen Smyth for her expert editing of the book manuscript.

Works Cited

Bartlett, Peggy F. and Geoffrey Chase, eds. *Sustainability in Higher Education: Stories and Strategies for Transformation.* MIT Press, 2013.

— *Sustainability on Campus: Stories and Strategies for Change,* Cambridge: MIT Press, 2004.

Duncan, David James. "Being Cool in the Face of Global Warming." Kathleen Dean Moore and Michael P. Nelson, eds. *Moral Ground: Ethical Action for a Planet in Peril.*

Trinity University Press, 2010, 434-439.

Johnston, Lucas F., ed., Higher Education for Sustainability: Cases, Challenges, and Opportunities from Across the Curriculum, New York: Routledge, 2013.

Jones, Paula, David Selvy, and Stephen Sterling, eds., *Sustainability Education: Perspectives and Practice Across Higher Education.* New York: Earthscan, 2010.

Leiserowitz, A. A., and L. O. Fernandez. *Toward a New Consciousness: Values to Sustain Human and Natural Communities.* New Haven: Yale School of Forestry and Environmental Studies, 2008.

Orr, David. "The Four Challenges of Sustainability." *Conservation Biology* 16, 6 (Dec. 2002): 1457-1460.

Sterling, Stephen. "Higher education, sustainability, and the role of systemic learning." Peter Blaze Cocoran and Arjen E. Wals, eds. *Higher Education and the Challenge of Sustainability.* Boston: Kluwer Academic Publishers, 2004.

Wals, Arjen E.J., and John Blewitt. "Third-Wave Sustainability in Higher Education: Some (Inter)national Trends and Developments. Paula Jones, David Selby, and Stephen Sterling, eds. *Sustainability Education: Perspectives and Practice Across Higher Education.* New York: Earthscan, 2010.

Weissman, Neil. "Sustainability and Higher Education: Partners by Nature." *Liberal Education,* vol. 98, 4 (Fall 2012).

SUSTAINABILITY EDUCATION: A STUDENT PERSPECTIVE

Marshall Curry, Emily Dougan

Otto Scharmer, Senior Lecturer at the Massachusetts Institute of Technology (MIT) and co-founder of the Global Wellbeing and Gross National Happiness (GNH) Lab, argues that while immense amounts of energy and money have been poured into our educational systems, little investment has been made in "the single most important core capability for this century's knowledge and co-creation economy." That is students' capacity to "sense and shape their future." This book is an investment in students' futures that addresses the environmental and educational challenges of our generation.

The issues of sustainability permeate every facet of life. Sustainability requires educators and students to come together, under a variety of intellectual disciplines, to: a) connect with the natural world; and b) understand the complexity of problems and solutions that face our communities. Teaching sustainability encompasses more than scientific awareness. As the essays in this book make clear, such pedagogy requires an artistic, philosophical, systematic, and historical consciousness as well.

The essays found here function as valuable resources for current college students when encouraging their institutions to integrate sustainability into the curriculum. Students can draw on the chapters of this book to think creatively to integrate sustainability into their own educational trajectory, reference best practices, and improve accountability to their professors. Students can also access concrete ideas for research, service, and co-curricular projects that inspire community movements toward sustainable futures. These pragmatic tools for engagement are critical in dissolving the boundaries between pedagogy and action. They equip students with the skills to demonstrate independent investment in sustainability in their own communities, augmenting the framework provided by educators and contributing to the institution-wide commitment required for the redefinition of an educational system.

The essays collected here also provide a valuable introduction to what prospective students should look for in a college experience. Unlike any 'top 50 sustainability universities' list or admissions publication found online, this book provides a better resource by detailing specific philosophies, teaching styles, assignments, and projects offered at each institution.

More significantly, the book offers an alternative vision for what a college education ought to be about: preparing change agents and systems thinkers who are able to deal creatively and concretely with the multiple challenges posed by our non-sustainable practices. It provides an alternate road map for charting a course through higher education, pinpointing sites of innovation and classes that students can match with their own learning styles, career paths, and passions. At the same time, the book calls for deeper and more radical change to our entire educational paradigm.

Thankfully, among the calls for drastic change found here, there are also descriptions of hope for the future. Too often students are turned off by forecasts of doom in the face of environmental problems and left to feel helpless. As the quotes by students in these essays showcase, learning in the courses highlighted here is deep and transformative. Passionate students and staff should take this book and use it to find own niche as a change-agent, both within the system of higher education and within a new paradigm of sustainability education.

Marshall Curry received his BA in Sociology from Willamette University in 2013. He received a Mellon Liberal Arts Research Collaborative grant focused on ritual, sustainability, and community, and has presented papers on sustainability and education at the Oregon Higher Education Sustainability Conference and the Sustainable Agriculture Education Association annual conference. He was a Resident and Teacher Assistant with the Willamette Academy Summer Program in the summer of 2013 and is a Ford Family Scholar, Class of 2009.

Emily Dougan is an Environmental and Earth Sciences major at Willamette University with minors in Chinese and Geography. She recently studied abroad in Hong Kong and is currently conducting a research project on the management policies of national parks in southwestern China. She received a Mellon Liberal Arts Research Collaborative Project grant, interpreting and evaluating the importance of place-based education (2012), and a College Colloquium Undergraduate Grant, researching food deserts in Shanghai (2013).

I. Conceptual Frameworks: Sustainability's Challenges to Traditional Curriculum, Disciplinary Frameworks and Educational Paradigms

Learning Outcomes for Sustainability in the Humanities

Jon Jensen, Luther College

Abstract: This essay explores the question of what we expect students to know and be able to do as the result of successful education for sustainability. I start by defending the claim that teaching sustainability is not simply teaching *about* sustainability. Rather, the goal is to equip students with the skills and habits of mind necessary to move *towards* sustainability. Given this conception, what are the learning outcomes for teaching sustainability and how do innovative educators structure their courses to reach these outcomes? The specific focus is on identifying and critically evaluating learning outcomes for sustainability in the humanities since sustainability education is still perceived by many to be primarily the domain of the natural sciences.

Jon Jensen is an Associate Professor of Philosophy and Environmental Studies at Luther College, where he also directs the Environmental Studies program and the Center for Sustainable Communities. Jensen holds a Ph.D. in philosophy from the University of Colorado at Boulder and taught at Green Mountain College before joining the Luther faculty in 2002. He is the co-author of *Questions That Matter: An Invitation to Philosophy* as well as numerous essays in environmental philosophy and sustainability. Jensen is a board member of the Association for the Advancement of Sustainability in Higher Education (AASHE) as well as the Upper Midwest Association for Campus Sustainability (UMACS). He actively promotes education for sustainability through regional consortia and leads faculty development workshops on integrating sustainability in the curriculum throughout the country.

The Missing Sustainability Revolution

A sustainability revolution has swept through higher education in the last decade. Over 650 college presidents have signed the American College and University President's Climate Commitment (ACUPCC) and the Association for the Advancement of Sustainability in Higher Education (AASHE) boasts over 1,000 member institutions. While the impact is far from even across and within colleges and universities, nearly every school is delinquent in one key area: curriculum. In spite of the sustainability storm, what is taught in the college classroom has changed little in recent years. David Orr's observation from the 1990s that "we are still educating as if there is no planetary emergency" is still true today. Hard data on this is hard to come by, but the *National Report Card on Sustainability in Higher Education* concluded that, "between the years 2001 and 2008, the amount of sustainability-related education offered on campuses did not increase and may have even declined."[1]

The need for sustainability in the curriculum is increasingly recognized and change is happening, albeit slowly. One driver of this change has been the President's Climate Commitment. The ACUPCC is well known for its insistence that schools take immediate actions to reduce energy usage and set a date for carbon neutrality, but it also contains a requirement to deal with student education. Its list of requirements for Climate Action Plans includes a plan for "Actions to make climate neutrality and sustainability a part of the curriculum and other educational experience for all students."[2]

In response to this mandate, workshops have begun at campuses across the country – many led by graduates of the Sustainability Across the Curriculum Leadership workshops run by AASHE under the direction of Peggy Barlett and Geoff Chase.[3] These programs work, they are making a difference, and they need to be continued. But much more is needed. As sustainability advocates plot a strategy for moving forward, we should step back and consider bigger questions, such as:

- What would it mean to transform the curriculum of higher education – to have a sustainability revolution in what students learn as they earn their college degrees?
- What is meant by education for sustainability and how does it relate to current practices?
- How does education for sustainability work synergistically with other changes in higher education?
- How do we effectively prompt faculty to incorporate sustainability into their existing courses and design new courses with a focus on sustainability?

This essay approaches these bigger questions by focusing on student learning outcomes. My aim with this focus is two-fold: to better define what is meant by education for sustainability and to help faculty understand how they can incorporate sustainability into their courses.

What's the right question?

One of my greatest teachers was a man who I only met a couple of times and whose impact was primarily in the form of a single question. A "weed science" professor at a land grant university, he focused his work on revising his discipline's traditional approach by reframing the questions. Instead of asking, "What chemical will kill weeds most effectively?" he urged researchers to ask larger, more holistic questions; the paper he was working on was entitled simply, "What's the Right Question?"

"What's the right question?" is vital to ask as we seek to infuse sustainability into the curriculum. It is tempting (and common) to start discussions of sustainability education with the following questions: What is sustainability? Do we all agree on what sustainability means? What is happening now to expose students to sustainability and where can more be done? What information do we need to provide to teachers so they can teach about sustainability? While these may be interesting questions, all of them share a set of assumptions about education and sustainability—for instance the idea that faculty transmit information to students so they can understand what sustainability is—that need to be challenged.

I believe that we need to ask different questions and that we need to move beyond the notion of education *about* sustainability. While clearly it is important to raise awareness of environmental issues, to use sustainability examples in courses, and even to talk about the concept of sustainability, this exposure approach is clearly not sufficient. Rather, our goal ought to be to equip students with the skills and habits of mind necessary to move *towards* sustainability. Given the urgency and complexity of the problems we face, it is not enough for students to simply know about a problem; they must be able to solve it, or at least to contribute to efforts to solve it. It is not enough for students to know "content;" they must also cultivate the skills, values, and inner dispositions that will enable their knowledge, their will, and their sense of hope to evolve to meet new challenges. One of the central claims of this paper is that teaching sustainability is not primarily teaching *about* sustainability, but instead teaching students how to move *towards* sustainability.

We need to ask questions about transformation—transformation of students to be sustainability leaders and transformation of society to a new model and a new way of understanding and living out the relationship between humans and the planetary systems on which we depend. I believe our core question needs to be: *"How can we educate our students to be leaders in a sustainability revolution?"*

Questions about teaching are as important as questions about sustainability. With any sort of curriculum change it is crucial to move from discussion about what we teach to what students learn. At a basic level, this is the difference between focusing on inputs versus outcomes—on what the teacher puts into the course versus what students get out of the course. "What do I want to teach my students in this course?" Is a fundamentally different question than, "What do I want my students to learn in this course?" The former looks at inputs: What will the students read? What lectures will I give? What information will I provide? The latter focuses on outcomes: What do I want my students to know and be able to do as a result of this course? How will their perspective or values change? Where do I want my students to be at the end of this course in terms of knowledge, skills, values, disposition, or perspective?

When we apply this distinction specifically to sustainability we get different questions. Instead of asking, "How should we teach *about* sustainability?" We should ask: "How should we teach *for* sustainability?" Instead of asking, "What do I want to teach my students about sustainability?" We should ask, "How can I foster in my students the knowledge, skills, and values necessary to be responsible citizens of communities striving for a more sustainable world?" This last question is vital: we need to make sure that we do not place too much emphasis on knowledge at the expense of skills and values. With sustainability it is not just, or even primarily, what the students know, but what they do, how they see the world, what they do after graduation, and even who they are as people. Focusing on learning outcomes pushes teachers to ask these questions in ways that are unlikely to happen when our primary focus is on inputs such as texts and topics.

A learning outcomes approach to integrating sustainability throughout the curriculum is preferable for at least four reasons. First, it connects education for sustainability to a larger trend in higher education—assessment—and the drive to clearly define and measure outcomes as a way to define the value of a college education and evaluate progress on achieving the desired outcomes. By linking sustainability to this larger movement, we build allies and gain momentum that would be impossible without connecting this work to assessment in general.

Second, this approach allows for individual faculty and departments to determine for themselves how sustainability fits with their courses and their teaching style. No one is telling the chemistry faculty what to teach; it does not feel forced from the outside. Rather, we are asking individuals to determine for themselves what they want students to be able to do. This is empowering, not limiting, and it creates buy-in and deeper investment. Third, a learning outcomes approach fosters reflection on pedagogy as well as content. This gets us to ask *how* we will teach something, not just *what* we will teach. Once the focus is shifted to student outcomes, discussion of pedagogy is inevitable and innovation is almost ensured. Finally, focusing on learning outcomes works. When faculty ask the right questions about student learning and sustainability, incredible things happen in the classroom and beyond.

A Graduate's Sustainability Toolbox

Perhaps the best way to illustrate the learning outcomes approach is with the phrase, "Begin with the end in mind." While popularized by Stephen Covey as one of his "seven habits of highly effective people," it can work equally well when thinking about transforming education. In this case, the end is our graduate, or the student who has completed a particular course. And not just any graduate or any student, but our prize graduate, the one who is a model of what we hope for all our students. What would we want to say about our very best student? How would we describe not only what this student did in college but also what he or she is capable of now? What knowledge would this person possess? What values or habits of mind would manifest in his or her work and personal interactions?

Since the work of sustainability is fundamentally about change—about fixing things that are broken in our culture and society and creating things that are new—I like to think of sustainability as analogous to carpentry or perhaps to being a handyman. Like a good handyman, sustainability change agents are capable of seeing what is broken and having a sense of how they might begin to tackle the problem and create new solutions. But seeing what needs to be done is only a start; the handyman who can't fix the problem is worth little, similar to the doctor who can diagnose my illness but can do nothing to heal me. Likewise the handyman must have the skills, as well as the tools, to fix the problem and the creativity to come up with new solutions.

We might think of our graduates in a similar way. Do they have the ability to see what is broken in a community (or our society), have an intuitive sense of what needs to be fixed, and the creative and analytical skills to come up with new solutions? Do they have the tools they need to start working on creating more sustainable communities?

My contention is that it is our job as sustainability educators to fill the toolboxes of our students so they are prepared to address the challenges of the day and lead the sustainability revolution to transform society. Sustainability learning outcomes are simply one way of articulating the set of tools—the skills, perspectives, disposition, knowledge, and values—that our students will need as they face the challenges of the twenty-first century. Consider the following categories and questions that might help to frame up the discussion of what "tools" our graduates need:

- Sustainability Literacy: What do our graduates need to know to be effective change agents who understand the challenges we face and have the knowledge needed to address these challenges?
- Sustainability Skills: What skills are essential for the next generation of sustainability leaders?
- Sustainability Virtues: What virtues will graduates exhibit if we have been successful in education for sustainability?
- Sustainability Perspectives and Dispositions: How will students see the world? What dispositions will guide their behavior as they encounter challenges?

The important work is to ask the questions and to engage in dialogue leading to a shared understanding of the goal, the desired endpoint for our students. The answers to these questions will, of course, change based on the institution, the course, the professor, and the context. But these broad questions are important for clearly indicating the direction of education towards sustainability that is shaped by learning outcomes.

Below are drafts of some of the tools—the learning outcomes—that I see as most important for successful education for sustainability, organized by the categories outlined above. Since all learning outcomes are specific to the teacher, the course, the institution, and even the particular situation, no comprehensive list exists. I offer these not as definitive answers, but with the hope that they provoke your own thinking about the learning outcomes for your own courses and your own institution.

This list is not merely my own, but the result of collaboration with faculty colleagues from across the country and from many disciplines. I have been fortunate to work with two different groups who worked on sustainability learning outcomes in a formal way in addition to much informal collaboration. In 2009, AASHE convened an ad hoc group of faculty to work on student learning outcomes for sustainability, resulting in a short, unpublished document called the Sustainability Education Framework.[4] In 2010, a group of faculty from schools in the Associated Colleges of the Midwest (ACM) gathered to work collaboratively on education for sustainability resources, including learning outcomes, with a specific focus on creative assignments for integrating sustainability into introductory courses within major disciplines. These two experiences shaped both my teaching and my thinking about what it means to educate for sustainability and the learning outcomes that can best frame this work. The lists below reflect the input of many others and hopefully will provoke your own thinking.

Sustainability Literacy: Ecology and Society

Students will comprehend the structure and function of natural and social systems and the ways in which humans are dependent upon resilient and healthy ecosystems.

Perhaps nothing is more foundational to sustainability than a basic understanding of the natural systems that are the foundation for all life. Ecology is at the heart, but students also need basic literacy about all aspects of the biosphere; equally important is a foundational understanding of the economic and political systems that structure human society. These, however, must not be seen as separate from the natural systems on which we depend. Sustainability literacy demands a deep understanding of the interdependence inherent in systems.

Sustainability Skills: Problem Solving and Systems Thinking

Students will comprehend systems dynamics, including feedbacks, limits, and leverage points and will be effective problem solvers, integrating knowledge and methodologies from different disciplines to craft creative solutions to real world problems.

We need graduates who are effective at solving problems. Not simple, one-dimensional problems, but the complex, evolving challenges we face as a society. They must be adept at seeing the problem, gathering and synthesizing the necessary information, devising options, and evaluating the options to determine the best course of action. To be effective problem-solvers, students must be effective at systems thinking. We need students who have a systems perspective and are able to apply that perspective in a wide range of situations, moving beyond reductionist thinking to see the big picture and the leverage points for change. It is not enough simply to determine a possible solution; one must also be able to implement that solution. The growth in problem-based learning is perhaps the best sign of progress in this area.

Sustainability Virtues: Respect and Humility

Students will exhibit virtues such as respect, humility, and empathy as they model sustainable lifestyles and collaborate with others to address community challenges.

Skills are not enough when faced with a crisis of character and culture. We need graduates who show respect for all life, as well as a deep commitment to work for change. We need a new generation of leaders with humility and empathy, who recognize their place in communities and the world. Any talk of virtues, character, or morality will make many people uncomfortable but I think we must not shy away from the moral dimensions of sustainability or education. The objective is not to force values on students or tell anyone how to behave. Instead, students must see for themselves the implications of dominant cultural values as well as the alternatives that exist. This is neither indoctrination nor religious education; it is merely a recognition that creating a more sustainable society is fundamentally a moral imperative and thus our response must specifically address the moral dimensions of the problem with appropriate learning outcomes.

Sustainability Dispositions: Agility

Students will be flexible and adaptable—able to learn quickly, adjust to new situations and work effectively in a rapidly changing world.

Heraclitus's observation that one can never step into the same river twice is particularly relevant with the rapidly evolving nature of both the problems and the solutions relative to sustainability. Effective sustainability leaders must be adaptable, not locked into a certain way of thinking or doing things, but open to and welcoming of change, adjusting tactics to fit the new situation. Like the agile athlete who can adapt to changing conditions, sustainability graduates must be capable of easily adapting to a changing world.

Again, these learning outcomes are suggestive, not definitive, and certainly not meant to apply to all courses. What is crucial is that we move beyond the notion that education for sustainability is teaching about sustainability and instead recognize the need to teach for sustainability. This shift both reframes the conversation and opens up new possibilities. Most importantly, it helps us as teachers to ask the right questions as we think about our courses, programs, and assignments. These are questions not so much about content, awareness, or knowledge, but about skills and dispositions, virtues and perspectives, and the outcomes we hope to see in our best graduates.

The list above may seem short on "content" since typically learning outcomes place the greatest emphasis on knowledge: What will students know after this course or major? I have intentionally not taken this approach. One of my primary contentions is that knowledge and information are not the key to sustainability education. Simply put, information is not the answer; in fact, it might be the problem. As Wendell Berry and others have suggested, humans need to recognize and accept our fundamental ignorance as a starting point for right relationship with the Earth. If we are, as Wes Jackson has argued, "billions of times more ignorant than knowledgeable" no amount of additional information will rectify this situation.[5]

This is not an argument against education or an apology for the denial characteristic of so much of our culture. Rather, it is the recognition of the realities of the human condition and a call to make a fundamental shift in education in general and especially sustainability education. This does not mean that we stop teaching content, only that we are clear that content is a means, not an end.

Sustainability Learning Outcomes for the Humanities

What is the role of English, philosophy, history, art, and other humanities disciplines in education for sustainability? What sustainability learning outcomes fit in this area of higher education?

For some, these may seem like odd and misplaced questions since they may fail to see any role for the humanities. Aren't the natural sciences and environmental studies the places where we teach about sustainability? What could Shakespeare or Descartes, painting, or foreign languages have to do with sustainability? Hopefully, the list of learning outcomes from the previous section dispels this misperception. In fact, I would argue that there is likely more of a fit with education for sustainability in what is traditionally delineated as humanities and social sciences than for the natural sciences.

In asking about learning outcomes *for the humanities* it is not my intention to reinforce the traditional "silos" of higher education and thus perpetuate the dangerous and false perception that learning can be divided into categories. Some of the best learning takes place in interdisciplinary courses between the humanities, sciences, and social sciences and more needs to be done to foster cross-disciplinary collaborations. At the same time, no matter how hard we work on sustainability throughout the curriculum and build interdisciplinary programs and courses, it is also true that the traditional division of disciplines, departments, and majors will persist for some time. Therefore it makes sense to think about learning outcomes that might be a particularly good fit for the humanities. Here I outline a few of the ones that I see as most important for faculty and courses in the traditional humanities disciplines, again with the goal of provoking individual thought, not dictating necessary content.

Place

Students will have a sense of place rooted in an understanding of the natural and cultural history and the unique challenges of living in this place.

Like politics, all sustainability is local. Even with global problems like climate change, sustainability must be firmly rooted in specific places and informed by a real and meaningful connection to place. Many students "go away" to school and thus find themselves in a new and unfamiliar place. Sustainability education must be rooted in a study of the particulars of a place—the natural history as well as the way that humans have interacted with the land there—while also teaching students how to learn about and connect with place. This can be a particular challenge for higher education since the "rootless professors" are often disconnected from place themselves.[6]

Deep Causes

Students will understand the deep causes of environmental and social challenges through historical and cultural lenses.

The humanities have a central role to play in helping students move beyond narrow views of what is causing contemporary problems to see things through a different lens. A historical perspective is essential to understand how we got here and why most quick fixes are destined to fail. Likewise, a full view of the religious, philosophical, and cultural assumptions behind policies and practices is a vital part of any successful long-term response.

Community

Students will have a critical appreciation of the centrality of community and the complexities of environmental, social, and economic relationships.

At its core, sustainability is about relationships, and communities are the fundamental unit of sustainability. Students must come to understand the deeply problematic implications of the individualism that pervades contemporary society and the basic fact that there is no such thing as sustainability for individuals. Like the others, this is a "big idea" with rich opportunities for teaching students about the types of communities, including core ideas like Aldo Leopold's "land community."[7]

Communication

Students will be able to effectively communicate orally and in writing with key decision-makers and stakeholders about complex challenges and solutions.

The ability to communicate effectively is as important to sustainability as to any other pursuit. Without effective communication, it is impossible to inform other people or even formulate a coherent plan, let alone convince others to help in executing that plan. Teaching communication skills is something we do relatively well in higher education already, though much more could be done to focus our work on the contemporary sustainability challenges of the day and the vital need to communicate clearly about complex and controversial issues to a wide range of audiences.

Storytelling

Students will understand the importance of stories in shaping our culture and will be proficient at telling compelling stories about the future.

There are few skills more important for sustainability than the ability to tell compelling stories. No effort to enact fundamental change is likely to be successful without a good story behind it. Furthermore, students need a clear understanding of the role that stories play in our lives and how they, often unconsciously, shape who we are, what we do, and what we see as normal or acceptable. As Wallace Stegner said, "we live in stories and everything that we do is shaped by stories." Without an understanding and critical examination of the stories that shape our culture and our lives as well as a new set of stories, told in powerful and persuasive ways, we have little hopes of moving towards a more sustainable society.

Observation

Students will be keen observers, able to see clearly the world around them in all its complexity.

The ability to see clearly, to see the whole system, and to see what is invisible to others is essential. I mean observation in several different senses. Actual physical observations – seeing nature in the midst of human domination, hearing birds, smelling the soil after a rain, feeling the humidity in the air as the weather is about to change. Observation is the key to connection, and our disconnection from the natural world is at the heart of the unsustainability that permeates our society. Sustainability leaders must also be keen observers in a more systemic sense, seeing the systems behind contemporary challenges with "an eye" for leverage points for change. The twin pillars of obliviousness and self-absorption are far too common in today's society and we must train a new generation of observers to make way for new possibilities.

We have, then, this beginning list of some learning outcomes for the humanities:

1. Students will have a sense of place rooted in an understanding of the natural and cultural history and the unique challenges of living in this place
2. Students will understand the deep causes of environmental and social challenges through historical and cultural lenses
3. Students will have a critical appreciation of the centrality of community and the complexities of environmental, social, and economic relationships
4. Students will be able to effectively communicate orally and in writing with key decision-makers and stakeholders about complex challenges and solutions.
5. Students will understand the importance of stories in shaping our culture and will be proficient at telling compelling stories about the future.

6. Students will be keen observers, able to see clearly the world around them in all its complexity.

This list is neither final nor complete. At best, any list of potential learning outcomes should be provocative, suggesting interesting possibilities to explore and questions about what and how we teach. What do my students know and what are they able to do after completing my course now? What do they need to know and be able to do in order to respond to the challenges of the twenty-first century? What learning outcomes might capture the intersection between these two questions? What would it mean to reshape my course to meet these learning outcomes?

Lingering Questions

Throughout this essay I have focused on questions and thus we should address a couple of likely remaining questions before concluding. Perhaps the most likely, lingering question is the most common one uttered in assessment work in general: How will you measure *that*? This is a common criticism of the sorts of learning outcomes outlined above and a likely objection to sustainability education because of the difficulty of designing evaluations.

While evaluation is important, we must remember that the primary purpose of developing learning outcomes is not for assessment purposes. The primary purpose is to improve student learning by focusing on our goals, the things we think are most important. When I hear objections to learning outcomes on the basis of measurement concerns—How will you measure *that*?—I respond with a statement: If this is important, let's find a way to measure it. My contention is that evaluation concerns should come later and that we should be careful not to eliminate important outcomes because of initial concerns over measurement. As we think about measurement, we would do well to remember that sustainability education is a process and not a onetime event. At its best, looking at learning outcomes is an iterative and adaptive process where we draft outcomes, work to apply them to a course, see how we did, and learn and adapt as we move along. When seen as an adaptive process, concerns over evaluation are clearly premature. Why should I be worried about measurement and evaluation prior to thinking about how I might incorporate this into my course?

Concerns over evaluation also need to take into account the need for more creative and applied assignments, not simple assessments. The old fashioned model of education where we teach students "stuff "and then test them on whether they know the "stuff," clearly does not fit with learning outcomes that emphasize skills and dispositions. When the question is, "What do I want my students to be able to do?" and not, "What do I want my students to be able to repeat on an exam?" the focus clearly shifts to a different sort of assignment. It forces us as educators to think outside the box in a healthy way, and it clearly emphasizes the qualitative nature of evaluation over the quantitative, as it should.

A second lingering question has to do with the traditional orientation of the humanities toward exclusively intellectual activities like discussions and writing. Is it time for more "hands-on in the humanities?" Focusing on creative assignments pushes us to consider the value of having students working with their hands, not just their heads. What is the role of "hand work" in education for sustainability? If, as I have argued, we would do well to think of education for sustainability as more of a craft than a content area, as being more like carpentry than history, then perhaps the old adage that we learn by doing is appropriate here as well.

We have long recognized that hands on experiences in labs enhance science education. The same can be true for all types of education for sustainability, including in the humanities and social sciences. The examples I have been exposed to are many and varied: An intermediate German class integrates exposure to sustainability with hands-on work by building model wind turbines—with all the instructions and interactions in German. This simple activity deepens their learning of the language; students must understand the language well enough to follow the directions, which can be a challenge for many native speakers while simultaneously engaging hands and sharpening their problem solving skills. Pedagogically, it is a win-win since it is great language learning but also good education for sustainability that engages the whole person—head and hands—not just the brain. An ethics class uses food and agriculture as a case study to look at different ethical approaches incorporating hands on work on farms as a way to "make it real" for the students who can see food production as an abstraction. An anthropology course has students build and test their own simple hunting devices, such as an atlatl, in order to have a greater understanding of the culture they are studying. In all cases, the "hand work" deepens learning in the traditional subject area while engaging the whole person and infusing sustainability into the curriculum.

A final question that must be addressed here relates to the audience for our work and the need for leadership development as one central element of sustainability. How do we balance literacy and leadership—sustainability education for the many versus sustainability leadership development for the few? Ultimately, we need to reach all of our students with a certain level of education for sustainability. In the words of Luther College's commitment, we must "make sustainability a part of every student's learning experience." While this alone is a large task, we cannot ignore the importance of developing a new generation of leaders for the sustainability revolution. Thus, leadership is an important learning outcome for sustainability. While rarely associated with the humanities, here too there are connections that must be recognized and developed. Humanities courses can not only expose students to great leaders—fictional as well as real—but can provide opportunities for students to develop their own leadership abilities. The same sorts of projects mentioned earlier provide valuable practice in being leaders on campus and in the community.

Teaching Hope

Our graduates could have all the technical tools and skills in the world, but still be unable to address the challenges we face as a society. This points to another dimension to education for sustainability that we must not overlook, a piece of the puzzle that is crucial to achieve our objectives. We must leave our students with a sense of hope, a belief that the problems can be fixed, that they can make a difference, that they can and must get to work. What I am describing is an attitude, a disposition, an underlying sense of possibility and necessity that must be cultivated in our graduates if we are to be successful.

I refer to this as teaching hope and I see it as simultaneously the most important and most challenging dimension of education for sustainability. In thinking about this we should begin by acknowledging the challenge. How do we educate our students for sustainability without leaving them hopeless? How do we instill in our students a sense of possibility and promise, as well as a motivation to get started on the "Great Work" of our generation? How do we give them the confidence to tackle daunting challenges with determination and good humor? As a teacher there is perhaps no set of questions that I find more vexing than these.

To say that one of our goals should be for students to leave our classrooms and schools with a hopeful disposition puts plainly on the table the role of emotions in learning and makes explicit the evocative role of the best education. What do I want my students to feel after taking my course? This may seem like an odd question but I contend that it is one that we must ask. If they know a lot about sustainability, have the skills to work for change, but are paralyzed by hopelessness, have I really been successful? Is it really enough simply to focus on skills and knowledge and ignore the emotions and dispositions that shape so much of our behavior? My answer is a clear "no," so I offer one more learning outcome.

Hope

Students will have a positive and hopeful vision for just and sustainable societies and have the disposition to work toward achieving that vision.

All teaching is an art but nowhere is this truer than with teaching hope. No formulas exist for meeting this objective, nor even any lessons plans. As with so much of the work of sustainability, we must make it up—build it ourselves, figure it out as we go. I cannot even imagine what my Director of Assessment would say about measuring whether or not my students have a "hopeful disposition," but that should never be an excuse for backing away from our convictions about what our students, and our society, need.

I certainly have no secrets but I offer four observations from my teaching. First, there is no quicker way to kill hope in students than to focus too much on all the challenges we face and the severity of these challenges. Yes, we must teach about climate change, but too much focus on it only backfires in the end and leaves students feeling powerless in the face of certain doom. Second, one of the most powerful tools for teaching hope is success. Students need to feel that they have agency and that their work makes a difference, that they can tackle a problem and solve it. Projects that allow students to experience success on a small scale are key to developing this sense of agency as well as to teaching problem solving skills.

Third, we must be conscious in working to connect our students to sources of hope. In his book, *Hunting for Hope*, Scott Russell Sanders catalogs the main sources of hope that sustain him and we would do well to have our students do the same. "What sustains us?" is a powerful framing question that makes explicit the tie to sustainability. This need for connecting to sources of hope is also one of the most powerful reasons to work on getting students outside and into nature. Whether we recognize it or not, we all take our life and energy from connecting with nature. We must also model this behavior for our students, since they learn from us how to see the world, how to approach problems, how to live and thrive.

Finally, I would suggest that we learn hope the same way that we learn most things, from other people. Thus, one of the most powerful teaching tools we have is connecting our students with hopeful people. Whether through interviews, guest speakers in courses, or any number of ways, we need to identify those who have the disposition we want in our students and determine how to connect our students to these individuals. Hope is contagious. It's like a virus in the air.

In the end, it is less important for us to know exactly how to teach hope and more important for us to ask how we create experiences that leave students with a disposition hopeful enough that they can become successful change agents for sustainability. Once again, asking the right question is the key. If we give our graduates amazing toolboxes of skills but leave them with a feeling of hopelessness and despair, we ultimately have failed.

Education for sustainability is fundamentally about questions. If we are able to ask the right questions about our courses, our programs, and our institutions, the changes will be dramatic. The ultimate change will be a different society, one that can and does sustain itself while also sustaining other species and all of life. That is a very different path than the one that we are on now. And the humanities will play a central role in getting us there.

Notes

1. Campus Environment 2008: A National Report Card on Sustainability in Higher Education, National Wildlife Federation report available at http://www.nwf.org/campus-ecology/resources/reports/campus-report-card.aspx

2. For more on the educational component of the President's climate commitment see "Education for Climate Neutrality and Sustainability" at http://www.acupcc.org/node/7347

3. For more information on AASHE curriculum workshops see http://www.aashe.org/events/workshops/curriculum. Barlett and Chase are the editors of *Sustainability on Campus: Stories and Strategies for Change*, published by MIT Press in 2004.

4. This document was never published but a draft is available by contacting the author at jensjo01@luther.edu. Given the diversity of institutions, courses, etc., it is nearly impossible to come up with a single list of learning outcomes applicable to all contexts. My goal here, as with the Sustainability Education Framework, is simply to provoke others to come up with their own lists, not to create a definitive list.

5.   For more on this perspective see *The Virtues of Ignorance: Complexity, Sustainability, and the Limits of Knowledge*, Bill Vitek and Wes Jackson, editors, University of Kentucky Press 2008

6.   For an interesting perspective on the way that hiring patterns and expectations in higher education tend to work against connection to place see Eric Zencey, "The Rootless Professors" in *Rooted in the Land: Essays on Community and Place*, William Vitek and Wes Jackson, editors, Yale University Press, 2004.

7.   See Aldo Leopold, *A Sand County Almanac and Sketches Here and There* (Oxford, 1949), especially the final essay, "The Land Ethic." For those who are not familiar with Leopold's work, it is a wonderful articulation of the need for a new perspective on the human relationship with and role within the larger "biotic community."

The Culture of Sustainability

Mark S. Cladis, Brown University

Abstract: My chapter emphasizes the *cultural* dimension of sustainability—the necessity of *sustaining* and *cultivating* various habits, virtues, dispositions, and practices that support the multifarious and interrelated aspects of environmental sustainability. I define sustainability as a cultural journey and virtue that disposes members of a culture to see, think, feel, and act in ways that uphold "the integrity, stability, and beauty" of the planet's interrelated communities. My chapter begins with a reflection on the relation between culture, cultivation, and sustainability, with particular attention given to "speed" in our culture and universities. I conclude with a case study of sorts—my own experiment with what I call *Slow Learning*, a commitment to deep engagement. I highlight pedagogical approaches that contribute to students' deep engagement with environmental course material, especially that which addresses sustainability. By slowing down the pace of a course, we create a gracious sense of time and space that is conducive to a thoughtful, reflective engagement that, potentially, leads to integrative and transformative education.

Mark S. Cladis is the Brooke Russell Astor Professor of the Humanities in the Department of Religious Studies at Brown University. His publications and teaching pertain to the history of Western political, social, and religious thought (including the relation between religion and the environment). He is the author and editor of *Public Vision, Private Lives*; *A Communitarian Defense of Liberalism*; *Elementary Forms of the Religious Life;* and *Education and Punishment: Durkheim and Foucault*. Currently he is completing a book, *In Search of a Course: Reflections on Life, Learning, and the Environmental Imagination.*

Trouble Ahead

A few days before New Year's Eve, the electronic road sign on Highway 95 flashed the words, DRIVE SOBER OR GET PULLED OVER. My five-year-old, who delights in rhymes, shouted the warning all day long: "Drive sober or get pulled over!" When we first spotted the sign, she had asked, "Daddy, what does sober mean?" "To be sober is to be wise. If you don't drive wisely, you'll get yourself and others into trouble." A few days later, we came upon a road sign that read, THERE MAY BE TROUBLE AHEAD. My daughter became suddenly quiet and still. "Is everything all right?" I asked. She replied from the backseat, "I'm looking out for Trouble."

Unlike my five-year-old, we as a culture are failing to take seriously the signs. Warnings abound, yet we fail to notice them, much less respond appropriately. How are we to get each other's attention? After a tragic accident in Poway, CA, the city offered free signs for its residents' front lawns: SLOW DOWN IN OUR COUNTRY TOWN. On a Sunday morning last October, a digital road sign in Winnipeg proclaimed, SLOW THE F--- DOWN. The *National Post* claimed the sign was "hacked by a digitally savvy mischief-maker." In my mind, though, I secretly hoped that it was the work of *The Association for the Advancement of Sustainability*. Knowing that slowing down is a fundamental step toward sustainability, members of this group—in my fantasy—took illicit means to get their fellow citizens' attention.

In this chapter, I write with the following assumptions: 1) achieving sustainability is largely a cultural challenge and as such requires cultural transformation; 2) achieving sustainability entails that we as a people slow down our pace, including our rates of consumption and production; and 3) the journey to sustainability must itself be sustainable; that is, it requires an accord of means and ends, of path and destination. After developing the idea of sustainability as a cultural challenge, I explore speed in American culture (broadly construed) and then in our students' university subculture. Along the way, I champion a form of embodiment—bodily attention, activity, and care—that correlates with slowing down. I conclude the chapter by arguing that the virtues and dispositions of sustainability need to be built into our pedagogy—into the designs, methods, and materials of our courses. I illustrate this claim with a case study of the *Slow Learning Movement* and of the course that emerged from it at Brown University, *Religion Gone Wild: Spirituality and the Environment*.

Sustainability: A Cultural Journey

When Lynn White claimed that, "since the roots of our trouble are so largely religious, the remedy must also be essentially religious," he was mostly right—if by "religion" he meant the pervading culture of a people (30). Environmental troubles arise as a result of our culture—our politics, economics, and religions; our social practices, habits, and beliefs. Yet environmental hope, too, springs from our culture—from the cultivation of aspects of our culture that are already present.

Our hope, then, is largely reformist in nature. A central part of our reformist task is the investigation and critique of culturally pervasive patterns and habits of making and keeping time. As a culture, we move too fast to notice or care about the environmental warning signs.[1] Moreover, our speed—in our private and corporate lives—is a fundamental cause of environmental degradation. Exploitative, high-paced speed in our financial and food markets, for example, brings immense damage to communities both human and non-human. In our private lives, high speed breeds anxiousness, dissatisfaction, and the inability to be attentive to social and natural plights and oppression. Our cultural velocity is simply not sustainable. It is essential, then, that we cultivate the capacity to slow down.

Now, sustainability is a vast abstraction with many possible meanings. To fabricate a single definition of sustainability to satisfy everyone in every context would be as unfeasible as it is unnecessary. Still, provisional definitions for specific projects are useful. Some emphasize the science of sustainability and study the biology, chemistry, or geology of ecological communities. Others emphasize the economics of sustainability and study trends in production and consumption. Some emphasize sustainable development, devising strategies to improve the quality of life of impoverished populations without denigrating natural ecosystems; still others examine prosperous nations and seek ways to limit their environmental footprint.

My approach will focus on the cultural dimension of sustainability—the necessary cultivation of habits, virtues, dispositions, and practices that support environmental sustainability in multifarious and interrelated ways. By emphasizing "cultivation," I draw attention to the *journey* of sustainability—an ongoing process that entails discovery, growth, and nurturing. Moreover, the journey is in every step, for every step is itself a destination sustaining a journey toward a richer future. The movement toward sustainability must itself be sustainable.

Think of sustainability, then, as a cultural journey toward a set of virtues (an evolving cluster of nurtured dispositions or capacities) that dispose members of a culture to see, think, feel, and act in ways that *sustinere*—that uphold "the integrity, stability, and beauty" of the planet's interrelated natural and social communities.[2]

While *virtue* may sound like a quaint term, it is in fact a radical one, insofar as virtues thread through the bones and sinews of a people, rooting them in their ways and manners. Transform a people's virtues and you have a transformed people. It's a moral tautology. Sustainability as a cultural journey, then, requires the transformation of virtues—of the hearts and minds of the young and old. How is such a transformation to take place? How are we to slow down, perceive the trouble ahead, and respond appropriately? Set up road signs? Sky writing? There are many ways, all participating in the cultivation of virtues and sensibilities that foster sustainable ways of life. Educators have a special role in this cultural journey, for educators have the privilege of working with students, and students, in turn, are instigators of change. They are journeyers.

Over- and Underemployment in American Culture

Students participate in a variety of cultures or subcultures. For sake of convenience, I write of a broad American culture and a university subculture.[3] Students dwell at the intersection of these cultures, and at that intersection they must undertake their journeys toward sustainability. A characterizing feature of these cultures is their fast pace, their high speed. I have mentioned the intricate connection between means and ends (journeys and destinations) in achieving sustainability. This means-ends relation poses a radical and promising challenge. It requires that we identify not only worthy ends, but also worthy means-ends pairs. The process of *slowing down* comprises one such fundamental means-ends pair. High speed is not sustainable. It denigrates "the integrity, stability, and beauty" of the planet's communities. We cannot afford the cost of high speed, if we calculate that cost in terms of consumption of fossil fuels; the loss of wetlands, crop diversity, topsoil, and fisheries; the high extinction rate of mammals; the clearing of forests; and the inordinate pollution of the air, water, and land. Additionally, our fast-paced culture precludes most of us from making time to attend to our surroundings, to engage unhurriedly with our environments, and to notice thus the deleterious changes to the natural and social worlds. Moreover, our pace precludes most of us from challenging such changes and promoting alternative, sustainable paths. For although it is lethal, our cultural speed is powerfully addictive.

At the personal level, it begins innocently. We sense that our capacity for joy and civic engagement declines as our schedules become increasingly frenzied. We tell ourselves, *I'll slow down later*—after I pass my exams, graduate, land that job, get that promotion, buy that house, put the kids through college, and retire. After I die. The commercial market responds to our addiction to overwork by prescribing time saving devices and measures supposedly engineered to mitigate our frenzy. Yet none of these comes with the warning: "Increased efficiency may be hazardous to your mental, physical, and social health." The danger lies not with any single time-saver, any one shortcut. Rather, the risk is their accrual by a life and a culture obsessed with maximizing performance. As each task takes less time, we multiply the number of tasks for which we feel responsible. Our hectic pace renders us unable to give sufficient care to, or draw meaning from, our work. And while we dash through our lives, we lose sight of good work—work that is both useful and beautiful, that honors both nature and culture, and that contributes to a sustainable *oikonomia*, to local and global housekeeping.[4]

Improved technology and the concept of "time-management" were intended to bring prosperity and leisure. Yet most families and communities have not experienced either, with real dollar wages declining and workweeks lengthening year after year. It is incontrovertible that, since World War II, North Americans have had less leisure time; we put in almost twice the hours at the workplace that we did fifty years ago. We consistently choose money over time, speed over slowing down.

The leisure time we do have we spend on TV and Internet entertainment. It seems incongruous to me that members of our high-speed culture watch a daily average of four and one half hours of TV and spend two and one half hours online. We curse the red light that delays us fifteen seconds, yet we insouciantly watch hours of TV— increasingly online—daily. It is as if we exist in two time zones: the frenzied, high-speed zone of our workday lives and the sluggish, insipid zone of our tele-recreation. This is less ironic than it seems; hectic work calls for intense recreation. Marx complained that religion is the opiate of the people, consoling them and easing their pain, but making them numb to the dysfunctional conditions that foster their need for metaphysical comfort. Today, TV, Internet, and video-game recreation is our people's opiate. It blinds us to our condition. It calms us by desensitizing. We therefore tolerate and indulge our opiated, disembodied state.

There are alternative routes to rest and stillness. A less busy workday might reduce our desire for intense TV and Internet entertainment. Some productive, if paradoxical, counsel goes like this: *Citizens, if you want more time in your life, do things the slow way.* If you have an especially busy week, try to walk to work instead of driving; cook an elaborate meal instead of buying prepared food; make plans with friends instead of staying overtime in the office; spend the weekend with a community group instead of the hopeless task of catching up on work. The idea is that, by slowing down, we will perceive and experience more time. Will we be as efficient and accomplish as much? Probably not, if measured by most standards of efficiency and accomplishment. Will we do what needs to be done with more grace and excellence? Yes, and with pleasure.

There are many ways to begin to slow down. As is often the case, the voluntary ways are less painful than the involuntary. A car accident can slow us down. A stroke can slow us down. So can a lost job. Economic recession teaches many of us to slow down the hard way. It is true that for some, the pink slip paves the way to a welcomed retirement. For others, it promotes an intentional, sometimes radical, desire for simple living. These people might buy books like *Possum Living: How to Live Well without a Job and with Almost No Money*; they might call themselves "freegans;" they might forage food, squat in old buildings, hop trains, and embrace unemployment. Mostly, however, we do not see the recently jobless celebrating new-found freedom. Mostly, they want their old lives back. Again, there is a world of difference between *wanting to* and *having to* slow down. The sixty-hour workweek never looks so good as when our hours drop to zero. While the pain of over-employment runs deep, the pain of under- or unemployment runs perhaps deeper still.

Speed, Disembodiment, and the University Culture

There are different kinds of pain that come from over- and under-working. As an educator, I have noticed how university students must rush through their days. They, too, have little time or opportunity to pay attention to their emotional, bodily, or intellectual states, much less to the conditions of the natural and social world around them. Their lives often vacillate between strenuous, hectic studying and excessive, hazardous partying. These modes of existence exact a heavy toll. Student Counseling Services at universities across America struggle to manage the increasing cases of depression, anxiety, and eating disorders. Additionally, the adults in these students' lives maintain their own form of manic living, and so provide little direction as role models.

But students also suffer from a form of underemployment. Students in residential colleges are sheltered to a large extent from menial or manual work—work that could bring daily opportunities for significant learning and health. I have in mind such tasks as cooking meals, cleaning rooms, or raking leaves. Keeping students from humdrum chores is intended to be a good thing. We wish to protect them from distractions, from drudgery, from alleged impediments to intellectual growth. In so doing, we treat our students as Disembodied Minds. We arrange everything so they can read, write, and think with great efficiency, unburdened by the tasks of Embodied Living (save, perhaps, walks to class or treadmill workouts at the college gym). In the process, students become sheltered from opportunities for spiritual and emotional maturation. They are denied, for example, the experience of washing dishes as a form of thanksgiving: there are dishes to wash because there is food to eat. Each plate, fork, spoon, and cup is an object to be treated mindfully; each can teach care and attention. For if a student learns to wash a bowl with great care, he or she can develop the capacity to read a sentence with attention.[5]

I think we are all mostly Cartesians—we, the members of university culture. To treat students as anything other than disembodied minds would require rethinking our curriculum and its relation to the practical, bodily matters of human affairs. In the ancient Mediterranean world, philosophy was a practice—a way of life—that greatly resembled what we today might call religion: comprehensive beliefs and practices that pertain to deep questions of human suffering, identity, purpose, and happiness. The practice of ancient philosophy addressed the cultivation of the whole person and her relation to community and society. Moral, aesthetic, economic, and physical dimensions of life were all addressed by this ancient philosophical or traditional form of education. Yet this approach often conflicts with that of the contemporary research university, in which almost any practical activity is held in suspicion.

The traditional approach is decidedly *material*. If we practiced such pedagogy today, moral inquiry would explore not only abstract questions about ethics or rights, but also practical issues pertaining to our students' relation to local public schools, prisons, and community service organizations. An aesthetic schooling would include classes not only in art history but also in the work of local artisans and in students' own artistic skills. Economics courses would develop not only theoretical economic models but also strategies to enhance the university's involvement with local businesses and farms, demonstrating local outcomes of national and global policies. And the physical would refer not only to string theory but also to such material activities as dance and meditation, on the one hand, and recycling, sustainable building construction, and composting on the other. This is what I am calling a *material* education in contrast to the contemporary university's *abstract* approach—namely, treating the student as a disembodied mind with little or no connection to a place, a set of passions, and a body. For all its fear of spirituality, the university is the most spiritual place on earth.

Speed and disembodiment travel together. The faster we move through our lives, communities, and land—literally and figuratively—the weaker our connection to our bodies, neighbors (human and non-human), and world. We cannot hold what we cannot slow down to touch. We cannot care for all those proper nouns that make claims on our lives—particular communities, places, or things—if we move so fast that they become common nouns, abstract and generic. Speed and disembodiment, then, work together against sustainability. How can we help our students to slow down and make contact—contact with their bodies, with their biotic communities, with their homes?

Role models can help. Offering students exemplars is a material, practical, and loving gesture. We can expose students to the hopeful lifestyles of individuals engaged in good work, simplicity, the arts, the earth, and meaningful sociability. Helen and Scott Nearing, for example, have much to offer. The final chapter in their *Maple Sugar Book* is titled, "A Life as well as a Living." In it, the Nearings reflect on the relation between the art of sugaring and the art of living:

> We wanted to make a living in about half of our working time—say four or five hours a day—so that we would be freed from the livelihood problem and enabled to devote the other half of our time to study, teaching, writing, music, travel. (238)

This is a deeply humane vision. It presents a profound challenge to our personal lives and also to the global market economy. By making do with less—by escaping the quagmire of consumer culture—the Nearings lived without debt, worked less, and enjoyed more. Indeed, they possessed more. They held time—time for quiet contemplation, social engagement, education, art, and travel. They adopted what they called the daily four-four-four formula: "four hours for bread labor, four hours for vocation (i.e., reading and writing), and four hours for social intercourse." This principle incites my fear, hope, and longing. It threatens my identity as one whose self-worth has been determined by productivity in my career. It offers freedom from that prodigious burden, "I am what I produce."

This lifestyle also poses a radical challenge to our fast, extractive global economy. If we slowed down and worked less, we would buy and borrow less, which, in effect, would put a brake on those global engines that would have us produce, consume, and pollute more. It would arrest, by gentle neglect, rapacious practices that threaten social and natural habitats around the globe.

I understand the Nearings' principle may sound unrealistic. Could all individuals or families opt out of consumerism, debt, and rampant careerism? Would we want to? And could global economies survive such simplicity? Yet, on the other hand, how realistic is the prevailing belief that our current way of life is sustainable, with its overconsumption and overproduction, with its laborious toll on life and love, on natural and social communities? We need alternatives. We cannot, of course, all head to Vermont with the Nearings and practice sugaring. Yet standing still for a moment and attending to alternative patterns of life can help us take steps to promote joy and health for our selves and planet.

Sustainability and the Slow Learning Movement

Another way to help students to slow down and make contact is to design and teach our courses in sustainable modes. In addition to imparting information about sustainability, can our courses operate as models of sustainable communities? Can we attempt to practice sustainability in the classroom as we learn and work to achieve it locally and globally? *Yes*. Given their fast-paced lives, students, like all of us, are deeply grateful for opportunities to pause, look around and within, and be present to the life that surrounds them. They are grateful to be reminded, to paraphrase Emily

Dickinson, how startling a thing it is to live. They desire to wake up to the world and to work in its care.

Several years ago, when I was a Carnegie Scholar in the Higher Education Scholars Program, I developed a project called *Slow Learning: Deep Engagement for the Sake of Transformative Education*. This project investigated pedagogical approaches that facilitate students' deep engagement with their courses and, in particular, with my course, *Religion Gone Wild: Spirituality and the Environment*. In this course—a study of religion, ethics, and ecology—students considered such fundamental issues as the place of humans in the natural world, environmental justice, and sustainable economic, political, and cultural ways of life. According to its syllabus: "'What is the relevance of this material to me and to my community?' will be an implicit, sometimes explicit, question in the course." But how exactly was I to give my students the opportunity for the material to make deep claims on their lives, to pose transformative questions of them? Out of this question, the *Slow Learning* approach developed.

First, I *slowed down* the pace of the course (literally and metaphorically speaking) in order to create a gracious sense of time and space that was conducive to deep engagement. By "deep engagement," I mean a thoughtful, thorough, reflective engagement with course material—the readings, the field trips, and the students themselves—for the sake of integrative and transformative education. I avoided creating a hectic syllabus comprising a vast number of topics and prodigious reading assignments. In so doing, I literally slowed things down. This in itself was surprisingly challenging for me. Assuming more is more, I had acquired the bad habit of trying to cover in a semester what had taken me years to learn.

Mainly, however, I *slowed down* by employing a variety of approaches and principles that afforded opportunities for deep engagement and therefore transformative education. These approaches and principles included:

- Varying the location of class meetings; paying attention to space.
- Slowing down or alternating the pace of the course (the number of topics and reading assignments on the syllabus, for example).
- Allowing more time for discussion (probably double the time).
- Modeling deep listening for students.
- Leading an occasional contemplative exercise that focuses on a particular course theme or question.
- Allowing spontaneity (being willing, for example, to allow the students to re-write much of the syllabus and even the exams).
- Trusting the students, for they are courageous and competent. For the most part, they already know how to listen and engage thoughtfully and deeply— and they can *lead* the class (including its professor) to new vistas.
- Having students keep a dynamic journal/learning portfolio, where they may express themselves in a variety of ways (for example, through drawings, maps, poems, musings, letters from parents and friends, emails between students).
- Using the journals as sites for students to respond to spontaneous questions such as: *What question does this material/course pose to you? Which piece of art at the museum grabbed your attention and why? How do you learn best?*

Midterms and exams can also be embedded in the journal; an exam, then, might last a couple of weeks or more.

- Concluding the semester with a class retreat, offering suitable time and space to discuss the broader significance of students' journeys in the course.

These are some of the specific pedagogical approaches that belong to what I fondly call the *Slow Learning Movement*.

When I read through the students' written work (especially their journals), I discovered that the students made implicit and explicit connections between *Slow Learning* pedagogy and their learning as multifaceted persons, as practitioners of the art of living. Additionally, they had grasped a relation between the *Slow Learning* student and "the strategic learner," that is, the learner who is engaged not only in course material but also in the process of reflecting on how we learn what we learn. I discovered, then, that there is a natural connection between the principles and approaches in *Slow Learning* and integrative and transformative education.

One of the most significant pedagogical acts, I learned, is simply to raise the issue of gracious time and space with the students. Interrogate with them the possibility of an environment characterized by slow time and dynamic, empathic space. By simply posing the challenge, our students will come to the course—to its material, to its discussions, to each other—altered. They will read differently, speak differently, and listen differently. They will learn differently. They will engage deeply. This is what my evidence suggests: *Posing the possibility of gracious time and space creates gracious time and space.* What kind of evidence did I collect? I employed a variety of assessment techniques, both qualitative and quantitative, including instant feedback response slips, pre- and post-course questionnaires (response scales as well as open-ended questions), and a variety of non-intrusive, course-embedded data gathering techniques. The most significant and helpful evidence for my project came from student reports on their learning. Giving credit where it is due, I conclude this section with the voices of a few of the students:

> "The Slow Learning Movement develops among students a sense of purpose and connectedness by integrating the learning process with the social and natural world, both near and far. Similar to gracious time, the movement involves gracious space, meaning that the class environment is conducive to learning and forming connections with other aspects of life." —Sabina

> "The slow learning movement brings the world to life. In a University environment, we are shielded from the rest of the world, yet the slow learning movement allows the outside world to creep back into our consciousness because we have time to slow down and reflect on what we are learning and how it applies to the outside world." —Dan

> "This class more than any other class has changed my life. The way I approach everyday life and my relationship with the world around me has drastically changed because of my deep involvement in the course." —Emma

Joy Ahead

If achieving sustainability requires a cultural transformation through the cultivation of dispositions, virtues, and practices that support environmental sustainability, if slowing down our pace and consumption are among these sustainable practices, and if the journey to sustainability must itself be sustainable, requiring an accord of means and ends, then we will need to rethink the manner and matter of our college and university courses. The very design and pedagogy of these courses must include and derive from sustainable practices. These practices model sustainable virtues that dispose students to engage deeply with the course material and its relation to biotic-social communities. Teaching in a sustainable *mode*—and not just teaching *about* sustainability—would pose a worthy challenge to the Cartesian university culture, for it would require that students be treated as embodied citizens with practical, physical lives.

It is, of course, also valuable to teach *about* sustainability, to give students useful information on the various obstacles and potential solutions that pertain to sustainability. There is no substitute for apposite content. But we also need courses that impart this content in the mode of sustainability. We need courses that not only relay the itinerary of the journey, but also initiate students to the journey of sustainability within the community of the course. The successful course becomes itself an occasion for sustainable living.

There are companies that specialize in customized warning signs. What sign would we create for our students? APPLY YOUR BRAKES FOR YOUR COMMUNITIES' SAKES. Or, TAKE YOUR TIME—YOU WILL ARRIVE. We could place our signs in strategic locations: on the bookshelves, along the walkways, inside the classrooms. To be effective, however, the signs need to be carried in the heart. They must be written on the soul. And as the warnings become part of our lives, their tone changes. From disapproving, external directives, they become inviting, pleasant mantras. The stakes are high and the challenges immense, but the journey is not grim. "Warning: Trouble Ahead." Yes, but together we can make of Trouble an enduring community of good work and joy.[6]

Notes

1. In this chapter, the "we" mostly refers to the U.S. and other post-industrial, affluent societies.
2. This definition is informed by Aldo Leopold's "Land Ethic" and his claim that "a thing is right when it tends to preserve the integrity, stability, and beauty of the biotic community" (224-25).
3. "University culture" and "broad American culture" will be used as empirically thin, constructed caricatures for the sake of bringing attention to some actual, social features.
4. For my allusion here to "good work" and to "*oikonomia*," see Wendell Berry's *Sex, Economy, Freedom and Community*, pp. 99 and 104.

5.   Berea College and Deep Springs College are two examples of institutions that recognize and address the problem of the "Disembodied Mind." Berea College, for example, has a "labor program" that provides all students with "experiences for learning and serving in the community and [that] demonstrates that labor, mental and manual, has dignity as well as utility." And Deep Springs College "operates on the belief that manual labor and political deliberation are integral parts of a comprehensive liberal arts education." "Labor" is one of the College's three mission pillars (the other two being academics and self-governance).

6.   I am grateful to Maggie Millner, my Brown University research assistant, for her expert editing and deep engagement with this text.

Works Cited

Berry, Wendell. *Sex, Economy, Freedom, and Community*. New York, NY: Random House, 1993.

Leopold, Aldo. *A Sand County Almanac and Sketches Here and There*. Oxford, UK: Oxford University Press, 1987.

Nearing, Helen, and Scott Nearing. *The Maple Sugar Book*. New York, NY: John Day Company, 1950.

White, Lynn. "The Historical Roots of Our Ecologic Crisis." *Ecology and Religion in History*. New York, NY: Harper and Row, 1974.

Historical Consciousness in an Age of Climate Change

Wendy Petersen Boring, Willamette University

Abstract: What does it mean to be "historically awake" in an era of climate change? How can the study of history contribute to students' desire and ability to move towards more sustainable ways of living? This essay explores these questions by reflecting on history as a cultural resource for students to draw upon, wrestle with, and hold with care as they form their own sustainability ethic. In order to sustain what is worth sustaining, we need to think historically as much as we need to think creatively, scientifically, humanely, and with vision. We need history that functions as a calling to that part of ourselves which will recreate and restore human and natural communities and that remembers the full range of ingenuity and wisdom we possess, individually and as a species. To be historically "awake" in the face of climate change entails understanding the ecological peculiarity of the present moment, our role as geological agents in planetary history, our past as species history, and the ways in which the notion of "sustainability" itself reflects both its deeper historical sources and its particular, contemporary historical context.

Wendy Petersen Boring, Ph.D., is an Associate Professor of History at Willamette University in Salem, Oregon, where she teaches pre-modern European history, women and gender studies, and sustainability studies. She served as Chair of Willamette's Sustainability Council for three years and currently teaches food systems and ethics at Willamette's Zena Farm Summer Institute in Sustainable Agriculture. She has presented nationally and regionally on integrating sustainability into the humanities and has published articles on sustainability pedagogy. Her research focuses on issues in late medieval philosophy, gender, and spirituality. She earned her Ph.D. in Religious Studies from Yale University.

"What kind of stories best serve in a crisis?...Which touch us most deeply?...Which might paralyze or polarize the same people? What are the differences between an empowering narrative and a paralyzing one? What are the mechanics and secret fuel of a story that directs us towards acts of courage, good sense, good humor, and hope?"

- David James Duncan, "Being Cool in the Face of Climate Change"

As environmental historian William Cronon has said, "sustainability" is firmly rooted in the prophetic tradition: "Change your ways!" it proclaims, or face dire consequences. From its origin in economic development frameworks in the 1970's and '80s in *The Limits to Growth* (1972), *World Conservation Strategy* (1980), and *Our Common Future* (1987), "sustainability" emerged as a critique of the economic inequities and environmental degradation wrought by what we commonly term "modernity." Historians have traditionally told the story of modernity in terms of increasing political, racial, and gender freedoms. "Sustainability" joins the ranks of post-colonial, feminist, and post-modern critiques of modernity, but it does so by exposing the illusions of an "unending frontier" that fueled global explorations, cultural and biotic exchanges, and resource-extraction systems that birthed the modern world (Richards). As Dipesh Chakrabarty suggests, from the perspective of climate change, the standard stories of modernity seem ever more problematic. It becomes clear that "the mansion of modern freedom stands on an ever-expanding base of fossil fuel use" (208). "Change your ways!" is thus not only a call for more just and sustainable practices, it is also a call to change the standard stories we tell ourselves—about who we are, where we stand, and how we got here.

Environmental historians, whether or not directly spurred on by the sustainability movement, have already begun to answer this call, offering increasingly sophisticated narratives of the transition to modernity (Burke, Pomeranz, Roberts, Goody, J.R. McNeil). Environmental history as a discipline has moved significantly beyond its early preoccupation with North America, wilderness, and crises, and expanded into the non-Western world. It is now inclusive of Africa, Asia, and South and Central America, offering nuanced accounts of relationships between human and natural systems across a diversity of time periods (*AHR* Conversation). Students and teachers of sustainability have much to learn from this work.

But here's the rub: we don't just need more and better environmental histories— although we surely do need these. We need cultural wisdom. As E.F. Schumacher observed, the problems we face in the transition to sustainability are not "convergent" problems solved by logic and method, but are instead "divergent" problems, formed out of the tensions between competing perspectives and interests, negotiated individually and communally in the public sphere (Prugh 7). As David Orr has compellingly urged, divergent problems cannot be solved by reason alone; they only can be transcended "by higher methods of wisdom, love, compassion, understanding, and empathy" (Orr, "Four Challenges," 1459; *Earth In Mind*).

I believe that to sustain what is worth sustaining, we need to think historically as much as we need to think creatively, scientifically, humanely—and with vision. However, we don't need history as nostalgia for a golden Eden in the past, or history as names and dates that fly out of the mind on the breezes of June, or history as academic specialization stored in silos in dusty warehouses.

We need a history that forms a central fiber of our identity and gives us a sense of purpose and vision for our collective future. We need stories that help us understand how we got to where we are—and ones that help us find our way forward. We need a living history—one that connects us to the past and one that we carry in our minds and hearts. We need stories of past failure and collapses, genius and collaboration, savagery and courage, sacrifice and love. We need history that functions as a calling to that part of ourselves that will recreate and restore human and natural communities, that bears witness to our capacity for both good and ill, and that remembers the full range of ingenuity and wisdom we possess.

How do you teach *that*?

This question has haunted me as I have gone about my work teaching pre-modern European history at a small, liberal arts college in Oregon. It has led me, among other things, to develop a course, "Western Civilization and Sustainability: Beginnings to 1650"—the only course in our curriculum that can boast of hosting an oxymoron in its title.[1] Increasingly, my questions over the past seven years have moved beyond those of relevance (Why study history in the face of sustainability challenges?) to ones of resonance: What does it mean to be "historically awake" in an era of climate change? What would it look like to cultivate a living historical consciousness as we face the challenges of sustainability? How can the study of history contribute to students' desire and ability to move towards more sustainable ways of living?

In what follows, I offer some points of reflection on teaching history with these questions of resonance in mind. These are by no means exhaustive. I see them as points of departure from which variations can emerge, not just for history, but for other disciplines as well. Each offers a point of dialogue between history and sustainability, where history offers unique perspectives and resources and sustainability "pushes back," reorienting questions and assumptions, energizing what it means to cultivate knowledge in the humanities.

History as Resource

Most broadly, as I teach towards sustainability, I find myself inviting students into a different relationship with time. As a culture we do not have a vibrant historical consciousness; we barely have any historical consciousness at all.

For history to be a living, breathing cultural resource, we need to experience the study of it as a profound, edgy, beautiful, authentic, and critical dialogue with the past, pursued with the aim of forming a personal ethic of sustainability. This feels to me like several steps beyond "making it relevant." It means I need to encourage students to see the texts, ideas, and narratives that we encounter in class as their inheritance, individually and collectively. It means I need to find ways to make ideas from the past come alive in student's minds, hearts, and imaginations, so that they can mix and match past and present and create new patterns of thought and new forms of understanding. It means finding patterns of teaching that understand history as a "resource" in a counter-cultural, counter-capitalist, counter-modernity way—not as something to extract, consume, and toss away, but instead something to hold with care, use well, and make our own.

There are a variety of practical ways to make this happen: pairing contemporary essays, films, and art with analyses of texts from the past, or assigning essays that ask students to use historical sources as resources for contemporary problems. However, I think that perhaps the most significant thing I do is to simply be intentional about taking a different approach towards fostering knowledge. Teaching history with sustainability in mind, I have found, is an exercise in cultivating knowledge that comes from somewhere and serves a purpose: from our living, breathing interaction with the ideas, individuals, and communities of the past, for the purpose of rumination that will spur the clarity and courage we need to restore natural and human communities.

Historical Peculiarity of the Present

To be historically "awake" in the face of the challenges of sustainability requires holding two different things simultaneously in mind, a kind of double take of the historical imagination which pans across a wide field of time. On the one hand, we need to fully grasp the historical peculiarity of the present moment, the sheer historical oddity of this era we now call the Anthropocene; at the same time, we need to see the present as embedded in a much larger story of species history and biological interconnection stretching back into deep time.

Environmental historian J.R. McNeill coined the phrase "ecological peculiarity" to describe the twentieth century's extraordinary use of energy and resources. While environmental change is as old as the earth itself, and humans have altered environments throughout our four million year career, there has "never been anything like the twentieth century" (3):

> such intensity, on such scale and with such speed...The human race, without intending anything of the sort, has undertaken a gigantic uncontrolled experiment on the earth. In time, I think, this will appear as the most important aspect of twentieth-century history, more so than World War II, the communist empire, the rise of mass literacy, the spread of democracy, or the growing emancipation of women. (*Something New Under the Sun*, 3-4)

Most students walk around with a list of environmental problems in their heads, or at least a general sense of environmental gloom/sin/collapse; but, few have a grasp of the historical uniqueness of the energy regime that supports our most common daily activities. McNeill underscores "ecological peculiarity" by placing the twentieth century in broader historical contexts, using history to disrupt the practices, institutions, and ideas we have normalized. We know, for instance, that we use a lot/too much energy, but to hear McNeill say, "No other century—no millennium—in human history can compare with the twentieth century for its growth in energy use.

We have probably deployed more energy since 1900 than in all of human history before 1900" (15)—makes us pause. Pair that with the fact in the 1990s the average global citizen deployed about 20 "energy slaves" (20 human equivalents working 24 hours a day, 365 days a year) but the average American used upwards of 75 energy slaves while the average Bangladeshi had less than one (15-16), and we begin to ask questions about who and what is being enslaved to provide the "mansions of modern freedom" we enjoy. We understand that we have enshrined "growth" as both a description and a virtue for the economy. However, learning that the world's economy in the late twentieth century was about 120 times larger than that of 1500 and that, on average, we have nine times more income per capita than our ancestors had in 1500 and four times as much income as people had in 1900 (7), prompts us to question the notion of growth we have normalized: How long can this go on?

From an energy standpoint, the historical peculiarity of the present flows directly from the point of transition to fossil fuels, which, as historian Edmund Burke points out, "shattered all previous human expectations of how much was too much" (44). Since the early nineteenth century, there has been a thousandfold increase in the consumption of fossil fuels worldwide (47). Viewed from the perspective of energy, the Industrial Revolution "constituted an unprecedented break" in human relations with nature and the environment (33). Viewed against the background of all of human history, "present levels of energy consumption appear deeply aberrant" (49).

"Shattered all previous human expectations," "thousandfold increase," "unprecedented break," and *"deeply aberrant"* function as historical wake-up calls. Our worldview, rather than being the most advanced, expansive, and civilized (as our educational institutions and media advertise) begins to feel oddly limited by its ecological peculiarity. The notion that we might want to look before the last two hundred years for some creative ideas begins to feel pragmatic, even compelling. The historical observation, "Things have never been this way before in the entire history of the human species," prompts a deeper pause. Space opens up for reflection. We begin to sense how our way of being in the world, our way of perceiving the world, our daily practices, are an aberration in the experience of our species. They are contingent, not necessary. In the span of the history of our species, they are brand new. We begin to sense just how creative we will need to be in the future.

At the same time, grasping the intensity and scale of the twentieth century makes us rethink the stories we have told ourselves about how we got here. As Edmund Burke argues in "The Big Story: Human History, Energy Regimes, and the Environment", if we want to tell a story that captures what is unique about the present, we need to rethink things as basic as the standard way we chop up time. Instead of Agricultural Revolution, Classical Greece, Roman Empire, "Dark" Ages, Renaissance, and Industrial Revolution, the human story ought to be told in terms of energy regimes, of which, Burke suggests, there are basically two: the age of solar energy (a renewable resource) from 10,000 BCE to 1800 CE, and the age of fossil fuels (a nonrenewable resource) from 1800 CE to the present (35).

We need to be reminded that before the Industrial Revolution, the only important converters of energy were biological ones: muscle power of humans, domesticated animals, wind and water, and the chemical energy stored in wood and biomass (11). Even at the outset of the Industrial Revolution in Europe (ca 1800), more than 70% of our mechanical energy was supplied by human muscle (11). We need to be reminded that slavery was the most efficient means by which the ambitious and powerful could become richer and more powerful. It was the answer to energy shortage (12): "Control over people was therefore a central feature of the energy strategy of most states and societies in the age of solar energy. Those able to organize large numbers of humans gained a major energy premium" (37). As a student put it, "The exploitation of the environment has paralleled the exploitation of humans. Our thinking about climate change and resource degradation needs to address the intersection of environmental and social justice."

Telling the human story in terms of energy regimes underscores the dangers inherent in the isolation of the developed world. The environmental feedback loops and bioenergetic limits of the solar energy regime—famine, disease, warfare, deforestation—were readily apparent within a generation or two and thus the systems were essentially self-correcting and self-limiting. This was true over the vast range of human history: "the rules of the energy game of the agrarian age remained in effect during the six and a half millennia of the classic agrarian age (5000 BCE to 1400 CE)...Empires rose and fell, to be sure. But the energy calculations remained much the same," a fact highlighted by the stability of human population levels (38).

The ecological peculiarity of the present asks us to rethink that most basic of historical categories: human agency. As Chakrabarty has pointed out, the reality of climate change in particular suggests that historians must grapple with an utterly new notion of the human—not merely biological agents, but geological agents:

> The science of climate change speaks of a new kind of agency on the part of humans: a geological agency. It is collective; planetary in scope; it is not immediately available to human experience though its effects are; it is a byproduct of what we have come to regard as civilization (which needs energy to be available aplenty and cheap). ("Human Agency in the Anthropocene" 36)

Understanding humans as geological agents means expanding our vision over a very large time scale, drawing from disciplines far from history, and grappling with the discrepancies embedded in the fact that, although we are not politically "one," we are "one" as a species who has "re-jiggered the climate system" (36). The implications for our story telling are immense. Clearly, we cannot tell stories about what it means to be human which cast the environment in a background role, or feature human actors on a stage empty of ecosystems and climate, or cast the actors that have led to re-jiggering climate as heroes, as some of our histories have done in the past. How do you envision yourself as part of a species that has collective agency on a planetary scale? What kind of story can you tell that is simultaneously an origins tale, a warning tale, and an ode to hope for change?

Species History

Grappling with our geological agency and ecological peculiarity are only part of what it means to be historically "awake." We also need to develop a historical consciousness that is attentive to our identity as one species within hundreds of millions of years of biological creativity. We need human history as "species history." To my mind, we need it on at least two levels.

On one level, we need to tell stories that reflect the reality of deep interconnection and evolution between biotic and human communities over a vast swath of time. We take the notion of the interconnectedness of the web of life as ecological fact in the life sciences; it is time to extend this frame of thinking more fully into the humanities and social sciences. As E.O. Wilson has argued, the social sciences and history have for too long been "blinkered by a steadfastly non-dimensional and non-theoretical view of mankind. They focus on one point, the human species, without reference to the space of all possible species natures in which it is embedded." We need species history to counter the limits and dangers inherent in anthropocentric focus, to articulate meaning for humans in terms of evolution, limits, and biological processes. "To be anthropocentric," Wilson says, "is to remain unaware of the limits of human nature, the significance of biological processes underlying genetic evolution, and the deeper meaning of long-term genetic evolution" (*In Search of Nature*, 99-100). We need, in other words, to figure out how to not be anthropocentric in the era of the anthropocene.

Species history as a story of humans embedded in a universe-long story of change, complexity, interconnection, and biological limits makes us pause and notice how our basic patterns as humans are part of the rhythms of a much larger, more than human reality. As historian William McNeill has said it, eloquently:

> Human beings, it appears, do indeed belong to the universe and share its unstable, evolving character...[W]hat happens among human beings and what happens among the stars looks to be part of a grand, evolving story featuring spontaneous emergence of complexity that generates new sorts of behavior at every level of organization from the minutest quarks and leptons to the galaxies, from long carbon chains to living organisms and the biosphere, and from the biosphere to the symbolic universe of meaning within which human beings live and labor, singly and in concert, trying always to get more of what we want and need from the world around us. ("History and the Scientific Worldview" 12-13)

Historians have begun to answer the call for stories that approach humans as one species embedded in a larger story. David Christian, for instance, in *Maps of Time: An Introduction to Big History*, argues for crafting "big history" to answer the "enduring questions that in former times creation myths addressed: Who am I? Where do I belong? What is the totality of which I am a part?" Although he points out dangers with "big history"—thinning out the narrative, errors resulting from reliance on other disciplines such as biology, cosmology, geology, and the hubris of "grand narratives"—Christian argues that it is time for a unified account of the way things came to be the way they are, to gather together the fragments of specialization into a whole, to tell a story of origins and purpose with power, to tell a story of the whole—and then proceeds to do so.

Brian Swimme and Thomas Berry in *The Universe Story* also tell species history as universe history, beginning with "the primordial flaring forth" fifteen billion years ago and chronicling the remarkable diversity, creativity, and interconnection that marks evolution. The story they tell offers potential hope in the face of our ecological peculiarity: mass extinctions and crises of environmental overshoot unfailingly become the occasion for radically new and creative forms of life to emerge.

Why do we need stories like this? Because they provide narrative frameworks large enough to make sense of both our ecological peculiarity and our geological agency. Because they cultivate humility, compassion, wonder, and hope. Because they challenge our assumptions about what it means to be human in precisely the ways we need. As my students put it:

> What if we challenged where "human" begins? A narrative of humans that includes the beginning of life itself, from the first cells, through the mass extinction of the dinosaurs, to our current state, could prompt a greater appreciation of our role in a global inter-species community, awe at the unlikely coincidences that got us here, and compassion for fellow species who have traveled the bumpy road of evolution and thrived alongside of us.

> We should begin with a nod to our cosmological genesis whose depth and complexity we may never fully understand. We need to be reacquainted with the language of evolution...it is humbling to recognize we are part of a much larger, longer, and often incomprehensible process.

We also need species history because it provides a counter to narratives structured by a framework of progress. Human history as species suggests ecosystem patterns of growth and decline based on available resources, not teleological narratives driving towards progress. As one of my students put it, this is "honest history:"

> In light of sustainability...an 'honest' history would avoid the tendency to totalize human evolutionary processes and would permit us to embrace new notions about what it means to *be human*. [It would] challenge the master narrative of a single, deterministic trajectory of human evolution that has led inevitably to 'civilization' and 'modernity' as we understand it today, and it would account for the co-evolutionary processes between humans, our cosmological beginnings, and our ecological surroundings.

As significant as the industrial revolution was, as game changing as climate change is, we cannot focus our historical attention simply on the last two hundred years. We need to telescope out, to find perspective from seeing ourselves as part of a larger story that is not, ultimately, about us, but instead about the resilience of life itself.

Big Questions, Species Answers

At another level, we need to cultivate "species history" by turning to our own species in search of wisdom. There is great power in "expanding the we" not only to the more-than-human world, but also to individuals and communities in the past. To do this, we need to do what the humanities do best: ask the big questions. What does it mean to be human? To love? To sacrifice? To die? To have compassion? To be a citizen? To form a just society? These questions need to be posed not theoretically as topics which humanities professors might ponder sitting in their offices, but instead practically, individually, to students sitting in their classroom chairs. What does it mean to *you* to be human? What kind of human are you afraid of becoming? What kind of human do you want to become? Students need to be invited to see their ancestors as extending beyond their own genealogical family to include a much wider human family from which they can draw insights, cultural critiques, humor, questions, observations and wisdom.

Which brings me to another reason why I continue to teach from the pre-modern past: because the texts covering this period provide a rich, diverse, and beautiful source for sustained reflection on precisely the kinds of things we need to be ruminating on—beauty, love, limits, justice, conflict, equity, wisdom.

The texts from the pre-modern past speak to us from the perspective of a different energy regime, and thus are just distant enough to provide perspective yet close enough to resonate. They bear witness to our capacity for both good and ill, they record the full range of ingenuity and wisdom we possess, individually and as a species, and they have the capacity to call to those parts of ourselves that want to recreate and restore human and natural communities. They give us, as a student put it, glimpses of "individuals who derive power by exercising restraint and who seek enlightenment by recognizing their place in the natural, social, and spiritual landscape."

To be historically "awake" in the face of sustainability is to see the history as shot through with resistance movements that articulate with cutting insight, generous vision, and wicked humor the dangers of a human life circumscribed by pursuit of power, prestige, and possessions and offer alternative visions of seeking meaning. These can be found throughout the historical record, cross-culturally and cross-temporally. But there is a particular kind of liberation that comes when students locate threads of resistance, of which they are usually unaware, embedded in the history of the very civilization that, as they often put it, is uniquely responsible for "getting us into this mess." The examples are many, but might include: Thucydides' critique of Athenian over reaching, lack of self-awareness, and the failings of empire; Plato's critique of glib rhetoric as enchanting a populous into pursuit of platitudes rather than truth; Plotinus's vision of the human as embedded in Gaia-like universe of interconnection and transformed by Beauty; St. Francis's critique of proto-capitalist, heavily managed landscapes and embrace of voluntary poverty; Bonaventure and Aquinas's critique of knowledge acquisition without epistemic humility; Dante's critique of greed and hypocrisy and vision of the power of love to transform and hold it all; and Thomas More's critique of the close-mindedness, cultural superiority, and unjust distribution of wealth of the sixteenth century.

Encountering these moments of resistance in their full historical and textual specificity sharpens our minds, helps us to see our cultural blind spots, probes our self-awareness, and gives us sharp eyed, wise companions for the road. On the flip side, teaching this history trains students to challenge the easy and superficial diagnoses and blame often found in contemporary critics. "Western Civilization" is far from monolithic; human behavior is more complex and adaptive than those who focus on contemporary culture often allow. After a semester spent encountering these texts, one student concluded, "a definition of what it means to be human must once again include limits on our desires and in so doing undermine the prefiguration that our history is bifurcated into the modern-secular and classical-spiritual worlds." This "is not an appeal to coercion but to *discipline* as an embedded part of the human experience."

Situating Sustainability

Finally, being historically "awake" entails developing a historically thick notion of the term "sustainability"—not only in the pre-modern past, but also in the recent past. As Carl Mitcham has pointed out, the concept of "sustainable development" arose in the 1980s as a compromise term designed to recognize the realities of competing interests. The World Commission on Environment and Development, faced with competing interests of environmentalists (who argued for limits to growth) and developing world economists (who argued for more development and growth to alleviate poverty), offered the notion of "sustainable development" to bridge the gap (317-324). "Sustainable development" as the triple bottom line of Environment + Equity + Economics, focusing on intergenerational equity, became a way to hold together what are, in fact, points of real conflict (324).

Mitcham takes us back even farther, noting that rooted deep in the Western psyche is an understanding of history as progressive, either toward a perfect future, or away from an imperfect past (312). As the notions of Paradise and Redemption fade away with the secularization of Western thought in the seventeenth and eighteenth centuries, they are replaced by scientific and technological progress as "an indefinite and continuous superseding of the past" that is headed not towards some definite future, but instead towards a future of never-ending progress, without limits (314). The notion of "limits to growth," which emerged in the 1970s, was historically significant in that it questioned this deeply embedded notion of progress. However, as Mitcham points out, the concept of "sustainable development" harbors the same progressive understanding of history that has haunted the Western psyche and justified limitlessness in the past. Often, "sustainable development" models simply make the idea of "limits to growth" the precondition to further and continuing growth (316).

It was in the 1990s that "sustainability" became ubiquitous, the "big, sloppy term for a big, complex subject" (Prugh 2) appropriated just as eagerly by conservationists and environmental activists as by corporate marketing teams. As William Cronon has argued, its popularity in the 1990s down to the present day can be attributed to a variety of factors. As mainstream environmentalism became attacked by those on the left (as indifferent to race and social justice) and those on the right (as in direct competition with economic growth and job protection), sustainability's triple bottom line, Equity + Environment + Economy, offered a way to continue the earlier conservation strands of environmentalism without the divide between nature and culture and simultaneously put social justice front and center. In a post 1989, post Cold War context, in which the old capitalism versus communism divide no longer resonated, sustainability moved in to fill the open ideological space, affirming a healthy economy as central and holding out hope that, in the future, the triple bottom line could be achieved. Further, the development of 'carbon' as the universal metric with a prophetic and moral imperative, and the message of individual and small community empowerment, brought concrete measurability along with confidence and hope. As Cronon points out, although it derives its chief moral force from global claims regarding resources and climate, the rhetoric of sustainability focuses on individual choices and institutions, which is empowering and confidence giving; it is not a 'downer.' Its call—we are on our way to a more stable, benign, and just way of living—resonates across the political spectrum ("The Riddle of Sustainability").

Even this much historical perspective breeds a healthy suspicion of the hidden ambiguities in the term. Its popularity alone should make us suspicious, coinciding as it does precisely with decades of vast over-consumption. As my students have argued, understanding the recent history of the term prompts the sorts of questions and observations that are critical to crafting a personal ethics of sustainability:

- o Is the triple bottom line simply modernity's version of the "you can have your cake and eat it too" mentality that got us into this mess?
- o Is it really possible to bridge the real competing interests between the "need for development" and the "need to conserve and restore?"
- o What is the difference between wants and needs, and who decides?
- o "Sustainability" must distinguish between developing and developed world differing levels of vulnerability to, experience of, and responsibility for environmental degradation.
- o "Sustainability's" focus on the individual is empowering but also dangerous in that it works by reinforcing our identities as private consumers. As Maniates points out, there are problems with the "individualization of responsibility." When "responsibility for environmental problems is individualized, there is little room to ponder institutions, the nature and exercise of political power, or ways of collectively changing the distribution of power and influence in society—to, in other words, 'think institutionally' (4). There is also nothing to show that all the individual efforts will add up to tip the scales towards necessary structural change.
- o To the extent that it promises stability, "sustainable development" is not historically savvy enough. Any vision of the future has to include patterns of growth and decline. We need to think in terms of resiliency, not stasis. It is also not historically informed enough: many human communities have lived sustainably prior to modernity and offer counter-paradigms and practices that could serve as resources.

- o "Sustainable development" seems to enshrine a "fairly recent version of Homo sapiens: the efficiency conscious individual" (Sachs 16-19) and eclipse others, particularly those of indigenous cultures.
- o "Sustainable development" models often seem to treat earth as a spaceship that needs a manual, which is "at the very least, at odds with traditional cultures" (Mitcham 323).

History as a mode of self-knowledge

A historically thick understanding of "sustainability" and critical recognition of its ambiguities, an awareness of our ecological peculiarity, a recognition of our geological agency, wrestling with the depths of our species wisdom, cognizance of our place in the beautiful, interconnected, unfolding complexity of the universe—these provide rich soil for developing a personal ethic of sustainability. As students "map" their sustainability ethic they work with the notion of what David Christian calls "Maps of Time"—a mode of doing history that functions a bit like creation myths did in their day.

The aim is not perfect, total, or complete knowledge but rather workable, indispensable knowledge:

> Knowledge systems, like maps, are a complex blend of realism, flexibility, usefulness, and inspiration. They must offer a description of reality that conforms in some degree to commonsense experience. But that description must also be useful. It must help solve the problems that need to be solved by each community, whether these be spiritual, psychological, political, or mechanical...In their day, creation myths offered workable maps of reality, and that is why they were believed. They made sense of what people knew. (11)

Historical consciousness as a map of where we stand in time "makes sense" of what we know in terms of what we can grasp of the whole. After a semester doing this, my students observe:

> Why study history in the fact of ecological crisis? We study history because there is no way we can possibly understand the fragility of where we are without a keen awareness of what we have inherited as a culture, as individuals, as a human community, in our blood, our psyches, our land... We reach to the past to interrogate the framework and cultural paradigm from which we operate and to cultivate a community of well-informed, determined, and compassionate thinkers.

> Because of this class, I have had to take responsibility for my thoughts and actions. I can no longer do something without viewing the system through a critical eye. I have learned it is okay to question what is around me, and have felt immensely empowered to do so. I have learned that being spiritual and being an atheist are not two conflicting ideologies. Because of this class, I

have seen the immense power in the human word. I have been moved to tears of joy and tears of anger and I am continually surprised at how deeply I was required to look into myself to answer the questions posed by the readings and my peers. Because of this, my study of ecology has taken on a whole new form.

How can the study of history contribute to students' desire and ability to move towards more sustainable ways of living? By offering a mirror. By telling stories that bear witness to our capacity for great good and ill, savagery and courage, sacrifice and love. By telling stories that feed the spirit and thus shape what we see. As David James Duncan has said, "life itself sometimes hangs by a thread made of nothing but the spirit in which we see...One of the terrors of being human, and one of the joys, is that for all our limitations and confusions, we have been given power" ("Birdwatching as a Bloodsport" 43, 47).

Notes

1.   Thanks to the students in my class, "Western Civilization and Sustainability: Beginnings to 1650," whose intelligent work has shaped my understanding of the craft of history and who have helped me reflect on what I do and why it matters, especially to those I quoted here: Carley Kwiatowsky, Alex Lanz, Victoria Binning, and Madeline McClelland. Thanks also to those who have been invaluable conversation partners over the years whose thoughts helped shape this essay, Lindsay Trant and Timothy Robb. Sincere thanks also go to my colleague, Dr. Leslie Dunlap, who signed up to take the class, for her intellectual companionship and her insightful comments on a draft of this essay. Thanks also go to Colleen Smyth and Emily Boring who did a terrific job editing the manuscript and preparing it for publication.

2.   For a Syllabus for "Western Civilization and Sustainability: Beginnings to 1650, please see Appendix C.

Works Cited

American Historical Review Conversation: "Environmental Historians and Environmental Crisis." Participants: Richard Hoffman, Nancy Langston, James C. McCann, Peter Perdue, and Lise Sedrez. December, 2008. 1431-1465.

Berry, Wendell. "Faustian Economics." *What Matters? Economics for a Renewed Commonwealth*. Berkeley, CA: Counterpoint, 2010.

Brown, Lester. *World on the Edge, How to Prevent Environmental and Economic Collapse.* Earth Policy Institute. New York, NY: W.W. Norton, 2011.

Brundtland, Gro., ed. *Our Common Future*. New York, NY: Oxford University Press and World Commission on Environment and Development, 1987.

Burke, Edmund and Kenneth Pomeranz, eds. *The Environment and World History.* Berkeley, CA: University of California Press, 2009.

Chakrabarty, Dipesh. "The Climate of History: Four Theses." *Critical Inquiry* 35 (2009): 197-222.

---. "Human Agency in the Anthropocene." *Perspectives on History*. 50.9 (2012): 35-36.

Christian, David. *Maps of Time: An Introduction to Big History*. Berkeley, CA: University of California Press, 2004.

Cronon, William. "The Riddle of Sustainability: A Surprisingly Short History of the Future." Unpublished public lecture, Reed College, April 17, 2013.

Duncan, David James. "Being Cool in the Face of Climate Change." *Moral Ground: Ethical Action for a Planet in Peril*. Eds. Kathleen Dean Moore and Michael P. Nelson. San Antonio: Trinity University Press, 2010.

---. "Birdwatching as a Bloodsport," *My Story as Told By Water*. San Francisco: Sierra Club Books, 2001. 31-48.

Goody, Jack. *The Theft of History.* New York, NY: Cambridge University Press, 2006.

Iyer, Pico. "The Inner Climate." *Orion Magazine*. Sept./Oct. 2008: 32-35.

Johnson, Trebbe. "Gaze Even Here." *Orion Magazine*. Nov./Dec. 2012: 67-71.

Kiser, Lisa. "The Garden of St. Francis: Plants, Landscape, and Economy in Thirteenth Century Italy." *Environmental History* 8.2 (2009): 229-245.

Maniates, Michael F. "Individualization: Plant a Tree, Buy a Bike, Save the World?" *Global Environmental Politics* 1.3 (2001): 31-52.

McNeill, J.R. *Something New Under the Sun: An Environmental History of the Twentieth Century World*. New York, NY: W.W. Norton, 2000.

McNeill, William. "History and the Scientific Worldview." *History and Theory* 37.1 (1998): 12-13.

Meadows, Donella, Club of Rome et al. *Limits to Growth*. New York, NY: Universe Books, 1972.

Meadows, Donella H., Dennis L. Meadows, and Jorgen Randers. *Beyond the Limits: Confronting Global Collapse, Envisioning a Sustainable Future*. Post Mills, VT: Chelsea Green, 1992.

Minteer, B. and R. Manning, "Appraisal of the Critique of Anthropocentrism and Three Lesser Known Themes in Lynn White's 'The Historical Roots of our Ecological Crisis'" *Organization & Environment* 18.2 (2005): 163-176.

Mitcham, Carl. "Sustainable Development: its Origins and Ambivalence," *Technology and Society* 17.3 (1995): 311-326.

Moore, Kathleen and Michael P. Nelson. *Moral Ground: Ethical Action for a Planet in Peril*. San Antonio: Trinity University Press, 2010.

Orr, David W. *Earth in Mind: On Education, Environment, and the Human Prospect*. Washington, DC: Island Press, 1993.

--- "The Four Challenges of Sustainability." *Conservation Biology* 16.6 (2002): 1457-1460.

Petersen-Boring, Wendy. "Western Civilization and Sustainability: Reflections on Cross-Pollinating the Humanities and Environmental Science." *Environmental History* 15.2 (2010): 288-304.

Pomeranz, Kenneth. *The Great Divergence: China, Europe and the Making of the Modern World*. Princeton, NJ: Princeton University Press, 2000.

---. "Putting Modernity in Its Place(s): Reflections on Jack Goody's The Theft of History." *Theory, Culture, Society* 26.7-8 (2009): 32-51.

Prugh, Thomas, R. Costanza, and H. Daly. *The Local Politics of Global Sustainability*. Washington DC: Island Press, 2000.

Richards, John R. *The Unending Frontier: An Environmental History of the Early Modern World*. Berkley, CA: University of California Press, 2005.

Rudd, Gillian. *Greenery: Ecocritical Readings of Late Medieval English Literature*. Manchester, UK: Manchester University Press, 2007.

Russell, Edmund. "Evolutionary History: Prospectus for a New Field." *Environmental History* 8.2 (2003): 204-228.

Sachs, Wolfgang. "A Critique of Ecology." *New Perspectives Quarterly* 6.1 (1989): 16-19.

---. *Global Ecology: A New Area of Political Conflict*. London, UK: Zed Books, 1993.

Schumacher, E.F. *A Guide for the Perplexed*. New York, NY: Harper & Row, 1977.

Sitarz, Daniel, ed. *Agenda 21: The Earth Summit Strategy to Save our Planet*. Boulder, CO: Earth Press, 1994.

White, Lynn. *Machina Ex Deo: Essays in the Dynamism of Western Culture*. Cambridge, MA: MIT Press, 1968.

Williams, Michael. *Deforesting the Earth: From Prehistory to Global Crisis, An Abridgment*. Chicago, IL: University of Chicago Press, 2006.

Williams, Terry Tempest. "Climate Change: What is Required of Us?" *Moral Ground: Ethical Action for a Planet in Peril*. Eds. Kathleen Dean Moore and Michael P. Nelson. San Antonio, TX: Trinity University Press, 2010.

Wilson, E.O. *In Search of Nature*. Washington, DC: Island Press, 1996.

World Conservation Strategy: Living Resource Conversation for Sustainable Development. Gland, Switzerland: International Union for Conservation of Nature and Natural Resources, United Nations Environment Programme, and World Wildlife Fund, 1980.

Justice and Sustainability: Inseparable Imperatives?

Steve Vanderheiden, University of Colorado at Boulder

Abstract: In the study of international environmental policy, concerns for sustainability frequently overlap with those for justice, understood in terms of equitable access to ecological goods and services. Whether in the context of natural resource management or climate change mitigation policy, the effort to maintain goods over time (as sustainability is typically understood) invites questions about access to those goods by persons and groups, largely as justification for sustainability imperatives but occasionally also in tension with them. Similarly, demands for justice or equity in access to environmental goods and services, or in exposure to the environmental hazards that result from their degradation, inevitably lead to questions about how those goods and services might be more sustainably managed. In this chapter, I examine the conceptual and practical overlap between imperatives of environmental justice and sustainability, considering how the study and teaching of each one of these interrelated concepts requires the other, as well as how the pursuit of each is complicated by the demands of the other. In the process, I consider how both have come together in recent international environmental policy efforts.

Steve Vanderheiden is an Associate Professor of Political Science and Environmental Studies at the University of Colorado at Boulder in the USA, and Professorial Fellow with the Centre for Applied Philosophy and Public Ethics (CAPPE) at Charles Sturt University in Australia. In addition to numerous articles and book chapters on political theory and environmental politics, he is the author of *Atmospheric Justice: A Political Theory of Climate Change* (Oxford, 2008), and is currently completing a book entitled *Doing Our Bit: Individual Responsibility for Climate Change*.

The concepts of *justice* and *sustainability* have been linked for nearly as long as the latter has served as the core imperative of environmental protection and natural resource management. Yet, the relationship between the two is neither obvious nor uncontested. As commonly understood, sustainability is a property that is reducible to facts alone, describing current resource use patterns as possible to maintain in perpetuity, relying upon no culturally specific value claims and connoting no imperatives of action. By contrast, justice irreducibly rests upon such value claims and issues imperatives to advance its directions. Even when applied to the same referent—the sustainable or just society, for example—the two concepts appear incommensurable. As Hume's account of the naturalistic fallacy reminds, one cannot validly derive *ought* imperatives from *is* statements. Fixing their gaze upon different features and basing their assessments upon fundamentally distinct analytical frameworks, justice and sustainability have nonetheless been linked in environmental politics in ways that suggest an interdependence that bridges the fact-value divide, and informs our better understanding of each.

Understanding these links can enhance one's appreciation of the challenges that sustainability poses for social and political institutions, along with some core values and interest conflicts in contemporary environmental politics. This chapter will survey some political history and suggest two classroom discussion exercises designed to highlight those links, as they have developed through the international efforts at sustainable development and through the domestic environmental justice movement. In teaching about sustainability, especially political efforts to sustainably manage finite resources, where issues of distribution of those resources take on a practical urgency, its values basis becomes evident. Appreciating this basis, along with its relationship to justice, is crucial to understanding sustainability as an imperative. This chapter endeavors to assist in that understanding.

Dealing with Brundtland: Pretend You Are a Trust-Fund Manager

The document that was first and remains best-known for pairing the imperatives of sustainability with those of justice is the 1987 World Commission on Environment and Development's report *Our Common Future*, popularly known as the Brundtland Report, after its Chair, the former Norwegian Prime Minister Gro Harlem Brundtland. Following a UN mandate to encourage international cooperation in sustainable development, the report aimed to bridge developed country concerns for environmental protection (or *sustainability*) and developing country interests in economic growth that narrows welfare disparities between the global North and South (or *justice*, in an international sense).

While these objectives at the time were widely thought to be in conflict, as growth in the global South was expected to result in higher environmental impacts from increased production and consumption, the report aimed to reconcile those tensions through the idea of sustainable development, which it defined as "development that meets the needs of the present without compromising the ability of future generations to meet their own needs" (43). Here, the ideal of intergenerational justice or equity features prominently, casting sustainability as ensuring that the interests of future persons be given adequate weight in present decisions. At the same time, international or global justice within generations is also emphasized, as the report claims that "overriding priority should be given" to "the essential needs of the world's poor" in development decisions.

In order to emphasize the compatibility of justice and sustainability imperatives, the report calls attention to several ways in which poverty and environmental degradation are mutually exacerbating. It notes, for example, how poor peasants must rely upon the burning of wood for heat and fuel, speeding deforestation, as well as how the impacts of pollution and resource depletion often disproportionately harm the poor. Besides poverty itself, political inequality is also identified as a significant causal variable in environmental degradation:

> An industry may get away with unacceptable levels or air and water pollution because the people who bear the brunt of it are poor and unable to complain effectively. A forest may be destroyed by excessive felling because the people living there have no alternatives or because timber contractors generally have more influence than forest dwellers. (WCED 46)

In order to adequately address global poverty, the report suggests, development efforts must pay attention to environmental issues, or risk worsening the conditions of the world's least advantaged. And in order to adequately protect the environment, the report simultaneously suggests, poverty must be regarded as a leading environmental threat.

Rather than viewing development as inherently unsustainable, as environmentalists from the global North tended to do, or regarding environmentalism as inherently elitist, as anti-poverty activists from the global South commonly assumed, the report aimed to provide both with common cause in sustainable development. The vision it developed was one in which sustainable development becomes the core imperative of both environmental and justice movements, refocusing the development community on environmental issues and the environmental community on ones concerning anti-poverty efforts and political empowerment. For many, this represented an attractive solution to the North-South conflicts that had divided both constituencies.

Not everyone was convinced by the Brundtland Report's effort to reconcile these two imperatives, however. Critics noted that the report called for a five- to ten-fold increase in consumption levels for the world's poor, suggesting that the commission had jettisoned the concern with ecological limits that define sustainability in its effort to appeal to anti-poverty advocates (Daly). While not disputing that some forms of development could be sustainable, other critics note that the idea of sustainable development has become an empty concept since the Brundtland Report coined it, pointing out that it is now frequently used by corporations and other development interests as a greenwashing tool for unsustainable programs which have done as little to reduce poverty as they have to prevent pollution or resource depletion. Nonetheless, the report's influence on thinking about the relationships between environment and development, both inside and outside of the academy, has been profound. No longer can efforts at sustainable resource management be seen as categorically distinct from issues of social justice and, indeed, sustainability itself is now seen as entailing core commitments to intergenerational justice and, to a lesser but still important extent, greater global equity.

In teaching about sustainability, the role that justice or equity issues play in defining and constraining the concept can be illuminated partly by examining the political context and text of the Brundtland Report, which, as noted above, emphasizes links between them for both political and conceptual purposes, but also through several other exercises that challenge students to consider the various ways in which these imperatives interact. For example, the philosopher Bryan Norton suggests the metaphor of a trust fund manager as an illustration of how sustainability demands concern with equity along two dimensions (140-41).

Charged with managing the fund so that its principal is not drawn down and thus might be available in perpetuity, while also disbursing the proceeds from its interest among competing trustees within a generational cohort, the manager must balance the interests of whole generational cohorts, while also attending to equity issues within each. The manager must make some difficult decisions in allocating current funds, as each trustee surely prefers more than they would receive under a fair allocation, and indeed often believes that they deserve more than can be equitably given them. Of course, this task would be easier if the manager would dip into the fund's principal, rather than relying upon its interest, as whole generations, like each of their members, would prefer to have (and often come to think that they deserve) more than others. But failing to manage the fund sustainably would only ease the difficulty of ensuring equity within a generation of trustees at the cost of inequity among generations of them.

I encourage my politics and environmental studies students to consider this thought experiment as a model of the dynamic between these two equity dimensions of sustainable resource management by having them role play. Some are charged with the fund's management and others make competing claims on it at any given time and across different points in time. Finite resources in an ecologically limited world, combined with practically unlimited wants and rising populations, place stress on the environment and its capacity to yield the resources that serve human welfare.

Concerns for equity within a single generation thus complicate efforts to ensure sustainability: while it is tempting to promote greater equity by simply increasing the size of the pie to be distributed, this is no more a tenable solution for many environmental policy problems than it is for the fund manager, who must obey a constraint on how much of the resources held in trust can be spent in a given time period. Students may adopt one or more distributive principles as defining equity in the fund manager experiment—that all receive equal resources, that those accustomed to consuming more should continue to get more, that more should go to those of greater merit or needs, and so on—but the equitable solution is likely to be the one that most can recognize and support as such, even if they might prefer some inequitable outcome that benefits them personally. However students precisely define it through this exercise, equity offers itself not only as the most fair and acceptable means of sharing scarce resources, but also offers the most compelling account of sustainability imperatives. As the Brundtland Report emphasizes, it involves the effort to balance the needs of the present with those of the future, attending to both at once and seeking the fairest allocation of resources within as well as between generations.

Having considered this more abstract thought experiment, I then encourage students to consider more realistic practical issues affecting intergenerational equity, which is constitutive of the imperative of sustainability, rather than merely being instrumental in bringing it to fruition. While in the simpler experiment our fund manager might decide to allocate only each year's interest on the trust, thereby preserving the principal, interest rate fluctuations could make for widely variable annual yields (as with ecological productivity), which can make it difficult for trustees to form expectations about how much they might receive in upcoming years and thus make longer-term plans.

Cycles of boom and bust can led to profligate waste in good years and hardship in bad ones, as with real-world ecosystem services. With the benefit of long-term job security in her position, which is typically unavailable to elected officials on shorter terms in office (with electoral incentives that discourage deferred gratification), the manager might elect instead to disburse funds on five or ten-year rolling average rates of return, saving some surplus interest in up years and spending it in down ones. Some students may also predict near-term or further future windfalls on the investment, as with predictions that future technologies will make resources much more efficient to use in the future, perhaps as part of an argument for using more of those resources now, where it takes more of a given resource to produce some comparable amount of welfare. Issues also arise from population growth, if the children of current trustees will come to have claims on that fund in the future, and these can likewise be teased out through the fund manager metaphor.

This kind of thought experiment readily lends itself to classroom discussion, as students ponder the challenges faced by the fund manager and consider whether the metaphor applies to issues in sustainable resource management. Its application to sustainable development can be teased out if students think about how to manage natural and economic resources that might be used to promote development, with the goal of greater equity in life chances among members of this generation and the next. Although the relationship between national resource wealth and political development is complicated, students might be encouraged to think of the managerial responsibilities in terms of the captain of a lifeboat—as with past comparisons between sustainable resource management and allocation and command of "spaceship earth"—who can take on additional passengers, saving them through fairer allocation of scarce resources, without jeopardizing those already aboard in the process. The poor could more easily be lifted out of poverty by turning more land and renewable resources over to agriculture and industry, or by exploiting more nonrenewable mineral resources, as this would narrow existing gaps between the global rich and poor by raising the position of the latter. While such a development strategy would likely meet less political resistance among developed states than would calls for global redistribution of access to a fixed stock of resources, it would also be less sustainable.

Instructors might draw further parallels between the fund manager metaphor and the task of the Bruntland Commission in international politics: perhaps the manager is employed by and requires the consent of the more affluent trustees in any plan to increase the shares paid out to the poorest ones, and cannot afford to alienate the former while seeking a proposal that could also be accepted by the latter. Gro Harlem Brundtland herself was put in a difficult spot when asked to lead the World Commission on Environment and Development, tasked with developing consensus between the global North and South on imperatives of development and environmental protection that at the time were thought to be at odds. Students could be asked to consider why the former Prime Minister of an affluent and oil-rich Scandinavian state was chosen by the UN Secretary General for a role on an advisory commission for the development of poor and typically resource-poor states, and to consider what constraints she faced in crafting the report given the various constituencies that she was required to serve. Finally, they might be urged to consider the role of future trustees in the politics of sustainable development, given that their consent cannot be meaningfully given or practically sought, leaving their interests least well protected of all in this negotiating process.

A Historical Approach to Teaching Bullard: How EJ Became Intertwined with Sustainability

As critics have noted, tensions remain between the ideals of justice and sustainability. These can also be illustrated through the presentation of some political history, combined with an exercise that requires students to think through those tensions. The political history is of the U.S. environmental justice (or EJ) movement, which has, for the past two decades, noted the causal links between race, class, and environmental vulnerability. Accounts of the early movement are widely available and worth teaching for a variety of reasons, but here the focus is on the developing relationship between the two imperatives that movement leaders came over time to embrace as constitutive of the demand for environmental justice. When first paired through early EJ campaigns, justice and the environment enjoyed a marriage of convenience, with each bringing some instrumental political resources to the other but without a coherent vision of how mutually-reinforcing the two could be. Over time, the framing of environmental campaigns in justice terms, along with a focus on environmental issues in social justice efforts, yielded a far more sophisticated understanding of the relationship between equity and sustainability than either could suggest on their own. The presentation of this history can assist students in appreciating the development of its key ideas.

The justice-based analyses of environmental problems that spawned the movement originated in a campaign to keep a toxic waste facility from being located in the middle-class African American Houston neighborhood that was home to sociologist Robert Bullard, whose wife was organizing the community against the site. Their legal strategy was to challenge the decision on Fourteenth Amendment equal protection grounds. For this case, Bullard began what would become the first scholarly EJ study, documenting patterns of disproportionate race and class impacts of exposure to toxins, hoping to demonstrate statistically that Houston was unequally protecting its citizens through its pattern of past site selection. Their goal was not to promote either equity or sustainability in a broad sense. Had they prevailed in their legal challenge, the production of hazardous waste near Houston would have been unaffected, and its risks would likely have been displaced onto less powerful and more vulnerable others.

Although this legal strategy was unsuccessful—the court required proof of intent to discriminate on racial grounds, which is nearly impossible to document, rather than merely patterns of discrimination, which Bullard's research clearly demonstrated—its core claim extended the ideal of equity to exposure to environmental hazards. The justice claim, which made this an EJ campaign rather than a NIMBY[1] effort, asserted that no one should be made more vulnerable to environmental harm on account of their race; that the hazards that society produces through polluting processes ought to be more equitably distributed among persons and groups within society. Framing the disproportionate exposure of poor communities of color to environmental hazards as unjust and an illegal form of discrimination, the domestic EJ movement went on to embrace civil rights legal strategies and political tactics in other campaigns. Each time, it made the ideal of equity its centerpiece, condemning as unjust the environmental policy decisions that proposed disparate race and class impact.

While clearly seminal in what would become the domestic EJ movement, one aspect of this early claim about environmental justice is somewhat troubling from the perspective of sustainability. More equitable exposure to the environmental hazards that a society produces may solve the justice problem, as defined here, but does little to minimize the environmental problem to which Bullard was originally opposed in a local sense, and would later oppose in a more universal sense. Successful resistance to locating a toxic waste facility in any one neighborhood might result in the facility being moved to a more politically unempowered one, following the path of least resistance. So long as the EJ movement retained this "not in my backyard" strategy and vision, its vision of justice would not be a sustainable one. But the domestic EJ movement did not retain this myopic vision, evolving instead into a full-fledged environmental movement, opposing the creation of toxic wastes as well as inequitable exposure to its hazards. As Bullard famously recounted, the original aim of "not in my backyard" was transformed through EJ campaigns into one of "not in anyone's backyard," working to reduce the creation of toxic wastes and improve standards for their storage rather than redirecting the location of their disposal (Agyeman, Evans, and Bullard, Ch. 1). In so doing, the movement's vision of justice became attached to a broader vision of sustainability.

What can this historical anecdote offer to the teaching of sustainability? Its lessons are several, and can be drawn out through studies of EJ movement history as well as first person accounts by leaders like Bullard. First, it shows how, where issues of distribution occur in environmental policy-making, concerns for justice often come to require some commitment to sustainability, once the root causes of the injustice are fully explored. Avoiding exposure to environmental hazards is prudent, but neither just nor sustainable in itself. The same concern can become a justice campaign by adopting a more critical perspective, as the EJ movement did, with aims to prevent such hazards from exacerbating existing disadvantages, broadening its purview from mere prudential concern with one's own welfare to a more enlightened and altruistic regard for social justice. But even a justice-based analysis can be shortsighted unless it also aims to prevent environmental hazards from endangering anyone, not simply distributing vulnerability more widely, as the movement also did. Having a vision for society that is both sustainable and just—in this case, of a world in which social processes do not produce waste products that would subject innocent victims to pollution-related illness or death—can avoid shortcomings associated with only one of these ideals, speeding the evolution of that vision into a genuinely useful set of social norms, upon which defensible law and policy might be constructed.

Second, it shows how a powerful new idea can be developed and transmitted from a more narrowly focused setting into broader and related settings, when it comes to be viewed as rectifying an error or omission in an existing idea. One impact of the past two decades of EJ campaigns is that mainstream environmental groups now take positions on and devote resources to EJ issues, having recognized their prior failure to acknowledge justice issues in relevant environmental policy areas. The Sierra Club, for example, has gone from taking anti-immigration positions that antagonize social justice goals to running a program on "Environmental Justice and Community Partnerships," with the stated mission: "To discuss and explore the linkages between environmental quality and social justice, and to promote dialogue, increased understanding and appropriate action." Its interest in justice issues may be partly strategic, aiming to build coalitions between mainstream environmentalists and EJ constituencies, and partly group image maintenance, as the charge of elitism made against the environmental movement hindered its efficacy. It may also be partly the result of the new critical lens that EJ movements have provided for the analysis of environmental threats. This lens, first applied by the domestic movement to toxic waste exposure, has now been applied to a variety of other issues, including access to goods, like food, water, and green space, as well as exposure to hazards. It has also become global in scope, emerging as the dominant discourse in campaigns for "climate justice" in the development of international climate change policy.

Sustainability as Value-Laden: Teaching Ecological Footprint Effectively

Justice and sustainability thus converge within EJ campaigns and theories, where the concern for one is now taken to require a concern for the other, but how can this convergence inform the teaching of sustainability? Sustainability is sometimes cast as a descriptive but value-free tool, and therefore one that need not be explored in its normative foundations or contested in its prescriptions. But sustainability is an inherently value-laden concept, as applied to the way that societies manage their environments and resources, and must be viewed as such, if it is to be properly understood. Generically, the idea of sustaining a thing is purely descriptive, passing no judgment on what should be done, with its value wholly dependent upon the thing to be sustained. Even a sustainable society might be regarded in this way, as sustaining an evil society cannot be a good thing, although it would be better if the evil society was an *environmentally* sustainable one. Herein lies the source if its value. Without committing the naturalistic fallacy, deriving an *ought* prescription from an *is* description, and without erroneously vesting nature with some metaphysically dubious value, environmental sustainability acquires value by virtue of its essential connection to the ongoing enjoyment of good lives, which are themselves valuable. Regardless of whether or not a thing is good and should be sustained over time, *environmental* sustainability is inherently good for, without it, opportunities for good lives diminish, and probabilities of indubitably bad things (famine-related suffering, resource conflicts, etc.) increase.

When Mathis Wackernagel and William Rees began touting their innovative concept of the *ecological footprint* as a yardstick for measuring sustainability, they, too, insisted that the manner in which footprints were calculated and presented was purely descriptive, and did not smuggle in any claims about values that would need to be defended as such. Since then, they have softened their denial of the value-laden nature of footprints, drawing several policy prescriptions from them in their seminal *Our Ecological Footprint*. Most students probably have some familiarity with the idea of an ecological footprint—which measures the demand for ecological goods and services that persons or groups create through their consumption patterns, usually in terms of the ecologically productive land that comprises their "footprint" on the planet—or one of its derivative concepts, like water or carbon footprints, but few have likely considered how the ecological footprint as a measurement tool can connect imperatives of justice and sustainability. Presenting footprint data in certain ways can make these connections more explicit, thereby enhancing the role that justice or equity concerns play in holistic analyses, like footprint calculating.

Students might be encouraged to find one of the several footprint calculators that are readily available on the Internet, and to critically explore it. Besides calculating their own footprints, they might seek information about what in their footprint is being measured and what is not, and see how their footprint can go up or down by changing their answers to the various survey questions. They might also consider how value questions arise from the way that data are presented, critically reflecting upon whether some ways of presenting data are more objective or complete than others, or what other data would they need to reach defensible judgments about what sustainability requires. Some calculators, for example, compare individual footprints to averages, which convey mild normative content about how one's individual environmental impacts compare to compatriots'. Averages comparing footprints of Americans to residents of other countries, developed and developing, convey still more, as expected gaps (e.g. between the U.S. and India) are wider than many expect, and unexpected gaps (e.g. between the U.S. and France) are significant. But none of this comparative data yet conveys any prescriptive content about sustainability: merely knowing that my footprint is fifteen times that of the average Indian does not, in itself, tell me that it is unsustainable, or indicate any connection that my large footprint has with the smaller ones I compare it to. And while it may document significant inequity in access to ecological goods and services, it offers little reason for finding these to be unjust.

More revealing are calculators that also present data about the ecological capacity of various regions or the whole planet. Learning that, for example, the average American uses 5.1 hectares of ecologically productive land to support their consumption patterns, whereas the average Indian uses only 0.38 hectares, helps students note a wide disparity and invites consideration of the social and cultural drivers of ecological demand that partly account for it (Wackernagel and Rees).[1] But value judgments begin to emerge when students learn that there are only 1.3 hectares of such land available for each living person, and that we need to devote over 80 percent of the earth's biologically productive land to supporting human consumption. My footprint is four times what is sustainable if everyone consumed at the same rate. So where does this leave everyone else, and indeed the planet? Learning that average footprints are 1.5 hectares—more than 10 percent higher than sustainable footprints—portents future harm resulting from unsustainable global consumption patterns, raising issues of intergenerational justice (Vanderheiden). More striking are the international implications of data presented with this context. Our planet has a finite capacity to support life, and footprint data suggests the need to find more equitable ways to share the resources that we have, within and between generations. Getting average footprints down to 1.3 hectares, as is required by the imperative of sustainability, presents a monumental challenge, especially given the earth's growing human population and shrinking ecological capacity. As critics of the Brundtland Report and climate justice advocates have argued, greater equity within the constraints of sustainability, rather than growth itself, offers the necessary conditions for a just and sustainable world, where humanity as a whole lives within its ecological means, and the planet's resources are more fairly shared.

Students might be challenged to come up with principles for allocating the planet's ecological capacity among its various claimants, defending their decisions in terms of values that others could accept. If current average footprints exceed what is sustainable, how can the resulting degradation of ecological capacity be justified to future generations? How might I defend my footprint of 5.1 to an Indian whose footprint is 0.38, but who aspires to many of the benefits of development that make mine so much bigger? Could I claim to be *entitled* to this much, if it entails that many others have footprints that remain at or below minimal subsistence levels indefinitely, with no hope for a better life for themselves or their children? Perhaps most illuminating and explicitly prescriptive are the footprint calculators that measure impacts in terms of the number of earths that would be required if all consumed at the same rate we do.[3] Implicitly importing ideals of equity into its presentation of data, my footprint of four earths immediately raises the obvious point that we have only one planet, and that anyone consuming over the sustainable average necessarily affects others, whether by leaving much less than a whole earth for contemporary others to consume or by degrading the planet's ecological capacity through overconsumption. Like the fund manager metaphor, exploring ecological footprint calculators and using footprint data to set up an exercise in sustainable resource management issues can reveal the justice or equity issues embedded in sustainability imperatives, challenging students: first, to acknowledge the role that they play, and then to try to draft and apply defensible principles of justice for sustainable resource allocation decisions.

The point of the thought experiment is not necessarily to find a solution to the conflict over scarce ecological resources, but rather to highlight the role that equity plays in defining the terms of that conflict. Given ecological limits, and assuming constant population and the absence of technological innovations that make current living standards possible at a quarter of their current ecological cost, problems of equity emerge as soon as students contemplate potential paths to sustainability. Failing to live within our ecological means is itself an equity problem, since unsustainable consumption patterns leave future persons worse off, but there are no paths to sustainability within our generation that don't raise obvious equity objections as well, except for the significant contraction of ecological demand. Indeed, equity issues are inextricably related to sustainability imperatives, as should now be evident. While ostensibly reducible to facts alone, rather than to values, sustainability imposes constraints on the efficacy and durability of efforts to pursue or maintain social values like justice. What good is the establishment of a just society if it is also unsustainable, imposing costs onto others beyond its boundaries and condemning its own citizens to a future of increasing scarcity-related insecurity? Indeed, why protect the human environment for the ostensible benefit of vulnerable others, only to treat them unjustly in the process? Pragmatically, how can environmentalists hope to persuade others that they really care about environmental threats to the well-being of the poor and vulnerable, while callously ignoring other kinds of threats to that same well-being, or resisting the imperative to make the fair treatment of all central to everything that we do? Appreciation of the links between justice and sustainability, brought out through such exercises and discussion, should help students to better understand both concepts in their separate contexts, but more importantly as linked together.

Notes

1. Acronym for "not in my backyard."
2. These are 1995 data, and national average footprints have changed significantly since then, but are presented here because they can be found in Wackernagel and Rees (1996), and illustrate a relationship between equity and sustainability that has not changed.
3. Redefining Progress uses this data presentation format in their footprint calculator (http://myfootprint.org).

Works Cited

Agyeman, Julian, Robert Evans, and Robert D. Bullard, eds. *Just Sustainabilities: Development in an Unequal World*. New York, NY: Earthscan Publications, 2003.

Daly, Herman E. "Sustainable Growth: An Impossibility Theorem." *Valuing the Earth: Economics, Ecology, Ethics*. Eds. Herman Daly and Kenneth N. Townsend. Cambridge, MA: MIT Press, 1993. 267-73.

Norton, Bryan. "Environmental Ethics and Weak Anthropocentrism." *Environmental Ethics* 6.2 (1998): 131-48.

Vanderheiden, Steve. "Two Conceptions of Sustainability." *Political Studies* 56.2 (2008): 435-55.

Wackernagel, Mathis, and William Rees. *Our Ecological Footprint: Reducing Human Impact on the Earth*. Gabriola Island, BC: New Society Publishers, 1996.

World Commission on Environment and Development (WCED). *Our Common Future*. New York: Oxford University Press, 1987.

Building a Pedagogical Toolbox:
The Nuts and Bolts of Infusing Sustainability into Humanities and Social Sciences Courses

Sharon M. Meagher, University of Scranton

Abstract: While the call for curricular attention to sustainability has been made often and widely, there exist real obstacles to infusing sustainability issues across the curriculum. Much of the literature on infusing sustainability into the curriculum highlights key obstacles (see, e.g., Pesonen 2003; Cullingford 2004; Dawe, Jucker and Martin 2005), but overlooks one that merits particular attention; namely, the fact that faculty often simply do not know how to infuse sustainability issues into their courses. By this, I mean that faculty members often lack the pedagogical tools and strategies necessary to incorporate sustainability into their courses successfully. In this paper, I discuss how the University of Scranton has successfully addressed this obstacle by developing and presenting a "typology" of pedagogical strategies that faculty have used to infuse sustainability into a wide range of social science and humanities courses. This typology serves as a model that others can use to find and adapt strategies that will work for them.

Sharon M. Meagher, Ph.D., is Professor of Philosophy and Chair of the Department of Latin American Studies and Women's Studies at the University of Scranton. Meagher also serves as the co-facilitator of the University's sustainability curriculum workshops. Meagher's research and teaching interests focus on urban issues and women and development in the global South. She is the co-founder and chair of the Public Philosophy Network, an organization that fosters and supports publicly engaged social action and research projects that involve collaboration between philosophers and various public partners. Meagher's publications include *Philosophy and the City: Classic to Contemporary Writings* (SUNY Press, 2008) and *Philosophical Streetwalking* (SUNY Press, forthcoming).

Following quickly on the heels of Northern Arizona's Ponderosa Project and Emory University's Piedmont Project,[1] the University of Scranton was one of the first institutions to develop an annual faculty development initiative aimed at infusing sustainability into the curriculum. We began the initiative in 2005 by inviting the Piedmont Project's co-facilitator Peggy Barlett to co-lead a workshop on our campus with my colleague, green chemistry expert Michael Cann. I participated in that workshop and became Mike Cann's co-facilitator the following year. Over the years, we have developed and expanded the sustainability workshop and made it our own. The features that are most unique to our workshop include the use of short, daily online readings for eight days prior to our first meeting, and follow-up reports from participants the following year. Faculty participants explain how they infused sustainability into one or more of their courses during the academic year, highlighting what worked, what did not, and what they plan to do in the future. These presentations encourage faculty to follow-through and make curricular changes and also provide pedagogical models that faculty in the current workshop might imitate.

To insure that the latter is possible, I have listened to my colleagues' presentations over the years and developed a "toolbox," or typology, of pedagogical strategies that they have utilized to successfully infuse sustainability into their courses. We have found this to be the missing piece of the puzzle in most sustainability curriculum initiatives. While some time is rightly spent on sustainability concepts and the formation of course goals and objectives, too little attention is paid to the most obvious issue—just how do instructors make changes to their courses without sacrificing existing content that they deem important? In this essay, I offer my most recent typology, drawing on examples from my colleagues' courses in the humanities and social sciences. The toolbox was built from an analysis of infused courses covering the entire scope of disciplinary and interdisciplinary courses offered at most universities, and thus might be shared profitably with colleagues in other disciplines.

Participant evaluations of our workshops consistently have shown that the key to most faculty members' success in infusing sustainability into their courses has been this workshop component. Faculty members learn by listening to their colleagues' presentations, followed by an analysis and discussion of them, using the framework of the pedagogical typology that I have developed. The typology has expanded over the years as my colleagues find new and inventive ways to infuse sustainability into their courses.

In the eight years that I have been involved with the project of infusing sustainability into the curriculum, much has changed. In the early years, we often assumed that faculty members might be resistant to sustainability concepts and/or skeptical about the need to infuse sustainability into the curriculum. We also worked with faculty members who had little or no knowledge about sustainability but were interested in learning more. We always have taken a "just in time" strategy, offering a faculty development workshop as a voluntary opportunity for faculty who at the time have some interest. We also pay a stipend to communicate that the university values this effort. Some eight years later, we continue to find faculty members interested in participating in the workshop, but now they are much more likely to enter the workshop with some substantive knowledge about sustainability and some passion for infusing sustainability into the curriculum.

While faculty attitudes and knowledge have changed over time, the challenges to infusing sustainability into the curriculum persist. A growing number of faculty members want to incorporate sustainability into the curriculum, but most still lack the pedagogical strategies and tools that they need to be able to do so effectively. There are a growing number of resources for faculty in terms of discipline-specific content that instructors might inject into their courses, including a massive syllabi repository.[2] But few instructors are interested in substituting someone else's syllabus for one that they may have spent years developing themselves; most want to figure out ways to incorporate sustainability into their own course plan.

The challenges to infusing sustainability into courses are many and varied, depending on the discipline and the instructor's teaching methods. Increasingly, outside accreditation bodies dictate course content in ways that appear to leave little room for new topics. While outside accrediting standards are generally not an issue in the humanities and social sciences, those of us who teach in those disciplines face other constrictions. Some courses are taught from a common department syllabus and most social science and humanities courses must meet general education or other curricular mandates that seem to leave little room to maneuver. A combination of pressures external to the course and internal to the demands of the instructor and discipline challenge most instructors to find room to incorporate sustainability into their courses. Given these obstacles, workshops that aim to infuse sustainability into the curriculum must provide instructors with pedagogical tools and models.

There is a growing literature that addresses sustainability literacy components as well as corresponding learning goals and objectives—both across the academy and in specific disciplines. Several other chapters in this book contribute to that cause. A few recent papers have argued for the use of more participatory pedagogies when teaching about sustainability.[3] Our instructors often note that sustainability issues engender more class-based discussion and we have encouraged faculty members to utilize more participatory pedagogies. But here I wish to focus on what we see as the gap in the literature on infusing sustainability into the curriculum—the lack of concrete discussion of practical pedagogical strategies, tools, and techniques needed if faculty members are to incorporate sustainability into their courses.

My primary contribution to the discussion has been to categorize different types of strategies into a typology that is useful to other faculty members. The presentation and discussion of the typology is but one component of the workshop. It is important for faculty development workshops to facilitate discussion about sustainability and related concepts, with the goal of developing some larger objectives and goals for infusing sustainability into the curriculum. The background readings and much of the presentations and discussions in our own workshop focus on these goals. The current typology includes fourteen strategies that may be utilized alone or in combination. We continue to encourage creativity and the development of new pedagogical strategies, so the typology may expand in coming years.

Figure 1 summarizes the typology; a narrative explanation of each pedagogical strategy illustrated by instructors' examples (with the discipline identified in parentheses) follows in the subsections below. Near the top of Figure 1 are those pedagogical strategies that are most difficult to implement but richest in sustainability content; near the bottom of the pyramid are strategies that all instructors can easily incorporate. However, those strategies near the base of the pyramid should *not* be construed as the "foundation" for those at the top. Rather, they are strategies that all instructors, minimally, can and should include in any and all of the courses that they teach. The strategies listed at or near the top are those most likely to have a wider impact, reaching out to create institutional change. Even smaller changes can have a big impact, cumulatively, as students learn about sustainability in a wide range of courses over time. In any given instructor's approach or university, there is often movement between the strategies listed; instructors may (and often do) combine any number of the pedagogical strategies listed, sometimes within a single course. And there is room within the college or university for courses that incorporate different combinations of strategies.[4]

Pedagogical Strategies for Infusing Sustainability into Courses

Figure 1. Typology of Pedagogical Strategies for Infusing Sustainability into Courses

Design new courses

While our main goal has been to infuse sustainability into the existing curriculum, participation in the workshop has motivated some faculty members to develop new courses as they identify gaps in existing curricular offerings. The development of new courses clearly allows for the most leeway in terms of pedagogical strategy, as faculty members are not restrained by existing course content and requirements. Janice Voltzow (Biology and Latin American Studies), for example, participated in the sustainability workshop so that she could develop a course that integrated her interests in biology and Latin American studies, developing a new course called "Environmental Issues in Latin America." Sustainability tied the two interests together. David Dzurec (History) created a new course on environmental history, although he began his sustainability infusion efforts by integrating environmental issues into his general education course on American history. Jessica Nolan (Psychology) teaches a new course on environmental and conservation psychology, but she also integrates sustainability into most all of her other courses. New courses can and do add to our curricular efforts, yet we do not expect that this can or should become the predominant strategy. Most of the new courses fulfill general education requirements and are available to all students.

(Re)cast central questions of the course in terms of sustainability

In some courses, "sustainability" can become a central focus or concern of an existing course. For example, I regularly teach a course called "Philosophy and the City," in which we explore fundamental questions regarding cities and citizenship from the perspective of key figures in the history of Western philosophy. Before my participation in the sustainability workshop, the central question that guided the course was "what is the good city?" For philosophers, answers to that question necessitate that one consider environmental, political, and social dimensions of city life. Yet I found that students did not grasp the concepts of "the good life" and "the good city." Recasting the course in terms of sustainability and shifting the central question from "what is the good city?" to "what is the sustainable city?" enabled students to connect contemporary concepts and vocabulary to key ideas in the Western philosophical tradition. Moreover, it allowed them to trace philosophers' relative attention or inattention to environmental issues, and also to understand the interdependence between social and economic dimensions of sustainability, especially as they bear on urban life.[5] Lastly, a philosophical examination of sustainability and the city equips students to critically assess the current use of the term "sustainability," providing philosophical and historical critical contexts (Palmer).

Another example in which the main question of the course was recast in terms of sustainability is a senior capstone course taught by my colleague Jan Kelly (Communications). Historically, students who enrolled in the annual department capstone course were free to choose any project they wished, but since her participation in the sustainability workshop, Kelly has focused the annual theme of the course on sustainability and civic engagement. Kelly has found that the theme has helped students find capstone projects that they are passionate about. Student evaluations of the course have skyrocketed since she made the change.

Introduce curricular module(s) or units

In some cases, instructors have chosen to re-focus or add one unit of the course that is specifically devoted to sustainability issues. In a course on nonfiction writing, for example, Joseph Kraus (English) decided to refocus one unit of the course on non-fiction nature writing and its connection to the sustainability movement, beginning with Rachel Carson's *Silent Spring*. In his course, "Catholic Social Thought," Patrick King (Theology) included a two-week curricular module on stewardship that had been developed by Catholic Relief Services' Global Solidarity Network Study E-broad Program. King also utilized other pedagogies, including the use of guest speakers, to integrate the unit seamlessly into his course.

Thread questions/issues throughout

Sometimes it is more effective to raise questions concerning sustainability throughout the course rather than appear to "ghettoize" the issues as if they are unconnected to other things. In a course entitled "White Color Crime," David Friedrichs (Sociology and Criminology) has woven in environmental concerns throughout the course, asking questions like whether business and other leaders who are responsible for ecological devastation should be understood as white collar criminals. Daniel Haggerty, Matthew Meyer, Christina Gschwandtner, and Ileana Szymanski (Philosophy) ask their students enrolled in Ethics to apply each of the major moral theoretical traditions that they study (utilitarianism, virtue theory, and Kantian deontology) to sustainability concerns and assess each tradition critically in light of how well or poorly the tradition attends to sustainability issues. For example, Kantian approaches to ethics tend to be strong at evaluating interpersonal relations, but quite weak at grasping moral problems involving the environment. Sustainability, therefore, provides a unifying theme for the course, allowing students to make connections between course units and encouraging them to compare and contrast traditions. Sustainability also allows students to connect Western moral reasoning to issues of contemporary and urgent concern.

Add or refocus service or experiential learning projects

In courses that include service or experiential learning projects, it is often possible to refocus those projects so that they address sustainability issues. In several cases, the University of Scranton campus also served as the experiential learning site so that the course has a direct impact on students and employees. Jessica Nolan (Psychology) teaches a Conservation Psychology course in which students assessed the impact of Earth Week and the campus farmer's market on student behaviors; they develop new research-based service learning projects each time the course is taught. Mary Beth Holmes (Communications) now encourages her Video Production students to find campus-based "clients" who require educational videos on sustainability, which in one case resulted in a particularly fruitful partnership with the campus librarians to reduce student printing waste. For their final project in their senior communications capstone course, students of Jan Kelly (Communications) implemented an off-campus housing recycling program that received regional news attention (O'Malley). The University also organizes an annual Earth Day fair that features course-based student projects led by faculty who participated in the sustainability workshops.

The Latin American Studies and Women's Studies programs developed new short-term study abroad courses and have increasingly focused them on sustainability. In the course "Women and Development in Latin America (Women's Studies and Latin American Studies), students travel to rural Puebla, Mexico to work with indigenous women's cooperatives in an area threatened by deforestation and loss of language and cultural traditions. The co-op has developed several projects that are starting to show results in reversing some of the threats, including an eco-tourism, educational youth hostel (where we stay) and a wood-saving stove construction project. Our students learn to build the stoves, but also learn why they are so important for the sustainability of the Totonac indigenous culture and environment. Of course, the ecological footprint of international air travel is quite large, and we discuss this issue, too, weighing and balancing those costs against the benefits of the travel for both the Totonac people and our students.

Introduce sustainability as parts of lectures

Faculty members teaching sequenced courses with pre-determined content often found that they are, nevertheless, able to include sustainability concerns by integrating the issues into parts of lectures throughout the course. Many have found that doing so has made it easier for students to make connections between sections of courses that otherwise seemed unconnected, since the theme of sustainability was introduced in various units. In their courses on the bible, for example, Will Cohen and Brigid Frein (Theology) periodically raise questions about biblical interpretation, pointing out ways that various biblical quotations have been misused to defend a doctrine of human dominion over the earth. David Dzurec and Katy Meier (History) have developed specific questions about various sustainability concerns for their lectures in a two semester course, "The History of the United States," helping students understand the relationship of social, environmental, and cultural factors on various historical movements and events. For example, particular attention is paid to the environmental impacts of war, and well as the environmental impacts of colonialism and Westward expansionism. The instructors also trace the history of the environmental and sustainability movements in the U.S.

Add some directed lectures or lessons

Another technique (again, used most often by those teaching courses or sections of courses with pre-determined content) is to add a few lectures on sustainability throughout the course, as they are relevant and connected to the material at hand. Richard Larsen's (Theater) set design work focuses on the use of sustainable design and building practices; he has integrated lectures on such professional practices in his technical theater courses. Joseph Cimini (Criminal Justice and Sociology) includes lectures and workshop sessions on sustainability in his gerontology course, helping students see the connection between sustainability and quality of life as we age.

Add new writing, research or project options

Rather than mandating sustainability as a course topic, some faculty members have success in providing assignment options that focus on sustainability. Susan Méndez (English), for example, offers her introductory writing students the option of writing their essays about sustainability on campus. In advanced courses that require research or projects, some faculty have found it helpful to add sustainability as a new topic on which students are encouraged to work. Ileana Szymanski (Philosophy) teaches a course on philosophy of food, presenting students with numerous opportunities to reflect and write on sustainability issues. Linda Ledford-Miller and Robert Parsons (World Languages and Cultures—Spanish; Latin American Studies) call attention to sustainability issues in Latin America by providing students with an assignment option requiring students to survey resources in the Latin American Network Information Center[6] database and then write and/or present a synopsis of one of the sources. In all cases, the faculty members provide students with sufficient background on sustainability so that they can make informed choices about assignment topics. In this way, all students gain some exposure to sustainability issues. Furthermore, students share their work with the rest of the class, so those who focused on sustainability issues teach the rest of the class something about the topic.

Bring in classroom guests

Mark Murphy, the University of Scranton's Assistant Director of Utilities and Plant Engineer, is the University's sustainability "guru" for the campus physical plant. He always makes a guest presentation at our faculty sustainability workshop, as few know the extent of the University's sustainability efforts on the operations side. Mark also speaks to classes as few students are unaware of the physical plant's sustainability efforts. As workshop facilitators, we help faculty find other appropriate outside persons and resources, and faculty also find their own. Recent courses have featured a wide range of guest speakers who work on issues such as fracking, clean river initiatives, environmental policy, and social sustainability and interdependence.

Add field trips or add site visits

Students cannot grasp the concept of sustainability unless they recognize the importance of place. Field trips and walking tours can literally ground students' appreciation of the local place where they are studying and living. I regularly take students in my first year seminar and upper level "philosophy of the city" course for walking tours of neighborhoods adjacent to the University, highlighting sustainability issues ranging from student garbage production at off-campus housing to recognition of environmental justice issues and who has access to parks and nature.[7] I have also done walking tours for other colleagues' classes in other disciplines, and a walking tour is also part of our sustainability faculty development workshop. Other instructors have included field trips to the local coal mine (for courses ranging from local history to the "Theology of Rest and Work") and to other sites such as sustainable farms.

Focus on professional standards and sustainability

Our faculty members who teach professional and pre-professional courses are finding that increasingly their professional ethical codes now address sustainability issues and thus can be used to introduce students to key concepts. Margarete Zalon (Nursing), in a course on nurses' professional responsibilities, highlights the ANA Code of Ethics for Nurses and its attentiveness to sustainability concerns. As professional organizations integrate sustainability issues into their own ethics standards, it becomes both easy and effective to draw these new standards to the students' attention; moreover, we have educational responsibilities to insure that our students are aware of the most recent standards and codes of professions for which they are preparing. Philosophy professors teaching professional ethics courses also can use these professional codes as resources in their teaching.

Change Classroom and/or Laboratory practices

Faculty members have added new standards and practices for laboratory and classroom use to encourage students to minimize waste disposal. Other faculty members have moved more assignments online and/or moved to administering quizzes and other short assignments on the backs of printed paper and paper scraps. Professors pay attention to whether lights are necessary in the classroom (although most of our buildings now employ automatic light sensors and light harvesting systems).

Develop co-curricular projects in conjunction with courses

Yamile Silva (World Languages and Cultures, Spanish; Latin American Studies) teaches introductory level Spanish language courses that limit the extent to which she can introduce sustainability issues, since the courses are taught exclusively in a language new to students. But she developed an evening film series that highlights sustainability issues in Latin America, introducing students to the culture and geography of the area and raising awareness that sustainability is a global and shared concern. The film series was open to all members of the community.

Through "hidden curriculum"

Changing classroom and/or laboratory practices are specific examples of what more broadly can be called the "hidden curriculum." Peggy Barlett introduced this term to me during her workshop presentation at the University of Scranton in June 2005, and we have made very good use of it in our seminars.[8] "The hidden curriculum" refers to the way we teach our course and the examples we choose to use. In content-focused courses, as well as those that concentrate more on development of skills and research methods, faculty members have a variety of choices in how they conduct their courses and examples to use.

Instructors can raise considerable awareness about sustainability issues by limiting the amount of paper they use, encouraging recycling, and utilizing other sustainable practices in their classes. In addition, instructors can use examples that routinely and matter-of-factly ask students to reflect on issues concerning sustainability. For example, statistics instructors can find data sets linked to numerous sustainability issues for students to use when learning various methods of analysis. Our instructors have been developing cases that pointedly do so in ways that encourages students to think about sustainability. Instructors teaching "Research Methods in Psychological and Behavioral Science" always need problems for their students to research, so they can practice methods that they learn in the class. Dr. Christie Karpiak and Dr. Galen Baril (Psychology) published some of their findings on student attitudes and behaviors towards the environment.

Most all instructors teaching these courses participated in the sustainability workshop and now assign students projects to collect data regarding campus sustainability efforts, developing their research and analytical skills. Thus, by focusing on some courses ignored by most sustainability curriculum initiatives, we have been able to close the loop, and connect our educational commitment to our sustainability commitments regarding our physical plant. Hopkinson, James, and Van Winsom argue that there needs to be better synergy between various institutional operations and sectors. We have found that the social and behavioral sciences can play a strong role by providing behavioral data on issues such as garbage generation by recycling attitudes that drive campus sustainability policy and planning decisions.

By emphasizing the educational value of "the hidden curriculum," we involved faculty members who teach many courses that most institutions would think irrelevant to sustainability education. We have not just included them; we have also made faculty members more aware of the choices they make in classroom management, their own behaviors, and their use of examples and projects.

Conclusions

The complexity of sustainability demands multi- and interdisciplinary approaches, and yet academic institutions still remain organized primarily around individual departments. While this is very much the case at the University of Scranton, our workshops are organized for faculty members in all disciplines. In fact, one of the selling points of the workshops is that faculty members enjoy having the rare opportunity to hear what colleagues in other departments do and to learn from each other. As Chase and Rowland argue, "one way to help faculty move toward sustainability is to provide opportunities for them to step outside the boundaries of their discipline and departments, talk to each other, share ideas and insights, and see themselves as essential participants in a larger project (97)." We have furthermore found that faculty can and do learn pedagogical strategies for infusing sustainability into their courses from colleagues in all disciplines. The workshop also has engendered a number of fruitful interdisciplinary course initiatives, such as a course called "The Physics of Theater" that utilizes sustainability concepts learned from physics to inform lighting and set design.

With a well-structured faculty workshop that values faculty time and expertise, colleges and universities can quickly infuse sustainability into a wide range of courses and have a large impact for a minimum cost. While faculty members are each other's best resources, it is important to focus not only on sustainability issues but also on pedagogical strategies. Many well-meaning and interested faculty members do not know how to weave sustainability into their courses, given the content and other demands placed on them. By hearing from faculty who already had success in doing so, and by providing a typology that summarizes the variety of pedagogical approaches taken by our own faculty, sustainability workshop participants get the support necessary to integrate sustainability issues successfully into their own courses.

Notes

1.   See "The Ponderosa Project: Infusing Sustainability in the Curriculum," by Geoffrey Chase and Paul Rowland, pp. 92, 97.
2.   The American Association of Sustainability in Higher Education (AASHE) 2005-12 provides numerous examples of courses and sample syllabi on its website at: http://www.aashe.org/resources/curriculum-resources/, but access to many of those databases is restricted to individuals whose institutions are AASHE members. The Disciplinary Associations Network for Sustainability (DANS) http://dans.aashe.org/content/resources provides a database of syllabi and resources organized by discipline and is open to all.
3.   See chapter three of Cotton and Winter's "'It's Not Just Bits of Paper and Light Bulbs:' A Review of Sustainability Pedagogies and their Potential for Use in Higher Education."
4.   Thanks to Wendy Petersen Boring for both suggesting the inclusion of a figure or table and also engaging in a conversation about the graphic's strengths and limits; our exchange is included in my discussion of the figure here.
5.   See Sharon M. Meagher, ed. *Philosophy and the City: Classic to Contemporary Writings*. Albany, NY: State University of New York Press, 2008.
6.   Latin American Information Network Center database. http://lanic.utexas.edu. Last accessed 11 Nov. 2012.
7.   Guidelines for conducting walking tours can be found at my website: http://philosophyandthecity.org/coursematerials/walkingtours.html(accessed 1/29/13).
8.   See also Cotton and Winter, Box 3.2.

Works Cited

Chase, Geoffrey W., and Paul Rowland. "The Ponderosa Project: Infusing Sustainability in the Curriculum." *Sustainability on Campus: Stories and Strategies for Change*. Eds. Peggy F. Barlett and Geoffrey W. Chase. Cambridge, MA: MIT Press, 2004. Print.

Cotton, Debby, and Jennie Winter. "'It's Not Just Bits of Paper and Light Bulbs:' A Review of Sustainability Pedagogies and their Potential for Use in Higher Education." *Sustainability Education: Perspectives and Practice Across Higher Education*. Eds.

Paula Jones, David Selby, and Stephen Sterling. New York, NY: Earthscan, 2010. Print.

Hopkinson, Peter; James, Peter; and Van Winsum, Adam. "Learning by Doing: Environmental Performance Improvement in UK Higher Education." *The Sustainability Curriculum.* 2004. 78-92. Print.

Karpiak, Christie P. and Baril, Galen L. "Moral Reasoning and Concern for the Environment," *Journal of Environmental Psychology* 28 (2008): 203-208. Print.

O'Malley, Denis J. "U of S Recycling Moves to Off-Campus Housing." *The Scranton Times Tribune* 4 Dec. 2010: A4. Print.

Palmer, Clare. "Sustainability and Philosophy." *The Sustainability Curriculum: The Challenge for Higher Education.* Eds. John Blewitt and Cedric Cullingford. London and Sterling, VA: Earthscan, 2004. 241. Print.

Shifting the Metaphor: Designing 21st Century Curriculum Based on the Principles of Living Systems and Sustainability

John Gould, Drexel University

"We also pour considerable amounts of money into our educational systems, but we haven't been able to create schools and institutions of higher education that develop people's innate capacity to sense and shape their future, which I view as the single most important core capability for this century's knowledge and co-creation economy."
\- C. Otto Scharmer, 2009

Abstract: If sustainability is to be an integral part of rethinking the organization of multiple disciplines, then it is necessary to surface the mental models underlying our present curricular structures. Assumptions presently underlying design of most schools are based on the factory model, which raises two essential questions: 1) How can using the concepts of sustainability and structure be used to create a shift in our present thinking about schools and learning; and, 2) What will move schools to a more naturalistic way of designing learning environs, focused on nurturing the development of a sustainable future for our students? Upon collectively exploring these questions, we can begin to design innovative curriculum to prepare future students and teachers. This essay begins with an overview of the concepts of sustainability and structure, as found in systems thinking, and ends with a conceptual framework for thinking about possible new designs for a 21st century curriculum based on sustainability. These concepts are used to stimulate a dialogue about the essential questions that result in a shift, moving from the twentieth century metaphor of schools as "production-lines" to one of schools as "seedbeds" and students as "seeds," based on principles of systems thinking and ecology.

John M. Gould, Ph.D., is Associate Clinical Professor and a Director of Ed.D. in Educational Leadership and Change at Drexel University, Philadelphia. He is also a senior associate of the Sustainability Collaborative—a burgeoning group rallying around the call for universal sustainability. Gould spent more than 30 years in K-12 education, with positions ranging from classroom teacher to superintendent of schools. He is grounded in systems thinking and has a strong commitment to the concepts of sustainability and leadership.

Introduction

If one thinks of the humanities and social sciences as exploring the human condition through the study of society and the behavior of its people, then these disciplines can be significant for understanding of how sustainability can lead to educational change. Sustainability is thinking about humankind's relationship with the environment and how economic development impacts the environment. The relationship between ecological and economic activities throughout this planet, as Jeffrey Sachs argues, is now cast in terms of sustainable growth and development, social justice, and gaps between rich and poor. These issues are important concepts underpinning one's understanding of why sustainability, at all levels within the educational system, is critical to needs of the next generation. To actualize this understanding, a key can be found in developing new metaphors for the activity of schooling.

Today, the critical drivers in developing these metaphors are advances in informational technologies, the evolution of neurosciences, genetics, nanotechnology, robotics, and changes in the structure of work. For example, Kurzweil defines a future period during which the pace of technological change will be so rapid, its impact so deep, that human life will irreversibly transform. The energy of this change is exponential growth. He shows in practical terms that the technological advances we saw in the last twenty years of the Twentieth Century will only take fourteen years to develop in the first twenty years of the 21st Century (2014); and after that it will only take seven years to advance twenty years (2021)!

These activities are greatly impacting the world of our students by affecting the future of work and the quality of life on this planet. All of these advances are increasing the complexities of a person's daily activities within any organization. This complexity is causing both personal and organizational angst, because our traditional methods of leadership and organization are no longer applicable to the emerging realities of the 21st Century. As educators, the question that we face concerns whether we think of sustainability as a subject to be taught or as an underlying principle in helping to design new learning environments for this emerging world. Coupled to this question is the prevalence of reductionist thinking that leaves one with the dilemma of thinking systemically about our students' future but acting within silos of past thinking.

So, why is this important? Why should you, as an educator, care? If you do not, you will abdicate your responsibility in preparing the next generation to live in their future instead of yours! In his book, *High Noon*, J. P. Rischard identified twenty global issues that must be addressed, within the twenty years after 2003, if we are to survive as a sustainable civilization. These issues fall into three categories: 1) how we share our planet with each other; 2) how we share our humanity related to social and economic ideas; and 3) how we deal with legal and regulatory issues affecting our global behavior (65-66). Within these categories, key issues are identified, such as climate change, water deficits, global infectious diseases, population distribution, poverty, biotechnological rules, illegal drugs, terrorism, and intellectual property rights. These are some of the issues facing our children's future. We must prepare them to understand these problems in order for them to find the solutions within their future. We must ask if our present K-20 structure is designed to deal with the complexities of these issues.

Sustainability and Structure—What They Are

In order to design educational systems that can address Rischard's global issues, it is important to understand two critical concepts: sustainability and structure. Reflecting on assumptions and values found in them will lead to new avenues for addressing these issues.

Sustainability

Sustainability has become one of those words used by many different people and organizations. It has become a "catch-all" phrase popular within the media and political discourse. The problem is not with the word, but in what could be called a "shallow" understanding of its underlying concepts and principles. Michael Fullan defines this shallowness: "the terms travel well, but the underlying conceptualization and thinking do not" (10). This lack of understanding the deeper assumptions that underlie sustainability has led organizations to base daily operations on non-sustainable practices. In developing a deeper understanding of sustainability, in order to find new metaphors for school design, it is important to innovate around learning environs focused on the future. Five definitions, based on Lester Brown, Michael Fullan, Peter Senge, Robert Lattimer, and John Ehrenfeld, set a context for understanding how sustainability can underpin a new design of curriculum and schools.

Lester Brown, one of the world's leading thinkers in sustainable development, famously defined a sustainable society as one that satisfies its needs without diminishing the prospects of future generations. This simple and eloquent definition has shaped much of the discussion in today's literature pertaining to sustainability. It sets the moral purpose for our actions. He argued that this moral purpose creates the need for new skills that "will thoroughly challenge the educational and training facilities of universities, corporations, and government agencies" (9).

To address this challenge, an understanding of the interrelationship between the economic and ecological needs of a community must emerge. Fritjof Capra points out that, in order to build " a sustainable society for our children and future generations, we need to fundamentally redesign many of our technologies and social institutions so as to bridge the wide gap between human design and the ecologically sustainable systems of nature" (99). He continues by saying "a sustainable human community is one designed in such a manner that its ways of life, businesses, economy, physical structures, and technologies do not interfere with nature's inherent ability to sustain life" (230).

This definition presents a dynamic process that human communities are in coevolution with nature, instead of a static state. To utilize this dynamic in the process of rethinking the design of our schools, Peter Senge suggest that three guiding ideas are needed for creating a more sustainable future:

1. There is no viable path forward that does not take into account the needs of future generations;
2. Institutions do matter;
3. All real change is grounded in new ways of thinking and perceiving ("The Necessary Revolution" 9-10).

These three principles set the stage for school systems to rethink the present assumptions and values that underlie how they are structured and carry out their daily operational practices.

In the field of educational change, Michael Fullan defines sustainability as "the capacity of a system to engage in the complexities of continuous improvement consistent with deep values of human purpose" (p. ix). The concepts of social justice, collaboration, equality, and creativity in fostering the common good are some of the deeper values that a school engenders beyond just the acquisition of information. This definition enhances Capra's sense of social responsibility.

Robert Lattimer's concept of universal sustainability broadens our traditional thinking of sustainability as environmental issues and their relationship to the economy. Universal sustainability is about creating new patterns of relationships with oneself, others, and nature; it is about thinking more deeply about these relationships and the systems we create as humans. A primary assumption of universal sustainability is a need to cut across organizational boundaries of the economy, political systems, science and technology, social systems, and education.

In economics particularly, universal sustainability builds a strong case for rethinking the underlying assumptions related to our present definition of capitalism. This rethinking impacts the direction and the purpose of organizations as they interact globally. In education, the understanding of these cross-boundary expansions is important to the redesign of the present K-20 curricular structures.

Finally, John Ehrenfeld defines sustainability as "the possibility that humans and other life forms will flourish on earth forever" (49). The intriguing aspect of this definition is the word "possibility." As he points out, the word "possibility" is not a present-based word, but it gives us the chance "to visualize and strive for a future that is neither available in the present nor may have existed in the past" (49). This definition is different than the other four because it is based in the idea that, as humans, we have potential to bring forth the future, based on what has yet to be satisfied. He argues that the "future is the possibility out of which one lives and acts in the present" (50). Understanding this process of bringing forth our personal and group aspirations is critical in redesigning curriculum and schools.

By combining beliefs and assumptions found within these definitions of sustainability, one can begin to envision new educational frameworks that integrate sustainability as a guiding principle for the curricular innovations and leadership needed to change structural organization of our schools. Common to all five definitions, the following principles can be found: 1) development of possible futures; 2) commitment to a deep set of human values that support the future; 3) acknowledgement that structures found within institutions are important organizing processes for human interaction; 4) understanding of cross boundary thinking; and, 5) most importantly, realization that new ways of thinking are critical to meet the needs of future generations.

Structure

Coupled to the definition of sustainability is the concept of structure. Structure is critical to understanding systems thinking. Donella Meadows defines a system "as a set of things interconnected in such ways that they produce their own pattern of behavior over time" (2). In a general sense, structures shape the behaviors of people over time. Structures always intersect with the humans within the organization. This is important to understand because, when a new structure is imposed on people, many times it will fail, because the process didn't include everyone affected by its development. In looking at how the word structure is used within educational organizations, one thinks of organizational charts, schedules, curriculum design, contractual arrangements, and policies. These structures shape the way people within the school go about their daily routines and activities. After a period of time, the influence of the structures is no longer overt and one loses sight of why and how the structure was created in the first place. For example, within the K-12 structure, why do we have grade levels, tracking, and nine months of schooling?[1]

This lack of understanding leads one facing rigid, immovable objects within the organization. Think of the meetings where people say "we can't do that because the policy or schedule will not permit us to do that." Robert Fritz points out that because "we fail to understand the powerful nature of structure, we are less able to create new and desired outcomes" ("Corporate Tides" 15). This inability to understand the dynamic nature of structures on behaviors within schools is what leads to a continuous cycle of reform effects that do not change the system. Fritz defines structure as:

> an entity (such as an organization) made up of individual elements or parts (such as people, resources...reward systems, departmental mandates... workload/capacity relationships, and so on) that impact each other by the relationships they form. ("Path of Least Resistance")

Building off this definition, one realizes that the present structures within our schools are the same as they were one hundred years ago, even with greater access to information through the Internet. In particular, the way curriculum is organized, the day is scheduled, and how the school building is physically laid out, schools are basically the same as they were when this writer went to school 58 years ago! This is why we continue to see the "pendulum-swing" between different educational practices and theories; the K-20 structure stays the same, no matter how powerful the new ideas!

For example, look at the two images below (Fig. 1), one showing the structure of most schools today and the other a representation of the Internet. What are the underlying assumptions about learning and the patterns of relationships among teachers, students, information, and the world at-large found within each?

Figure 1: Structures Affecting the Flow of Information and Patterns of Relationships

The image of the schoolhouse shows the present curricular structure as boxes that house content information (disciplines) and grouping patterns of people (grade levels). This structure shapes our present realities of what a school should be. Look at how media reinforces this structure in popular movies and television shows like, *"Ferris Bueller," "Welcome Back Kotter,"* and *"Glee,"* to name a few. These images blind us from seeing the emerging future needs of our children.

The image of the Internet shows a different structure. Given the evolution of social media through the Internet, it is creating possibilities for new patterns of relationships among teachers, students, content area experts, and the community to emerge. In looking at the structures of the Internet and our schools, one needs to ask how congruent they are; how do their assumptions for a new reality demand that we prepare students to demonstrate understanding and the application of information in a globalized workplace? By not surfacing the assumptions found in schools, the consequence is that we lose sight of why the school was designed in the first place and, therefore, we try to make "new ideas and practices" fit the "old structure." Just think about the millions upon millions of dollars spent to integrate technologies into the classrooms. What has really changed in the fundamental, daily operations of a school?

It was stated above that, taken collectively, the definitions of structure and sustainability underpin how educational organizations can begin to rethink the present mental models that are driving our K-16 schools. The way we are willing to utilize them in our thinking and conversation will either enhance or block the development of innovative structures for sustainability learning in the 21st Century. Tension between the current realities within the school and Ehrenfeld's possible futures creates energy to think of new metaphors for schooling.

The Present Metaphor: The Well-Oiled Machine

Robert Pirsig once pointed out in his famous book, *Zen and the Art of Motorcycle Maintenance*, that if a factory is torn down but the rationality which produced it is left standing, then that rationality will simply produce another factory. Today, the American educational system is at a crossroad. We are still driven by a series of assumptions based in thinking that arose out of the eighteenth century Enlightenment. This period was influenced by Descartes's rationalism and the Newtonian concepts that human organizations functioned as a machine. This is a very powerful metaphor in how our organizations are shaped. In the forward to *The Living Company,* Senge describes that "The machine metaphor is so powerful that it shapes the character of most organizations. They become more like machines than living beings because their members think of them that way" (x). The machine greatly influenced the development of twentieth century industrialism, sparked by Fredrick Taylor.[2]

Efficiency and standardization are important concepts found in the principles of scientific management. Using the lens of a "well-oiled machine" creates a sense that, in order to keep an organization functioning efficiently, the individual parts need to be monitored so that nothing will go wrong. This mindset has led to the development of a management structure based in a top-down power model. In a world where complexity is minimized and easy to control, this model works well. The job of those in charge is to maintain its efficiency. A major assumption about people within this model is the distinction between "mental" work (smart people) and "labor" (not so smart). Management is about command and control with "time and motion" studies needed to reduce work activities to their smallest parts. The result was a reductionism of the system and a fixation on the parts while losing sight of the total system. For the twentieth century, the system worked very efficiently.

The effect of the machine metaphor on the teaching and learning process led schools to design curriculum in order to sort students to become industrial managers (a few) and workers (the many). In looking at the evolution of educational systems, the need for conformity, standardization, and efficiency in pedagogy and organizational operations become the hallmark of our present system. The structural outcomes were compulsory education, the development of high schools, standardized procedures in teaching and learning, tracking of students, separation of knowledge into discrete subjects, and anathema hierarchical management of schools. Efficiency and standardization are very powerful "mindsets" within our present culture; they shape how our society "sees" school. These mindsets limit the flexibility and adaptability within the schools to deal with the complexity and changes related to the future of work and living in the 21st century.

Even with the evolution of informational technologies, today there is still a belief that information should be "pushed" at students because they are "empty vessels" that need to be filled. Students are not able to develop critical thinking until their heads are filled with basic information. Bloom's[3] taxonomy has created a linear mindset about the structure of information. For example, individuals can't think mathematically until they master basic computational skills. What this mindset creates is a belief that learning is about getting the right answer on a test.

A classic example in America is the Federal legislation No Child Left Behind (NCLB). The aspiration of NCLB to give every child a quality education is a great societal goal but, after twelve years, implementation has been a disaster. More and more children are being left behind and ill prepared for a highly competitive, globalized economy. The competitive rating of schools by communities, states, and countries reinforces the "right answer" mentality. The unintended consequence is the development of a student attitude that it is more important to get the right answer in school than it is to deal with the complexities of applying information to real world, complex situations.

Why? We have what de Geus calls no "memory of the future" (35), which is necessary to truly create schools that can embrace universal sustainability. These memories are developed when schools can nurture possible futures and the actualization of what we can create. The present realities of kindergarten to graduate school reform demonstrate this lack of a "memory of the future," because most reform efforts create memories of the past, locked into our twentieth century metaphor of the industrial factory. What the mind has not experienced before, it cannot see. In not seeing forward, there is very little discussion of the nature of deep change, how to bring it about, and what does it mean for schools and their communities. If we can begin to nurture what Senge calls a positive future, where we are living in the question of "what we want to create," then we can innovate for the schools needed in the 21st century and beyond.

Shifting the Metaphor: Living Systems as an Organizing Principle

De Gues introduced the concept of the "*living organization*" in his study of why there are very few large organizations that are more than 100 years old. He states, "like all organisms, the living company exists primarily for its own survival and improvement: to fulfill its potential and to become as great as it can be" (11).

Related to Michael Fullan's definition of sustainability above, de Gues identifies four key components that underlie the living company. The first is that an organization needs to be sensitive to the environment in which it exists. When this is a fundamental operating principle, the organization is in a continual state of learning and adapting to its environment. Second, there is a focus within an organization on building a sense of community and a persona of itself, to create its identity within the environment. Third, the organization builds constructive relationships with others within the environment and within its own structure. This leads to tolerance of different views and decentralization within its own internal culture. Finally, the fourth component is related to its ability to sustain its own growth and evolution as an organization.

Understanding the tension between the aspiration for the future and the current realities within the organization is the key for any organization to be sustainable. New metaphors for schooling that shift from those of industrial-age thinking to ones relevant to the principles of sustainability and ecology are the catalysts for change.

Building on the concept of a living organization, Capra believes that, to ensure a sustained future for our children, there needs to be an understanding that, as humans, we need to think of our organizations as living systems. He states:

> Understanding human organizations in terms of living systems, i.e. in terms of complex nonlinear networks, is likely to lead to new insights into the nature of complexity, and thus help us deal with the complexities of today's business environment. (100)

This concept is not just related to the business environment but any human organization, in either the private or public sector. It underpins development of a conceptual framework to shift from our present machine metaphor to one based on flexibility and adaptation to the environment. Sustainability is embedded in the understanding of networks of relationships that give rise to continuous change in living systems. Three key processes are found to underlie the natural process of change within any living system: adaptability, diversity, and creativity. How these are found in nature is through the dynamic process of continuous transformation of the parts within living systems.[4] A living system continually creates/recreates by adapting its structures through "web-like" networks with its surroundings. Adaptability, diversity, and creativity are the processes that can help us develop new metaphors for how to structure schools and curriculum based on living systems.

How would we design schools that are not based on a metaphor of a "production-line" found within a factory? How can we bring into sync the ideas within sustainability to innovate schools? What would be the underlying assumptions found within a metaphor that would nurture our thinking about schools in the future? How would information (content) be organized to actualize 21st century skills? These are the necessary questions to begin the dialogue about the future both within and outside the school systems. This will lead to the creation of redesigned schools with new assumptions based in the possibilities of the future. So, this new metaphor may be: *the school is a seedbed and our children are seeds*.

The underlying assumptions to actualize the metaphor of the seedbed should start with the following:

1. Generative-centered learning allows for the development of the intrinsic interest of students;
2. Learning is based on the diversity of intelligences and styles;
3. Understanding is manifested through a demonstration of the interdependency and change within the world, instead of just finding the right answer on a static test;
4. Conversations are inclusive among all who are involved in the learning process;
5. Education is seen as a vital part of the web of social relationships that link people and communities together;
6. Informational technologies would be utilized to enhance development of new relationships among different disciplines, leading to development of a sense of one's place within the ecosystem.

These assumptions are based in systems thinking and the understanding of living systems that focus on the ideas that: a) there is no path forward unless the needs of future generations are understood, and that b) new patterns of thinking and perceiving drive educational innovation.[5] It also means, as Senge states, "simply stepping back and seeing patterns that are, when seen clearly, intuitive and easy to grasp" (The Necessary Revolution 23). Thinking in systems allows one to "see" the possibilities across boundaries that presently block our ability to innovate new metaphors for our schools.

Schools As Seedbeds: Rethinking the Structure

Knowledge, innovation, critical thinking, entrepreneurship, and creativity are the real capital of this emerging world.[6] These are the skills that every student needs to master, based on their own aspirations for the future. These skills must become the basic building blocks at the beginning of a child's first experiences in school, and continue to be part of their learning throughout their life. These skills do not match well to the present structure of schools.

Until there is a rethinking about the total school system structure, our children will not be well prepared to live and function productively, much less negotiate the present "high-stakes testing" mentality, because of mismatched organizational structures.

Based on the concepts and assumptions presented to this point, let's explore one possible innovative design structure driven by the concepts found in sustainability and systems thinking.

A Possible New Structure of Learning Spaces

Fritz points out that, if a structure remains unchanged in light of outside forces, then the behavior of people will continue their previous behavior. If there is a sustained structural change, then it will lead to overall changes in the behaviors to meet the needs of a new future. To begin thinking about a new possible structure (Figure 2) to meet emerging demands of the 21st century world, let's consider grouping children in three-year age bands, starting with age five and continuing through adulthood.[7]

These age bands are contained in a *learning space*. This concept of a *learning space* is based on Kurt Lewin's view that social environments are dynamic fields of interactions of the people within them.[8] The content within each develops the humanities and social sciences as an integral part of nurturing in students what it means to be human in a technological age.

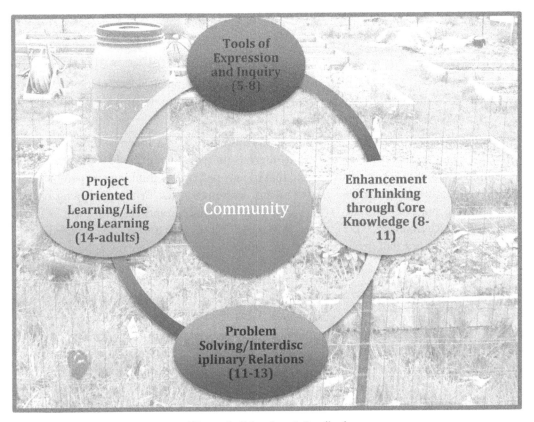

Figure 2. School as A Seedbed

The first *learning space* is called **Tools of Expression and Inquiry (5-8)**.[9] Children learn to communicate through using different forms of expression, and ask questions as they construct knowledge related to thematically-structured learning activities. The purpose of this band is to: develop literacy through notational systems adding color and sounds to letters and numbers, creating knowledge and understanding from asking questions, and developing the habits for creative thinking.

The second *learning space* is **Enhancement of Thinking through Core Knowledge (8-11)**,[10] where children learn how knowledge becomes organized into categories. Each content space is viewed as a specific way of thinking and interacting with their world. Information is structured intra-disciplinarily as students explore the different aspects of specific content, e.g. Social Studies and its sub-disciplines of history, economics, civics and government, etc.

The third *learning space* is called **Problem Solving/Interdisciplinary Relations (11-13)**. Students begin to manipulate the disciplines to find relationships and differences to problem-solve or construct new knowledge bases. The purpose for students is to expand their understanding of disciplines, pursue solutions to non-trivial problems, learn to value and integrate knowledge from multiple points of views, and create productive social relationships with others.

The fourth *learning space* is called **Project Oriented Learning/Life-Long Learning (14-adults)**. Students expand their knowledge in any given field(s) of inquiry. They specialize in their studies by directing their own learning and career development. The learning environment is structured to allow students to interact with mentors and partnerships within businesses, higher education, and community organizations. The purpose of this space is to: apply knowledge to "real" world situations; accept responsibility for continuous learning; realize learning as a collaborative process; and connect to a larger community, making us responsible for sustaining it into the next generation. This space changes the structure, of what we call high school, to a new structure that "opens" the schedule to develop new relationships with the organizations mentioned above.

This is a representative view of a future, life-long learning environment structured on the principles of sustainability, systemic thinking, and living systems. This structure is an example of Ehrenfeld's idea that possibility is not a present based word and gives us the freedom to explore the future in a very sustainable way.

A Deeper Dive Into a Learning Space

To illustrate how a particular *learning space* would develop, a sample project called the Rivers, Bays, and Ocean (RBO)[11] is used. The essential question underlying the RBO is:

Is it possible for regional watersheds and aquifers to lose their ability to supply geographical regions with fresh water?

The purpose of the RBO in exploring this question is to build understanding and action around the need to integrate ecological and economic priorities, to enhance quality of life within regional watersheds and aquifers. The curriculum is focused on cross-content learning activities that will nurture development of literate citizens to understand the problems identified by Rischard, and create skill sets to perform the work necessary to solve them.

This is accomplished within each of the *learning spaces* through the development of collaborative networks among government, non-profit organizations, businesses, schools, and communities. Each *learning space* is designed to leverage local resources to enhance lifelong learning related to these issues within watersheds. The curriculum is structured within the *learning spaces* to produce a "collective insight" about how given watersheds work and the strategic challenges they face, as a basis for coalescing diverse groups to think and work collaboratively. This "collective insight" will enhance the development of "prototypes" for schools and communities that are committed to creating a sustainable future for their children.

The focus of each learning space within the framework of the RBO is to:

- grow an ethic and practice of environmental stewardship;
- understand how to integrate ecological and economic priorities;
- enhance the quality of life for people within the watersheds;
- increase collaboration and thinking among government, non-profit organizations, and businesses to enhance student learning;
- understand the need to think regionally to solve complex ecological and economic issues; and
- regenerate the health of watersheds, ecosystems, and the human communities within them.

For example, looking deeper into the *learning space* of **Project Oriented Learning/Life Long Learning**, the environment is structured through networks of teams, both within the school and with "outside" groups. The students are not restricted to one learning environment and their schedule will be at multiple sites, depending on their developed program. These sites can be within a higher educational environment, a business, NGO, or other global learning networks. The environment will be blended, utilizing social media and MOOCs[12] to interact with experts within their field(s) of study. All their learning activities are designed to allow learners to apply their knowledge by demonstrating understanding and its application to meaningful activities. For example, individual students, or teams of students, work with their local legislator to draft laws or policy to protect their watershed.

Letting Go—Coming In

To conclude this essay on new metaphors for developing innovative curricular structures focused on sustainability, the idea of "letting go—coming in" is the starting point for our future. Scharmer developed the concept of "letting go—coming in" to explain that "tuning into something new requires that you must first let go of something old" (199).

The intent of this essay is to raise awareness that concepts such as sustainability, systems thinking, living systems, innovation, and creativity can help nurture a deeper understanding of why it is critical to think about education with new metaphors.

There is a need to move away from thinking about reform in education to innovation in education. Reform is improving within the present structure, whereas innovation infers the act of creating new system structures.

In looking at past reform efforts to change our schools, we keep coming up with schools that, for the most part, look like they did 100 years ago in both form and structure. Lattimer has, through universal sustainability, called for a new understanding of what 21ˢᵗ century capitalism needs to be. In the world of economic globalization, education is at the center of this evolution in thinking.

Until all sectors of society can begin to change our habitual patterns of thinking about what schools are, hopes for a future sustainable world are greatly at-risk. The problem we all must begin to consider is Russell Ackoff's warning - that the need to get the question right is the most important consideration.[13] If not, we will continue to do the wrong things righter and the more wrong they will become. In order to discover the right questions, we need to let go of the past and allow the future to come in.

Notes

1. See Tyack and Tobin's (1994) detailed historical perspective on how the present structure of schools developed in the United States.
2. *The Principles of Scientific Management*
3. Taxonomy of Educational Objectives Book 1: Cognitive Domain (1984).
4. For a more detail discussion see Capra's The Hidden Connections (2002).
5. See Senge et al.'s Schools That Learn: Updated and Revised (2012) for strategies to develop these and other assumptions to change schools.
6. See The Partnership for 21ˢᵗ Century Learning at http://p21.org/ and Young Zhao's World Class Learners (2012) for a deeper insight to these concepts. Zhao's web site is an excellent source for interaction with these ideas (http://zhaolearning.com/).
7. Each of the bands will have "primary learning directions" which are directly taught as specific areas of learning and activities. Also, there are "integrated content directions," which are integrated with the primary learning directions but not directly taught as a specific discipline. For example, in the first learning band, mathematics, reading, writing, speaking, art, music, and physical education are directly taught and are the focus of performance assessment. Systems thinking, science and technology, geography, civics and government, and history would be used to create the themes and "context" for the primary content areas. In the second band, mathematics, reading, etc. become the "skills" to express understanding and demonstrate performance of a specific discipline throughout the rest of the curricular structure.
8. Resolving Social Conflicts (1997). Also, see Scharmer's Chapter 15 on social fields for a deeper understanding of my development of the learning space.
9. Montessori, Dewey, Piaget, Gardner, Senge, and programs such as Reggio Emilia greatly influenced this writer's thinking about this framework, particularly the first band. Tools of Expression and Inquiry are critical because they students to develop the attitudes necessary for a constructivist K-12 system of performance accountability through project-based learning. Teachers are no longer in individual K-2 classrooms, but function as a "team" and work with a group of five to eight year olds.

10.   This space is designed based Howard Gardner's idea that the most important, irreducible, purpose of school-from elementary through high school- is to help students better understand the major disciplinary ways of thinking. This learning space is to help students to understand as humans we do organize information into categories called disciplines. This will help them to see how we think about and organize information, not to create separate silos of thinking.

11.   This curriculum was developed by the author and his colleague Dawn R. Sutton and is presenting being utilized in the development of a new form of Charter school in Pennsylvania. The project will link schools and communities within both the Delaware and Susquehanna watersheds.

12.   The World Is Open (2009). Also see http://mypage.iu.edu/~cjbonk/ for an overview of Massive Open Online Course (MOOC).

13.   See http://www.youtube.com/watch?v=MzS5V5-0VsA

Works Cited

Bonk, Curtis. *The World is Open*. San Francisco, CA: Jossey-Bass, 2009. Print

Brown, Lester. *Building a sustainable Society*. New York, NY: Norton, 1981. Print.

Capra, Fritjof. *The Hidden Connections*. New York, NY: Doubleday, 2002. Print.

deGeus, Arie. *The Living Company: Habits for Survival in a Turbulent Business Environment*. Boston, MA: Harvard Business School Press, 1997. Print.

Ehrenfeild, John. *Sustainability by design*. New Haven, CT: Yale University Press, 2008. Print.

Fritz, Robert. *The path of least resistance for managers*. San Francisco, CA: Berrett-Koehler Publishers, 1999. Print.

---. *Corporate tides: The inescapable laws of organization structure*. San Francisco, CA: Berrett-Koehler Publishers, 1996. Print.

Fullan, Michael. *Leadership and sustainability*. Thousand Oaks, CA: Corwin Press, 2005. Print.

Kurzweil, Ray. *The singularity is near*. New York, NY: Penguin Books, 2005. Print.

Lattimer, Robert. "Universal Sustainability: The Next Form of Competitiveness." *Competition Forum*. 9.2 (2011): 399-405. Print.

Meadows, Donella H, and Diana Wright. *Thinking in Systems: A Primer*. London, UK: Earthscan, 2009. Internet resource.

Partnership for 21st Century Learning. Framework for 21st Century Learning.

Pirsig, Robert. *Zen and the Art of Motorcycle Maintenance*. New York, NY: Bantam Books, 1984. Print.

Rischard, J. F. *High Noon: Twenty Global Problems, Twenty Years to Solve Them*. New York, NY: Basic Books, 2002. Print.

Sachs, Jeffrey. *Common Wealth*. New York, NY: Penguin Press, 2008. Print.

Scharmer, Otto. *Theory U: Leading from the Future as It Emerges*. San Francisco, CA: Berrett-

Koehler Publishers, 2009. Print.

Senge, Peter, et al. *The Necessary Revolution*. New York, NY: Doubleday, 2008. Print.

---. *The Fifth Discipline Fieldbook*. New York: Doubleday, 1994. Print.

Taylor, Frederick. *The Principles of Scientific Management*. Digireads.com Publishing, 2011. eBook.

Tyack, David and William Tobin. "The 'Grammar' of Schooling: Why has it been so Hard to Change?"*American Educational Research Journal*, 31.3 (1994): 453-479. Print.

Zhao, Young. *World Class Learners*. Thousand Oaks, CA: Corwin, 2012. Print.

Sustainability and Social Science Concepts

Robert Paehlke, Trent University

Abstract: A sustainability perspective changes our time horizon and shifts the place of value-laden concepts within inquiry, thereby influencing some key concepts in the social sciences. This chapter considers how teaching sustainability changes the way we understand many aspects of social science. We need first of all to consider the meaning of sustainability itself. In the end, sustainability is about maximizing human well-being over a multi-generational time period with minimum impacts on the living, natural world and a minimum of extractions of energy and materials from nature. It is about the full range of effects of our economic, social, technological, political and cultural lives as humans. It is this holistic focus that alters the meaning of many key social science concepts. The concepts considered in this chapter are: efficiency and productivity, citizenship, class and democracy. Thinking about how a focus on sustainability might affect these concepts teaches us a great deal about why and how they are important to our understanding of society and our common human future.

Robert Paehlke is Professor Emeritus of Environmental and Resource Studies and Political Studies at Trent University in Peterborough, Ontario, Canada. He is a founding editor (1971) of the Canadian journal/magazine *Alternatives: Canadian Environmental Ideas & Action.* He is the author of: *Some Like It Cold: the Politics of Climate Change in Canada* (Toronto: Between the Lines, 2008); *Democracy's Dilemma: Environment, Social Equity and the Global Economy* (Cambridge, Mass: MIT Press, 2004); and *Environmentalism and the Future Of Progressive Politics* (New Haven: Yale University Press, 1991) and edited *Conservation and Environmentalism: An Encyclopedia* (1995) and (with Douglas Torgerson) *Managing Leviathan: Environmental Politics and the Administrative State* (1990 and 2005).

Consideration of sustainability alters how we think about society. It influences the meaning of many concepts in the social sciences and thereby influences our teaching, potentially deepening our student's understanding of society. Sustainability focuses attention more directly on the concrete, everyday world—the world of food, shelter, transportation, human settlement, resources, health, nature, and climate. It also shifts our sense of time toward the future and our sense of space toward behavior and policies at the local and global levels, as well as the more familiar national policy realms.

This essay focuses primarily on four concepts: efficiency, class, citizenship, and democracy and suggests ways that social scientists might adapt these concepts for a world where sustainability is an important concern. Courses in political science, economics and sociology—particularly courses at the introductory level—might benefit from discussions of these adaptations. Today's students are attuned to sustainability in very practical ways. They worry that their futures are less secure than their parents' futures were. Social science concepts will be more interesting to them if discussions of those concepts incorporate such possibilities.

Sustainability—Broadly Defined

Sustainability can be broadly defined as the capacity to continuously produce the material basis for human well-being within the limits of a natural world of undiminished quality. Both policy initiatives and individual actions aimed at achieving greater sustainability require understanding society in terms of a "triple" bottom line—economic prosperity, social well-being, and environmental quality (Paehlke). In this view, economic prosperity is as much a means as an end, and human well-being—rather than prosperity or economic growth—is the more central objective.

At any given level of prosperity, individuals, communities, or nations experience widely varying levels of health, happiness, fairness, and education. Some minimum level of prosperity is obviously necessary for comfortable survival but, beyond that, considerable variability is found in the quality of life within each society that is obtained for each incremental rise of societal wealth. There is also variability in the degree of prosperity that is obtained from any given rate of energy and materials use. Compared to the United States and Canada, European nations, for example, use far less energy per person and achieve greater societal wealth from every unit of energy used, especially from fossil fuel energy.

How this is accomplished is affected by both personal behavior and public policy and is central to understanding how societies and economies function. The answer turns social science toward very practical, everyday matters: energy-efficient refrigerators preserve food using less energy than inefficient refrigerators. Public transit uses less energy per passenger mile than cars, lighter cars use less energy than heavier cars. Light can be produced with a small fraction of the energy used by incandescent bulbs. Recycled materials require less energy and virgin raw materials than materials produced from raw ore or trees. Almost every time any of these (and similar) things happen, environmental impacts are less per dollar of gross national product (GNP) or per quantity of material used.

We get more of what we want with less use of scarce resources. A wide array of public policies as well as corporate and personal initiatives can induce this transformation, sometimes called eco-efficiency. The hope regarding eco-efficiency is that adequate environmental protection can be achieved through such efficiency gains, rather than through actions that might limit prosperity. A more eco-efficient society is a more sustainable society.

Less familiar to most people is the second part of the sustainability equation. As important to sustainability as eco-efficiency are the differences in the effectiveness with which prosperity is utilized to create well-being. For example, one community might invest prosperity gains in health and education, obtaining greater societal well-being than a jurisdiction that spends a greater proportion of its wealth on junk food, military weapons, and "toys" for a few wealthy citizens. Thus a *double efficiency* is built into the triple bottom line. Societies can produce wealth from nature more, or less, efficiently and can produce well-being from any given level of prosperity more, or less, effectively.

Using environmental indicators, analysts can estimate how sustainably economic output and well-being are generated. The good news is that most economies are slowly becoming more efficient in terms of resource use per dollar of GNP. The bad news is that human numbers and total output are probably advancing at least as rapidly as this type of efficiency is improving; thus we are slowly imposing upon nature more and more. The challenge of achieving greater sustainability is to accelerate improvements in eco-efficiency and to find ways to get more health and happiness (or whatever else we take well-being to be) out of each increment of prosperity.

One way that might achieve the latter is to increase equity in the distribution of income (at least to the extent that extreme differences are avoided). Obviously, this is a politically charged assertion, but it is hard to argue that the opportunity for a few to acquire third homes or second yachts would produce more well-being than dollar equivalent opportunities for large numbers to be better fed or to acquire adequate shelter. Complicating the argument is that some kinds of goods carry much lower environmental impacts per dollar spent: most notably, education, health care, the arts, and locally produced organic vegetables.

Making sustainability a priority within public policy discussions and within public policy teaching could shift how citizens think about the world and how we think within social science. Economics and political science might well become more multi-dimensional. This shift might also more often incorporate discussions of values. As social scientists, we could preserve a reasonable level of detachment without avoiding the environmental and equity implications of public policies or the increasingly glaring implications of sustainability considerations for the core concepts in social science. We may well convey a deeper understanding of those concepts as a result.

Sustainability and Four Key Concepts:
Efficiency, Class, Citizenship, Democracy

Efficiency is important within economics and the study of public policy. Without a central focus on sustainability, efficiency would primarily be about the relative dollar value of economic inputs (especially human labor and capital) and outputs (products and services). With a greater emphasis on sustainability, efficiency comes to represent the amount of human well-being achieved for a given physical amount of energy and materials, as well as the extent of environmental impacts.

Social class, a central concept in sociology, provides a picture of the structure of society in terms of economic market position. Sustainability considerations, however, can open long-established systems of social stratification to rapid adjustment if key natural resources (such as oil, water, land or fish) are less available as a result of resource depletion, climate change or other environmental impacts. Sustainability *solutions* may also affect class and occupational patterns and the location of employment opportunities, reducing, for example, the number of extractive industry jobs and increasing the number of jobs in the design, manufacture, installation, operation and maintenance of renewable energy equipment.

Citizenship is understood as a set of rights and responsibilities linked to legal association with a nation state. Sustainability considerations can broaden the idea of citizenship in both time and space. Sustainability brings the needs of future generations to the fore and raises the question of how such concerns might achieve greater consideration within political processes. Sustainability also makes plain the importance of issues associated with our common global fate. Our obligations as citizens are stretched beyond national borders. Sustainability forces us, regardless of national citizenship, to address global concerns including climate change, global financial crises, the international movement of diseases and risks to ecological services.

Even our understanding of *democracy* is altered by sustainability considerations. Political efficacy is diminished when global decisions (or the lack thereof) and global outcomes render local and even national governments ineffective, if not powerless. Today's challenges, as well as today's economic organizations, operate globally and are not easily influenced by single nations, or even groups of nations.

Jean-Jacques Rousseau argued that democracy functioned best on a small scale, but the world has changed since his day. Many of today's greatest challenges require global cooperation, but there are few global opportunities for democratic participation at a global scale and few individuals who imagine having influence over global affairs. Sustainability has irreducibly global dimensions. The absence of global democratic institutions thus diminishes the sense of efficacy necessary for effective democracy and undermines national and local democratic institutions.

Sustainability thus adds new considerations to the teaching of social science. These could be addressed in an advanced interdisciplinary social science course or might simply provide new topics and perspectives for a variety of courses in political science, economics, and sociology. A greater appreciation of the changes is best seen in a deeper look at the implications for each of the core concepts identified.

Rethinking Efficiency

Efficiency and productivity are economic concepts. Productivity has primarily been used as a measure of output per worker hour. Efficiency is a measure of output per dollar invested or per unit of work time or of all inputs combined. Sustainability shifts the emphasis to outputs (in dollars or in met human needs) per unit of impact on nature (e.g. in terms of ecological damage or emissions into the air or water) and/or per amount of energy and material extracted. Efficiency in a sustainability perspective is very much about the efficient creation of values, especially as measured in terms of societal well-being.

Efficiency and productivity, as traditionally defined, are prone to being one-dimensional measures.[1] This approach usually assumes that a higher dollar output is always better and smaller dollar inputs (including lower wages) are always preferable. Sustainability forces a three dimensional approach, a triple bottom line. It matters how things are produced and used as well as the dollar value of the product. It matters especially what the long-term unintended consequences of production are and how economic benefits are used and distributed.

Germany gets a very high and rising proportion of its electricity from renewable energy sources, especially wind and solar. This is highly efficient in terms of resource use and air quality and human health, especially compared to coal. In contrast, while industrial agriculture is highly productive in terms of traditional productivity per farmer and per acre, and local, organic agriculture is deemed less productive in terms of work time and per acre, it may well be more productive per unit of fresh, healthy nutrition delivered. Such things as freshness and taste are not always easy to measure, but one measure might be the rapidly rising popularity of local, artisan-produced organic food, even though it may be somewhat more expensive.

Sustainability considerations may render economics a less exact science, but it makes it a far more interesting one—one less likely to prove wrong-headed in the long term by not thinking beyond the next few business quarters and one dimension.

Sustainability and Citizenship

Citizenship is about rights and duties. Sustainability considerations suggest the expansion of those rights to include a clean, safe and healthy environment. They also expand citizen duties to include not just political and legal activities, but politicization of our market behaviors as consumers, investors and employees as well. Food activist Michael Pollan wrote: "The wonderful thing about food is that you get to vote three times a day. Every one of them has the potential to change the world."

Sustainability also expands our understanding of citizenship both in time (at the intergenerational level) and in scope (at a global scale with regard to climate change and other concerns). It opens the question of global citizenship and the possible need for a global citizens' movement.[2]

Sustainability considerations alter the meaning of citizenship in a way that extends the concept's earlier evolution. Citizenship evolved from being centered on communities (city-states and principalities) to a focus on nation-states. Decisive events in this evolution included the consolidation of national power of the French and British monarchies, American independence and westward expansion, the unifications of Germany and Italy and, decisively for the establishment of the nation-state as the dominant political form, the mass decolonization that followed World War II.

One underlying impetus for the modern shift to larger scale citizenship was the industrial revolution. The industrial revolution led to massive increases in the output of goods and a resulting need to expand markets and trade. Multiple separate and autonomous principalities hindered trade with the imposition of varying bridge tolls, road use charges and duties. Larger governmental entities and uniform rules smoothed the way to continuing growth in production and trade.

The industrial revolution also altered the *content and meaning* of citizenship. During the first half of the twentieth century, the creation of the modern welfare state enhanced the meaning of citizenship dramatically. T.H. Marshall called this shift *social citizenship*, to describe the possibility that citizenship as a concept had gone beyond political and legal rights and duties to encompass minimum standards of economic well-being (Hobhouse).

Marshall, writing in 1950, argued that the basic rights of citizenship (within the United Kingdom) had evolved over several centuries (Marshall and Bottomore). Assured citizen access to hard-won legal and civic rights (freedom of speech, assembly, press, religion, as well as the right to own property, conclude contracts, and have access to justice) were expanded to include primarily political rights over the course of the nineteenth century, via the reform acts of 1832, the 1860s, and 1880s that gradually lowered property requirements for male suffrage.

The *civil and political* rights of democratic citizenship were then expanded to include basic *social* rights through the effective use of the other two rights. Industrialization, mass production, and citizen political action helped to advance and broaden prosperity. As Marshall put it: "The modern drive toward social equality is, I believe, the latest phase in the evolution of citizenship which has been in continuous progress for 250 years" (Marshall and Bottomore 71).

Sustainability adds a contemporary extension to citizenship's evolution from legal and political to social rights and duties that Marshall identified. It potentially adds environmental rights and protections to citizens' expectations of government. Two concomitant shifts come with this change. One, as noted, is a need for global decision-making regarding, for example, habitat, climate change and the long range transportation of pollutants. The other shift, equally important, is a broadening of citizen duties into economic realms—a blending of the economic and political realms. What we make and purchase and how we use and dispose of it becomes a part of good (or poor) citizenship. The increasing legalization of what are called benefit corporations looks to include corporate as well as individual citizens in this shift (Raskin).

Marshall's social citizenship and citizenship from a sustainability perspective are also linked in another way. While global economic integration has helped to raise many from poverty in once desperately poor nations, it has also been a factor in rising inequality within many nations. This greater inequality has undermined social citizenship. It also makes it harder to advance sustainability, as understood since the 1987 Brundtland commission report (World Commission on Environment and Development). Brundtland showed that economically desperate people are less likely to be environmentally-concerned citizens. Greater wealth and income inequality also concentrates political power and, in that context, pro-sustainability initiatives will be more easily resisted politically.

Social Class and Democracy in a Global Age

The core of the challenge of advancing sustainability is two-headed. Paul Collier articulated this challenge when he wrote: "Restoring environmental order and eradicating global poverty have become the two defining challenges of our era…if we fail in either we fail in both." This reality is daunting. The solution is at least in part political and, given limited resources and the scale of the problem, we need to find elegant, synergistic, cost efficient solutions. The challenge is, of course, complicated by the fact that economic growth can impose new environmental costs. We must learn how to avoid those costs and how to resolve both problems concurrently. Further, it would now seem that, without political mobilization, economic growth will not necessarily result in poverty reduction, especially in wealthy countries.

Guy Stallings has argued that a new class, which he calls the precariat, is emerging in Western societies. Those in the precariat are employed in even less stable positions than the old proletariat, the industrial working class. The working hours of the precariat are highly flexible and irregular (at an employer's discretion, often with little notice) and their employment itself is often prone to seasonality and is frequently less than full time. Work, often for more than one employer, may not provide enough income to establish an independent household. This new class is growing rapidly and is populated by the young, immigrants, and former industrial workers whose previous jobs have been 'off-shored.'

According to Stallings, the emergence and growth of the precariat could threaten both democracy and societal stability. In his view, the 'precariat' is a dangerous class because it is, for the most part, "disengaged from twentieth century political discourses" (3). Given these risks, he proposes that the political instability and thinning democracy associated with changing labor markets could and should be offset by modest, publicly funded, basic income stabilization grants, and by efforts to enhance deliberative democracy. Others have called such initiatives a negative income tax or a guaranteed annual income (Torgerson). Stallings links these policies to the need for citizen participation in democratic political processes. "Chronically insecure people," he notes, "make poor democrats" (6).

In contrast, Fukuyama observes that income polarization undermines earlier gains associated with globalization, in terms of global wealth distribution. Globalization, in fact, especially early on, has tended to increase social equity on a global scale, with incomes improving for many in rising nations such as Korea, China, Brazil, India, Russia and Mexico. However, at the same time, income equity has eroded within most countries, both in the rising nations and in those with fully mature economies (Stewart and Berry).

This rising internal inequality can undermine democracy by concentrating wealth and, with it, political power. It is thereby unsustainable. Ultimately, it could reduce the capacity to democratically advance either environmental protection or economic growth. Concentrated wealth, combined with the globalization of social and economic decisions seemingly beyond the reach of national governments, renders citizenship inadequate to the task (Paehlke).

At the same time, addressing sustainability can open opportunities to simultaneously address environmental and equity needs. Low cost aid or charitable opportunities exist to address global environmental challenges, especially within poorer nations. Black carbon (soot) emissions from kerosene cooking devices or lights used in poor nations can be replaced by low cost, environmentally benign carbon neutral alternatives. The alternatives are affordable to operate and can be manufactured near where they are used. Thus, simultaneously there is an equity boost and a significant environmental gain.

There is also a parallel opportunity in wealthy nations captured under the term "just transportation." Essentially, it involves increased tax subsidies to public transit. Getting people out of cars for some trips aids the environment and reduces carbon emissions. It is also a huge boon to the precariat, who would then be able to get to their multiple and ever-changing job shifts in varied locations, as well as to medical appointments and distant, lower cost food suppliers. Greenhouse gas emission reductions alone might well justify some level of subsidy; improved social equity is an important bonus.

To add one concrete example, Portland, Oregon added a twist to this policy by, until recently, making streetcars free to all within the downtown core (only those traveling to or from suburban locations paid a fare at that point to proceed). The result was positive for downtown businesses and also greatly diminished traffic within the core, since many drivers parked their cars and moved around the core by streetcar. Additionally, there has been a downtown building boom because people chose to live within the core. Thus the gain is threefold: the environment, social equity, and the economy were advanced simultaneously.

Sustainability and Democracy

Achieving sustainability requires widespread buy-in, active participation, and behavioral change among citizens. This requires, in turn, that democracy be highly stable and that citizens go beyond voting to a willingness to adjust everyday behaviors, not so much in response to detailed rules as in response to a reasonably comprehensive understanding of the reasons behind the need for change. People need to grasp some of the myriad ways they can adjust their living patterns in sustainable ways, with a minimum of personal inconvenience. Government policies need to make such adjustments affordable. Germans, for example, now use only thirty percent of the electricity per person of North Americans, with electricity increasingly produced from renewable sources. Such adjustments are not easily regulated; they come through citizen participation and a greater sense of efficacy and trust.

Sustainability needs *democracy* to be stronger—thicker in the language of political science (Barber). However, today's insecure employment status and sharpening polarity in wealth distribution may well be *weakening* democracy. To achieve sustainability, we may need to remake democracy itself. Someone must speak for the future powerfully enough to offset the voices that speak for entrenched interests that resist change. Bill McKibben makes a convincing case that a habitable world cannot withstand the burning of all of the oil that remains in the ground (McKibben). However, is leaving oil in the ground politically possible in any jurisdiction in the world, let alone most or all jurisdictions?

This would only be possible in democracies where wealth did not have a disproportionate voice. Political science classes might explore whether and how that could be possible (and to appreciate that, even then, the success of those who would speak for the future would be far from automatic). Economics and policy classes might explore how incentives and disincentives (and the global economic context) might be altered to allow nations to take bolder sustainability initiatives without placing themselves at an economic disadvantage.

Conclusion

Regardless of what views students might hold regarding sustainability concerns, thinking about social science in terms of those concerns can deepen their understanding of both social science concepts and today's society. Thinking about climate change or rising inequality begs questioning the possibility of citizenship rights and duties and democracy on a global scale. Those same concerns open questions regarding the multiple meanings of economic efficiency. Thinking about social class comes alive if students think about how their social position and economic prospects differ from those of earlier generations and why that might be the case. Teaching is more effective when classic concepts are tied to the everyday issues that students face.

Notes

1.   Other dimensions can be considered in, for example, cost-benefit analysis to the extent that they can be expressed in dollar values, but this is hard to do in the case of lost human lives or ruined ecosystems.

2.   See discussions on www.gtinitiative.org.

Works Cited

Barber, Benjamin R. *Strong Democracy: Participatory Politics for a New Age.* Berkeley, CA: University of California Press, 1984. Print.

Collier, Paul. *The Plundered Planet.* New York, NY: Oxford University Press, 2011. Print.

Hobhouse, Leonard T. *Liberalism.* Oxford, UK: Oxford University Press, 1964. Print.

Marshall, T.H., and T.B. Bottomore. *Citizenship and Social Class.* London, UK: Pluto Press, 1992. Print.

McKibben, Bill. "Global Warming's Terrifying New Math." *Rolling Stone* 19 Jan. 2012. Web.

Paehlke, Robert. *Democracy's Dilemma: Environment, Social Equity, and the Global Economy.* Cambridge, MA: MIT Press, 2004. Print.

Pollan, Michael. Interview with Michael Pollan on Oprah: Let's Vote With Our Forks. *Huffington Post* Mar. 30, 2010. Web.

Raskin, Jamie. "The Rise of Benefit Corporations." *The Nation* 8 June 2011. Web.

Stallings, Guy. "The Precariat: Why It Needs Deliberative Democracy." *Open Democracy* 27 Jan. 2012.

Stewart, Francis, and Albert Berry. "Globalization, Liberalization, and Inequality: Expectations and Experience." *Inequality, Globalization, and World Politics.* Eds. Andrew Hurrell and Ngaire Woods. New York, NY: Oxford University Press, 1999. 150-186.

Torgerson, Douglas. "Rethinking Politics for a Green Economy: A Political Approach to Radical Reform." *Environmental Issues and Social Welfare.* Eds. Michael Cahill and Tony Fitzpatrick. Oxford, UK: Blackwell, 2002. 4-21.

World Commission on Environment and Development. *Our Common Future.* New York, NY: Oxford University Press, 1987.

II. In the Classroom: Case Studies and Innovative Pedagogies

Multi-disciplinary Approaches to Sustainability Education

Dr. Francis Galgano, Dr. Paul C. Rosier, Villanova University

Abstract: This essay documents our experiences co-teaching Villanova University's first rendition of "Seminar in Sustainability Studies," the cornerstone of the University's new cross-college Minor in Sustainability Studies. The essay offers insights into the challenges and opportunities of co-teaching, of multi-disciplinary approaches to sustainability education, and of assignments reflective of the multiple places where sustainability education can occur. The essay also assesses the value of incorporating multiple partners from different disciplines and professional schools: Nursing, Engineering, Law, Business, and the Liberal Arts and Sciences. And it evaluates the risks and rewards of requiring students to develop a research paper that constitutes the bulk of their final grade and of incorporating local sustainability case studies.

Francis Galgano, Ph.D., is an Associate Professor and the Department Chair of Geography and the Environment at Villanova University, where he teaches an array of courses. These courses include Land Use Planning and Management, Global Positioning Systems, Geo-Technologies, Water Scarcity, and the Environmental Issues Seminar. He, along with two of his colleagues, recently published a paper titled, "Modeling Environmental Security in Sub-Saharan Africa" in the *Geographical Bulletin*. His most recent paper, "Water and Conflict: The Evolving Environmental Security Landscape" will be published in the *Middle States Geographer* in the spring of 2013.

Paul Rosier, Ph.D., is Department Chair and Professor of History at Villanova University. In addition to the Seminar in Sustainability Studies, he teaches a range of environmental history courses, including Global Environmental History (a core curriculum history requirement), American Environmental History, and a graduate course, Environmental History. His essay on American Indian environmentalism of the 1960s and 1970s—entitled "'Modern America Desperately Needs to Listen': The Emerging Indian in an Age of Environmental Crisis"—will be published in the December 2013 *Journal of American History*.

"We do not inherit the earth from our ancestors, we borrow it from our children."
- Native American Proverb
"To refuse the challenge implied by the triple bottom line is to risk extinction."
- John Elkington
"Universities must decide whether they will continue training persons for temporary survival in the declining Cenozoic period or whether they will begin training students for the emerging Ecozoic period."
- Thomas Berry

Introduction

In the spring of 2007, Villanova University president Fr. Peter Donohue joined hundreds of his counterparts in signing the American College and University Presidents' Climate Commitment, which put Villanova on a path toward climate neutrality and formalized Villanova's embrace of environmental sustainability that began in 1970 when it hosted Stanford University biologist Paul Ehrlich as its Earth Day keynote speaker.

The promotion of sustainability at Villanova was inspired by two main sources. The first was Villanova's Augustinian mission and the Stewardship principle of Catholic Social Teaching. The second was a 2005 United Nations' initiative entitled *A Decade of Education for Sustainable Development*, the goal of which is to change future generations' behavior and attitudes in order to create a more sustainable society (United Nations). This commitment to sustainability found form in two major institutional goals at Villanova: "striving to practice the principles of environmental sustainability and wise use of resources within the university community"; and "engaging in appropriate learning opportunities with the intention of creating a community whose members (students, faculty, staff, and graduates) are environmentally literate and responsible."

To institute these goals, Fr. Donohue declared the 2008-2009 academic year, "The Year of Sustainability," calling on faculty, staff and students to explore the multiple dimensions of sustainability—in the classroom, on the campus grounds, and in nearby communities. The Year of Sustainability culminated in the April 2009 International SustainAbility Conference, which featured a stirring keynote address by Robert F. Kennedy, Jr. and drew over 150 attendees (including several of this volume's authors) from Latin America, Europe, Japan, Australia, and the United States. In addition, faculty from all four of Villanova's colleges as well as its Law School organized panels, including a Nursing-Engineering collaboration, making it a truly University-wide and interdisciplinary event.

The Conference, organized by this essay's authors, had three main outcomes. First, it raised Villanova's profile as an institution committed to the practice and the teaching of sustainability, both locally and internationally; faculty and students from Bryn Mawr, Swarthmore, Drexel, Temple, and other schools either participated in or attended the sessions. Second, it highlighted recent efforts by faculty to integrate sustainability in the curriculum, an initiative that found expression in three panels. A panel Rosier organized examined ways of integrating sustainability into the Liberal Arts curriculum. Another panel emphasized the value of Integrating Sustainability into the Business School Curriculum. A third panel discussed the challenges of getting new faculty to buy into the sustainability imperative. The second and related outcome was that it raised expectations among Villanova faculty, staff and students to put into practice the multiple ideas shared at the conference. And finally, the conference and its discussion of curricular initiatives led to the creation of the Minor in Sustainability Studies (MSS), the product of collaboration between the two authors—Galgano (Geography and the Environment) and Rosier (History/Environmental Leadership Learning Community)—and Dr. Andrea Welker, an associate professor in the School of Engineering.

Inspired by the Conference and by the growing numbers of academic institutions that had initiated minors or majors in sustainability, Villanova launched the MSS in August 2011. In January 2012, the authors offered the first rendition of the Minor's foundational course, the Seminar in Sustainability Studies (hereafter Seminar). We developed the course, which is required for all MSS students, with the assistance of a Villanova Institute for Teaching and Learning (VITAL) grant. This essay documents our experiences co-teaching the Seminar and assesses the strengths and weaknesses of its constituent elements. The essay seeks to offer insights into the challenges and opportunities of co-teaching, of multi-disciplinary approaches to sustainability education, and of assignments reflective of the multiple places where sustainability education can occur.

We developed the Seminar within various frames, internal and external. First, Villanova has deepened its commitment to environmental offerings in recent years, forming the Geography and the Environment department, establishing the Environmental Leadership Learning Community for first-year students, creating a Masters in Sustainable Engineering program, and offering a wide array of environmentally themed courses in various departments and colleges. But with few exceptions of team-teaching across disciplines, most of the environmental courses are situated within and constrained by disciplinary boundaries. Recognizing the complexities and problematic nature of "sustainability," we sought to develop a course that crossed not only disciplinary boundaries within the College of Liberal Arts and Sciences, in this case between Geography and History, but within the University as a whole, in large measure because we were unequipped to elucidate crucial elements of sustainable problem-solving. Accordingly, we built into the VITAL grant funding for honoraria for Villanova professors as well as scholars from other colleges. Our intention was not only to draw upon the expertise of these faculty members, but also to build a sustainable network of teachers invested in sustainability education in the Seminar and to inspire them to incorporate sustainability components in their own courses. Broadly speaking, "Integrating sustainability into the curriculum," one of the charges of Villanova's Year of Sustainability and one of the highlighted themes of the Sustainability Conference, became a principal goal of the course.

Second, sustainability education is being offered more and more at American and foreign colleges and universities, as is interdisciplinary education. This volume of essays is evidence of the importance of sustainability education at many institutions. Indeed, a May 2012 article in the *New York Times*, entitled "Vocation or Exploration? Pondering the Purpose of College," highlighted the opinions of educators who support interdisciplinary curricula that combine "major elements of a liberal arts education and professional training." It cited the example of Sustainability, which "can be studied, for example, from the point of view of business, history, philosophy and politics" (Tugend). Given the seemingly inexorable expansion of the "green economy," a program that can combine the intellectual with the professional will definitely attract students jittery about unstable job markets. Such views of the role of colleges and universities in addressing the complex economic and environmental challenges of the twenty-first century validate our decision to develop the course as multi-disciplinary rather than simply as a conversation between history and geography, our comfort zones. Such an approach to sustainability is limited, focusing on social sciences and humanities but not incorporating business, engineering, or law and public health, equally important elements of sustainability education. Teaching sustainability, then, requires instructors to expand their own understanding of sustainability, the concepts and content of which are evolving rapidly.

With little time to promote the course, we enrolled only eight students. The eight students, most of them second semester freshmen, came from the schools of business, engineering, and liberal arts and sciences. We anticipate more students enrolling in our second offering of the course for several reasons: we will have more time to advertise the course; it is now required for all students adopting the Minor in Sustainability Studies; and sustainability education is generating more publicity nationwide.

Course Architecture: Four Units
(see Appendix A for syllabus and course flow)

Unit 1: Introduction to Sustainability Studies

In taking our pre-test asking them what they believed sustainability to represent in historical and contemporary times, most of the eight students identified sustainability with Native American traditions of living in harmony with the earth as well as recent trends in society stemming from the first Earth Day of 1970. To a certain extent, the answers were quite similar, drawing on familiar tropes of the Ecological Indian and assessing the history of sustainability as a relatively recent one.

Because of the young age of the students and their lack of college coursework in history and geography, we designed the first section of the course to provide an introduction to the two main disciplines via three sessions: Historical Perspectives on Sustainability, Geographical Perspectives on Sustainability, and Non-Sustainable Practices and Collapse: Three Ancient Examples. This final class of the introductory section enabled students to consider historical and geographical perspectives on sustainability via accounts of the collapse of Akkadian, Maya, and Anasazi civilizations.

Historical Perspectives

This first session established a framework for and vocabulary of sustainable ideas and practices from early Modern Europe to the 1960s, highlighting Europeans' pre-1600s normative constraints against mining the earth, the gendered ways in which they conceived of Earth as a mother giving and sustaining life, and the erosion of those constraints in favor of scientific imperatives to "penetrate" Earth's resources and harness them for the improvement of man. These themes, developed using a Carolyn Merchant article entitled "Mining the Earth's Womb" (drawn from her influential book *The Death of Nature*), reinforced for students that notions of sustainability have long existed in various forms and were the rule rather than the exception until the advent of the Scientific Revolution. In addition, the lecture covered protests against pollution in Great Britain and the United States during the Industrial Revolution, highlighting the Progressive era impulse to conserve resources for future generations and for national security—as President Theodore Roosevelt framed resource depletion in the early twentieth century. This context established a long line of reasoning within the United States for state and citizen action in the face of environmental crisis that found expression more fully during the 1970s.

The session also introduced students to a pantheon of American environmental thinkers, including Henry David Thoreau, who promoted solar, wind, and wave power in the 1840s; George Perkins Marsh, the first scientist to assert the idea of man's ecological "footprint" and the irreversible change that resulted; Ellen Swallow, MIT's first female student and instructor who popularized the idea of Oekology in *Human Ecology* (1910); Aldo Leopold, whose 1949 essay "A Land Ethic" produced a phrase that defined post-war environmental thinking: "A thing is right when it tends to preserve the integrity, stability, and beauty of the biotic community. It is wrong when it tends otherwise"; and Rachel Carson, whose 1962 book *Silent Spring* made public and popular the idea of ecology, redefined the "environment" as starting with the human body, and argued, thus, that by poisoning nature we are poisoning ourselves.

Geographical Perspectives

In the opening segment of the course, we presented our students with interrelating historical and geographical perspectives from which they could make sense of the broad and diverse subject matter found in sustainability studies. The geographical perspective offers a spatial vantage point—which complements the temporal–historical perspective—of sustainability and the processes that drive environmental stress. Unfortunately, many people associate geography with knowledge of maps, lengths of rivers, names of countries and their capital cities, and other such bits of elemental information (Getis et al.). Clearly, this type of factual knowledge has its place because it permits us to position events, locations, and phenomena in a useful spatial setting. However, knowing and understanding *why* the issues of sustainability exist in discrete places is significantly more important than just knowing where they are—that is the true relevance of a geographical perspective to sustainability studies (Mather and Sdasyuk).

Geography is much more than simply knowing place names, cartography, and locations. Geographers attempt to understand places and the interconnectivity between them. In the first unit we focused on understanding the nexus between people and their natural environment and the differentiation of sustainability issues across space (Roberts). To understand this nexus, we examined topics such as population, climate, biomes, net primary productivity, water, and human activity on the landscape so that our students could comprehend the interconnectivity of these issues across Earth space, and their influence on sustainable environments (Chapman et al.). Furthermore, these issues enabled us to introduce the geographic concept of scale and the relationship between human activity and natural processes in local places, and their relationship to global sustainability problems (Gersmehl, Wood).

The investigation of spatial variability—how and why things differ from place to place—gives purpose and methodology to sustainability studies. The geographic perspective is further defined by the study of how spatial patterns develop through time; thus an awareness of locations is only an important initial step in understanding why things are where they are, and what events and processes determine change and distribution over time. For example, contemporary sustainability questions may include: what are the salient processes that drive climate change and what makes it more severe from place to place?; why is population centered in four primary clusters in the world?; and what are the different process that drive desertification and what makes it more severe in one place versus another? These types of questions were embodied in the final lesson of Unit 1, in which we examined three case studies that illustrated non–sustainable practices and the collapse of ancient civilizations: the Maya, Akkadians, and Anasazi. These case studies were very helpful because they were a unifying method by which we could tie together the initial part of the course. Each civilization was separated geographically and temporally, but in each case their downfall was driven by non-sustainable use of water resources, each involving a different dynamic, level of environmental stress, and mechanism of collapse (Prugh et al.).

Unit 2: Environmental and Human Processes
The Water Problem (see Appendix A for map)

During the second unit we used three lessons to examine the nexus between human activity and process on the natural landscape: terrestrial ecosystems, population trends and globalization, and abrupt climate change. We used geographic and historical perspectives to link a set of fundamental concepts that united all of the disparate areas of sustainability studies, as well as to frame our inquiry to determine answers to the study of the landscape. In so doing, we used three critical questions employed in our analysis of sustainability: what is the environment like and how has it evolved over time?; why is it like this here, in a particular place?; and how will it affect sustainability? These questions were integrated into three case studies featured in Unit Four (Chester, Pennsylvania; Brazil; and China).

The examination of global water resources is perhaps the best example in this unit for illustrating the integration of historical and geographic themes. Recent statistics indicate that global water demand for irrigation, domestic, and industrial use will increase faster than the rate of population growth (Fagan). Furthermore, freshwater supplies are, geographically, highly variable and are not equitably distributed in a spatial sense; nor does its spatial distribution match population distribution. The water scarcity problem is further complicated because water does not lend itself to international trade and it is not practical or economical to transport from surplus areas to places of acute scarcity (Pearce). Water supply is often further eroded by water quality issues. Increasing populations require more irrigation and dams, both of which can adversely affect water quality. Thus, water passed to downstream users, even in water-rich regions, is typically contaminated (Butts, "Strategic Importance").

Water is a particularly challenging factor in the sustainability milieu, because it is an essential resource for which there is no substitute and the freshwater supply problem only promises to intensify in a greenhouse world (IPCC). Growing global population and its attendant economic demands means that the pressure placed on freshwater resources will grow inexorably. Today, about one billion people lack access to safe drinking water and this number is likely to grow to nearly three billion by 2050 (Gleick, "Volume 7"). Renewable freshwater is fundamental to human health, agriculture, and industry; but contemporary water demands are approaching the limits of a sustainable supply and shortages are already reaching crisis proportions in key places (Smith and Vivekanada). Only 0.036 percent of the world's supply is renewable freshwater; and by 2015, some three billion people (about 40 percent of the global population) will live in regions that are unable to provide sufficient freshwater to meet basic food, industrial and domestic needs (Gleick, "Water in crisis;" Postel and Wolf).

To put this into practical terms: ideally, on an annual basis, each individual needs about a cubic meter of water for consumption, about 100 cubic meters for personal needs, and 1,000 cubic meters to grow the food that a person consumes (Gleick, "Biennial report"). Thus, the minimum basic need is about 1,100 cubic meters, and accordingly, a country with less than 1,700 m^3 per capita is regarded as experiencing water stress, while less than 1,000 m^3 is considered as water scarce (SIWI). This is perhaps the best metric for illustrating the magnitude of the water shortage problem, because it demonstrates water supply as a function of population and demand. Appendix A (Figure 2) illustrates the geographic distribution of water–stressed and water–scarce states; it clearly confirms that chronic problems are highly concentrated in the world—including the Middle East, with the world's fastest growing population. In fact, the U.N. now considers thirteen states to be water scarce, and four of them—Israel, the Palestinian Authority, Saudi Arabia, and Jordan—are from this region. U.N. projections suggest that another ten states will be added to this list by 2025, to include Egypt, Ethiopia, Iran, and Syria: in other words, one third of the world's water-scarce states are located in this region. Clearly, population is the crucial variable, because every additional person requires over 1,100 cubic meters of new water every year, and the region's associated agricultural water needs present a near impossible challenge for Middle Eastern economies (U.N. "Water in a changing world").

Unit 3: Thinking Sustainably

We employed two field trips as a means of visualizing in the field the concepts that students learned in the classroom. The first, a walking tour of Villanova University's storm water system, was focused on a small-scale application of sustainable practices. This field trip was preceded by a lesson presented by Professor Andrea Welker from the College of Engineering, which addressed the larger problem of runoff and water management in the Philadelphia metropolitan area. Professor Welker took us on a tour of each of the storm water management systems emplaced on campus, which include rain gardens, permeable surfaces in parking lots and campus dorm areas, and runoff control that directs water to an artificial wetland constructed on campus.

On our second trip, we visited SAP America's headquarters (Newtown Square, Pennsylvania), the largest LEED certified Platinum building in the United States and the most highly rated in terms of energy efficiency, water management, and innovative design. Our students were able to visualize first-hand many of the concepts discussed in class as they toured a building that saves over one million gallons of water per year, along with a rainwater collection system that supplies upwards of 50,000 gallons of water for landscape irrigation and the flushing of toilets in some of the building's bathrooms. In addition, employee workspaces were designed to incorporate natural light; the builders used fallen timber from the campus to construct railings that were functional and attractive; and the building was heated and cooled by large geothermal systems. Such a tour can be conducted by virtually any class near a metropolitan area. Businesses such as SAP are eager to showcase their technologies and, by extension, their commitment to sustainability, for public relations, bottom line, or societal purposes.

This field trip was supported by two guest lectures—one on corporate social responsibility and the second on green science. Dr. Jonathan Doh, Villanova School of Business, presented a lesson on the ethical-moral responsibility of the corporate world to implement sustainable practices. Dr. Ross Lee, a chemical engineer recently retired from the DuPont Corporation (and an adjunct professor in Villanova's Chemical Engineering and Geography and the Environment departments), examined the practical underpinnings of the green science movement. Both lessons formed an important frame-of-reference for our students, because they linked moral/ethical issues with the practical, scientific aspects of green buildings and other sustainable programs in the corporate world.

Unit 4: Sustainable Functions

Throughout the course we posed additional questions related to the social dimensions of sustainability: who suffers the most from environmental degradation, and sustainability for whom? In considering these questions through the intersections of sustainability, ethnic studies, and globalization, we gave two lectures on the American and global environmental justice (EJ) movement, focusing on several key EJ case studies. They included the experiences of Latino farmworkers contending with health problems from exposure to agricultural pesticides, which connected well to our discussion of the issues Rachel Carson raised in *Silent Spring*, and to guest faculty lectures on sustainability, agriculture, and health. We also examined American Indians' and African-Americans' experiences with environmental injustices, on Indian reservations, which the federal government targeted for nuclear waste dumping, and in black communities targeted for biomedical and chemical waste dumping. Students read the "17 Principles of Environmental Justice" drafted by delegates at the 1991 First National People of Color Environmental Leadership Summit, an important document that catalogs the key themes of the EJ movement (Principles of Environmental Justice). Students extended this analysis to a global scale by considering the rise of the climate justice movement via a discussion of the "Principles of Climate Justice," drafted at the 2002 Bali Conference that brought together indigenous and environmental groups from around the world to discuss the ways in which the poor have suffered and will continue to suffer the worst impacts of climate change, especially in low-lying areas (Principles of Climate Justice).

Another course component emphasized the links between students' local environment and the national and international dimensions of sustainability. We explored the local via two field trips (mentioned above) and one of three case studies, which allowed students to put elements of their sustainability lectures into motion and into a broader context. The first case study supported our discussion of environmental justice. Students viewed a documentary film on the environmental problems of Chester, Pennsylvania, located fifteen miles south of Villanova's campus. *Laid to Waste*, produced by students of Drexel University (Philadelphia) in 1996, captures the health problems and political powerlessness of Chester's black community, which was targeted for corporate dumping and burning of chemical waste and municipal trash, including Villanova's.[1] Employing a local case study is especially important for engendering among our students an understanding of and empathy for those people who lack the privileges of most college students. This case was particularly useful, as Villanova students of the 1990s assisted Chester residents in the Campus Coalition for Chester, a reminder that students can and should link their education to service or professional responsibilities.

The other case studies explored the importance of China and Brazil to current global sustainability issues. China's population and its extraordinary environmental problems, which kill over half a million Chinese each year, have tremendous salience for understanding climate change, agricultural productivity, water shortages, and environmental justice. One of the course assignments required students to write a two-page sustainability profile of China using selected readings and an additional document they located. The students, who knew little about the pollution that dirtied the United States up until the 1970s, were struck by how polluted and unhealthy China is and how vulnerable its residents are to water shortages. China's environmental limits have resulted in its expansion abroad, especially to Africa and Latin America, raising significant concerns about how Chinese economic power will affect already impoverished communities in those regions. Students were also surprised at how powerful Brazil has become in producing agricultural commodities such as soybeans, most of which are exported to China, and how much pressure agribusinesses exert on the land base of the Amazonian rainforest, a key regulating element in the global ecosystem. Brazil becomes a useful site to explore the complex social, legal, political, and ecological dimensions of the rainforest—the tension between local, regional, national, and international claims to its resources has been and will continue to be an important element of this evolving story.

International case studies, and ideally a local one discussing questions of environmental justice or sustainable agricultural production, preferably combined with a field trip, can easily be integrated into introductory courses such as general education and core curriculum courses, as well as more advanced capstone courses. Exploring the global repercussions of China's and Brazil's environmental problems and initiatives would give students insight into international economic processes and pressures, the ecological role of rainforests in regulating climate change, and the environmental justice implications for ethnic groups in Brazil and China. Students can also explore other nations, such as Indonesia and India, that are trying to mediate the conflict between economic development and environmental protection that drives most debates on sustainability.

Giving students such case studies served two main purposes. One, it helped them integrate disparate lessons from the course into temporal and geographic frames, and two, it helped them conceptualize and design their research papers, which represented the bulk of their course grades. The assignment required each student to write a fifteen-page paper on an approved topic related to course themes. Half the students took a case study approach, writing on, for example, the social and environmental problems of deforestation in Indonesian rainforests and the impact of globalization on India's agricultural practices. In perhaps the best paper for the course, a student examined the prospects for renewable energy use in Sub-Saharan Africa. The student, a freshman in the Business School, integrated course concepts from different disciplinary perspectives and made a compelling argument based on a good range of sources that included the course's main text (*The Post Carbon Reader: Managing the 21st Century's Sustainability Crises*). Other papers explored the impact of climate change on small countries such as the Maldives and sustainable farming practices in the United States.

One of the unique aspects that we brought to this course was a lesson/laboratory that used a Geographic Information System (GIS) to study issues in sustainability. This was a challenging undertaking because we had students from diverse backgrounds and only two of them had any previous experience with GIS. Thus, exercises had to be developed such that they could be implemented during the scope of a single lesson. Nevertheless, we were able to implement this exercise and our students used various forms of geospatial data to illustrate county-level population changes in the United States and land-cover changes in the Chesapeake Bay watershed using satellite imagery. The exercises clearly captured the interest of our students and demonstrated to us the power and applicability of these types of data and analyses in a sustainability course. The session reinforced key themes of the course via the nexus of land policy, ecology, and demographics within a regional context. Students reported finding the GIS laboratory session quite valuable. We intend to further develop additional self-contained GIS exercises for use throughout the course.

Reflections

Although a challenging assignment, especially for first year students, the final paper (which served as a form of post-test) enabled the student to research a topic of their choosing (see Appendix A), tie together the intellectual strands of the course, and link the course to their field of study. To assist the students, we held a research information session with one of Villanova's reference librarians and reserved class time at the end of the semester for consultations and presentations; the library information session generated an online course guide that students could consult throughout the process. The research presentations reinforced the idea that students can learn from each other and expanded the course's list of subjects and case studies to supplement the main topics. Given the students' diverse set of disciplinary approaches and interests, the instructors permitted different citation styles and developed a grading standard to ensure fairness.

Incorporating guest lecturers into our course proved extremely valuable. We believe the students found benefit in learning about important sustainability topics and case studies from faculty with specialties in environmental law, engineering, nursing/health, business, chemistry, energy, and ethics. For our faculty colleagues, it was a chance to introduce themselves and their disciplines to students, who may take courses with them as a result. For us, it was a great opportunity to learn from colleagues as well as to encourage those professors to either expand their course offerings to include a sustainability-themed course or to integrate more sustainability issues into existing courses; we fully expect to reciprocate by guest lecturing in such courses. The downside to this approach is that students need to adjust to different styles of presentation and read a range of materials across multiple disciplines. But this is precisely the kind of training we believe is necessary to fully comprehend sustainability issues and to implement solutions in professional capacities. Introducing students to different disciplinary approaches conditions them to seek multiple perspectives. Another potential negative aspect to this approach is that guest speakers sometimes tend to miss the point of the particular lesson that they are presenting—in spite of prior coordination. We will attempt, in the future, to alleviate this potential problem by providing the guest speaker with a set of well-defined lesson objectives that they can focus on from their unique disciplinary perspective. In this way, we hope to mitigate the problem of off target lectures that we occasionally experienced during our inaugural course offering.

Nevertheless, judging from student comments, both formal and informal, they indeed found value in these various presentations. One student responded to our query about the value of the course by writing, "I enjoyed the numerous guest speakers; hearing several aspects of expertise was not only interesting, but allowed me to think in ways that I hadn't really before. The class also tremendously helped my researching abilities, along with writing scientific papers." One of the best students of the course, an Engineering major, explained the benefits of the multi-disciplinary approach, which combined humanities, engineering, health, law, and science, writing, "I very much enjoyed the course and I had to overload in order to take it. It was a really different type of thinking and a nice break from my engineering/science/technical courses."

In addition, given the strong natural ties between environmental history and geography, the course proved invaluable for both instructors of this Seminar. Rosier's teaching of environmental history, especially his new Global Environmental History designed for first year students, will incorporate geographical concepts, contexts, and case studies he learned from Dr. Galgano. Dr. Galgano in turn gained perspective on the social and even sacred ways in which different groups engage particular geographies and resources that shape and sustain cultural and political identity.

Note

1. A portion of the documentary can be viewed at: http://www.youtube.com/ watch?v=5Opr-uzet7Q

Works Cited

Aagaard, Todd. "Environmental Harms, Use Conflicts, and Neutral Baselines in Environmental Law." *Duke Law Journal* 60.7 (2011): 1505-1564. Print.

Butts, Kent. "The strategic importance of water." *Parameters* 27.1 (1997): 65-83. Print.

---. "Environmental security: a growing force in regional stability." *Modern Military Geography*. Eds. F.A. Galago and E.J. Palka. New York, NY: Routledge, 2001. 54–64. Print.

Chapman, A. R., R. L. Peterson, and B. Smith–Moran. *Consumption, Population, and Sustainability*. Washington, DC: Island Press, 2000. Print.

Economy, Elizabeth. *The River Runs Black: The Environmental Challenge to China's Future*. 2nd ed. Ithaca, NY: Cornell University Press, 2010. Print.

Fagan, B. "Fresh water supplies are going to run out, so what can we do to make the taps keep running?" *The Independent* 30 June 2011. Web.

Friedman, Thomas. "The Power of Green." *The New York Times* 15 Apr. 2007. Web.

Galgano, F. A. *An Environmental Security Analysis of Abrupt Climate Change Scenarios*. International Handbook of Military Geography, Vol. 2. Proceedings of the 8th International Conference on Military Geosciences, Vienna, Austria, 15–19 June 2009: 196–208. Print.

Gersmehl, P. *Teaching Geography*. New York, NY: Guilford Press, 2005. Print.

Getis, A., J. Getis, and J. D. Fellmann. *Introduction to Geography*. 8th edition. New York: The McGraw-Hill Companies, Inc., 2008. Print.

Gleick, P. H., ed. *Water in Crisis. A Guide to the World's Fresh Water Resources*. New York, NY: Oxford University Press, 1993. Print.

---. *The World's Water: The Biennial Report on Freshwater Resources*. Washington, DC: Island Press, 1998. Print.

---. *The World's Water, Volume 7: The Biennial Report on Freshwater Resources*. Washington, DC: Island Press, 2012. Print.

Heinberg, R., and D. Lerch. *The Post Carbon Reader Managing the 21st Century's Sustainability Crises*. Healdsberg, CA: Watershed Media, 2010. Print. [Course textbook]

IPCC (Intergovernmental Panel on Climate Change Working Group II). *Technical Paper on Climate Change and Water*. IPCC Technical Paper VI, 2008. Print.

Jiusto, Scott. "Energy Transformations and Geographic Research." *A Companion to Environmental Geography*. Eds. N. Castree, et. al. Blackwell Online, 2009. 533-551. Print.

Mather, J. R., and G. V. Sdasyuk. *Global Change: Geographical Approaches.* Tucson, AZ: University of Arizona Press, 1991. Print.

Merchant, C. "Mining the Earth's Womb." *Machina Ex Dea: Feminist Perspectives on Technology*. Ed. Joan Rothschild. New York, NY: Pergamon Press, 1983. Print.

Pearce, F. *When the Rivers Run Dry*. Boston, MA: Beacon Press, 2006. Print.

Postel, S. L., and Wolf, A. T. "Dehydrating conflict." *Foreign Policy* 18 Sept. 2001. Web.

Population Reference Bureau. *2011 World Population Data Sheet*. Web.

Principles of Climate Justice. *India Resource*. 2002. Web.

Principles of Environmental Justice. *EJ Net*. 1991. Web.

Prugh, T., R. Constanza, and H. Daly. *The Local Politics of Global Sustinaibility.* Washington, DC: Island Press, 2000. Print.

Roberts, Neil, and Chalmers M. Clapperton. "The Changing Global Environment." *Area* 28.4 (1996): 542. Print.

Roberts, N. *The Changing Global Environment.* Oxford, UK: Blackwell, 1994. Print.

Rubio, Julie Hanlon. "Towards a Just Way of Eating." *Green Discipleship*. Ed. Tobias Wright. Winona, MN: Anselm Academic, 2011. 360-377. Print.

SIWI (Stockholm International Water Insititute) "Water resources in the Middle East." 2009. Web.

Smith, D., and J. Vivekananda. *A Climate of Conflict*. London, UK: International Alert, 2007. Print.

Soffer, A. *Rivers of Fire: The Conflict over Water in the Middle East*. Translated by M. Rosovsky and N. Copaken. London, UK: Rowman and Littlefield, 1999. Print.

Steffen, W., et al. *Global Change and the Earth System: A Planet Under Pressure*. New York, NY: Springer, 2005. Print.

Tugend, Alina. "Vocation or Exploration? Pondering the Purpose of College." *New York Times* 4 May 2012. Web.

United Nations. "Water in a changing world." *United Nations World Water Development Report 3*. 2009. Print.

--- "A Decade of Education for Sustainable Development, 2005-2014." 2005. Print.

Wood, T. F. "Thinking in Geography." *Geography* 72 (1987): 289–299. Print.

Yardley, Jim. "Beneath Booming Cities, China's Future is Drying Up." *The New York Times* 28 Sept. 2007. Web.

A Willamette Valley Agriculture Wiki: Enhancing Place-based Sustainability Education and Creating Opportunities to Support Local Communities

Kimberlee J.Chambers, Pacific Northwest College of Art;
Sheridan A. Schlegel, Katy J. Giombolini, Jonnie B. Dunne, Willamette University

Abstract: Public access wikis on sustainability topics created by academic institutions can provide opportunities to enhance student learning and capacity building with local communities. We created a Willamette Valley agriculture wiki to provide students and educators with an opportunity for place-based learning exercises, allow for inexpensive publication of educational materials, break down barriers to knowledge acquisition, afford a venue for community capacity building, and encourage the sustainability of local agriculture. To assess the outcome of the wiki on student educational experience we conducted surveys with two sustainable agriculture-focused classes. The goals of these classes included helping connect students to their local landscape, providing innovative problem-based learning opportunities on sustainable agriculture issues, and exploring the spatial and temporal complexity of sustainability. The surveys revealed that students valued the experience of contributing their research to the wiki primarily for the knowledge sharing potential.

Kimberlee J. Chambers has a PhD in Geography from University of California, Davis where she studied traditional varieties of corn in Mexico, and a Masters in Ethnobotany from the University of Victoria in British Columbia. Her research and teaching interests span a variety of food and agricultural topics linked to conservation and sustainable community development. She is currently a research affiliate at Portland State University and an assistant professor at Pacific Northwest College of Art. Her research has been published in *Journal of Agriculture, Food Systems, and Community Development, Agriculture and Human Values, Journal of Ethnobiology, Journal of Economic Botany, The Professional Geographer, Renewable Agriculture and Food Systems, Cartographica, Native Plants Journal, The Singapore Journal of Tropical Geography*, and the *Canadian Botanical Association Bulletin*.

Sheridan Schlegel, the main developer of the wiki, attended Willamette University and majored in Global Health and the Environment, with an emphasis on agriculture and farm worker health. During her time at Willamette, Sheridan focused her studies on the intersection between healthy people and healthy environments and conducted research on Willamette Valley farm workers with the Salem Hospital's Community Health Education Center. She currently resides in Denver, Colorado where she works in youth and community development through the Beacons program affiliated with the Boys and Girls Club of Metro Denver. There, she provides health and wellness programing to under-served youth in low-income areas of Metro-Denver, incorporating food systems, nutrition, composting, and cooking into coursework. Sheridan is a co-author on publications in *Agriculture and Human Values*, and *Renewable Agriculture and Food Systems.*

Katy Giombolini majored in Environmental Science at Willamette University with a focus on sustainable agriculture. At Willamette, Katy researched local food in the Willamette Valley, involved herself with issues of food justice, and helped start the student run farm. Katy is currently the outreach coordinator for the Berggren Demonstration Farm and education coordinator for the Southern Willmatte Farm Corps--a beginning farmer training program. Katy has co-authored papers for *Journal of Agriculture, Food Systems, and Community Development, Agriculture and Human Values,* and *Renewable Agriculture and Food Systems.*

Jonnie Dunne majored in Environmental Science and minored in Geography at Willamette University. There he pursued several research interests, including local food marketing, agroecology, and Willamette Valley camas meadow ecology. He has since worked as a field technician in plant ecology research labs on Mount Saint Helens and the Mariana Islands. Currently, Jonnie is an AmeriCorps Stewardship Coordinator at the Bainbridge Island Land Trust, where he coordinates volunteers in monitoring and restoring 1,136 acres split among fifty land trust properties. Jonnie is a co-author on publications in *Agriculture and Human Values*, and *Renewable Agriculture and Food Systems.*

Key words: wiki, Willamette Valley, agriculture, capacity building, place-based learning

Open access wikis created by members of academic institutions have the potential to contribute to both the campus and the wider communities of which they are a part. We[1] created a Willamette Valley agriculture wiki to provide students and educators with an opportunity for place-based learning exercises, allow for inexpensive publication of educational materials, break down barriers to knowledge acquisition, afford a venue for community capacity building, and encourage the sustainability of local agriculture. We believe that public access wikis can be used as both a tool for teaching about sustainability and as a means for universities to help sustain local communities. A wiki focused on Willamette Valley agriculture offered an opportunity to support local sustainable agriculture initiatives and enhance equity through knowledge sharing. Our research focuses on the impact of using an open access wiki on students' learning experiences.

While wikis have been utilized in isolated environments within educational institutes and by the general community, there has not been significant research on connecting educational wikis with community use. What wikis have not done, therefore, is link community and educational knowledge to provide a space where the flow of information is accessible to those who are interested and not bound to any individual educational institution. By developing a wiki focused on Willamette Valley agriculture to be used by both members of the academic institution and the community in the region, we utilized the applications of wiki technology for both educational and community benefits. The potential for interaction between students and the surrounding area takes learning about sustainability beyond the walls of the classroom and provides opportunities for place-based education, giving their work greater context, meaning, and connection. The wiki contributes to the community by providing opportunities for information flow in both directions. While this wiki appeals to a particular agricultural growing region, it exemplifies the capabilities of a wiki site for educational use.

In what follows, we begin with a brief overview of how wikis have been used in the classroom and communities to highlight their potential (*Sharing Knowledge and Sustaining Communities*). We then explain our choice of a wiki sustainability topic and suggest considerations for selecting topics in other regions (*The Focus of a Community: A Willamette Valley Agriculture Wiki*). We include the steps we took in developing the wiki, use of the wiki in the classroom, and the assessment tools used to gauge student perceptions of the benefits and obstacles to using the wiki (*Making Links: A Wiki in the Works*). The discussion of our methods and results (*Wiki Benefits and Concerns*) highlights not only why this is an innovative and useful form of collaboration in both the classroom and community but the challenges that we faced in the development of the wiki, students concerns with using it, and obstacles to community members contributing. In the conclusion (*Conclusion: Food for Thought*), we review the relevance of the wiki for sustainability and place-based learning, knowledge distribution, breaking down the barriers between academic institutions and the communities that they reside in, capacity building, and community service, linking each of these to the potential for enhanced learning opportunities.

Sharing Knowledge and Sustaining Communities

A wiki has the potential to contribute to sustainability education by sharing of knowledge on sustainability related topics with the local community and through student design, development, and contributions to the site. Traditionally, the dissemination of academic works has been limited, despite the increase in open source and on-line journals. Additionally, student assignments often do not travel further than an instructor's desk. Traits of education such as these contribute to perceptions that academic institutions are separate entities from the communities in which they reside. Community wikis, however, may enable interactions between these entities and encourage students to engage more fully in their education.

With the advent of Web 2.0, specifically the wiki that allows for group interactions and user contributions, there has been an increase in the use of technology within the classroom (Lundin 433; Camihort 30; Cobus 24; Kane and Fichman 10). The knowledge that is gathered through classroom use of wikis has typically been constrained to those who are members of the site, isolating the work produced in the wiki from the general population (Lundin 434; Wheeler, Yeomans, and D. Wheeler 990; Camihort 30; Kane and Fichman 10). In addition to their role in education, public and community groups have used wikis (Chu 175; Leuf and Cunningham 21; Noveck 126); however, linking classroom and community through a public wiki has been underutilized.

By opening wikis to public access, instructors widen the audience for student works and educational institutions can disseminate information beyond the walls of the classroom, while also receiving greater input from community members. Wiki technology changes the roles of an author and a reader, as the wiki reader can become the author, editor, and publisher of any editable page of the site (Lundin 434; M. Cole 142; Koehler & Fuchs-Kittowski 410). With user editing, the goal of the wiki is continual contribution and the creation of a collective body of knowledge, thus making it a useful curricular tool for knowledge dissemination and creation (Koehler and Fuchs-Kittowski 410). Koehler and Fuchs-Kittowski argued that wikis could be used as a tool for community collaboration, resulting in a collective base of interdisciplinary knowledge (412). This communal information base is afforded because wikis enable ideas to be spread between the central wiki site and individual users, pairing the expertise with the experts (John and Melster 165; Noveck 117). The desire for a shared knowledge base drives community wiki contributions and, because of their appeal to a broad audience, these wikis tend to check and balance their own accuracy (Millard et al. 95; Cobus 24). The combination of these attributes with the goals of educational wikis can further the contributions to an individual wiki site.

The Focus of a Community: A Willamette Valley Agriculture Wiki

Each region has a unique sense of place, shaped by the physical environment and the human characteristics of the area.[2] Situating student learning activities in a bioregion helps connect them to the place where they live and provide real life context to their curricula. The human-environment interactions that form a particular identity of a region provide important opportunities for developing place-based wikis on sustainability. The creation of a Willamette Valley agriculture wiki, for example, provided an opportunity to link the diverse members of this community through one virtual network and create a venue for students, faculty members and staff to disseminate place-based research and writing that reaches a broader audience. Focusing on agriculture provided opportunities to address all aspects of sustainability: environmental, economic, and social.

The relationship between agriculture production in Western Oregon's Willamette Valley and the local food culture strongly influences the sense of place within the bioregion. Because of the environmental, economic, cultural, and social contributions that agriculture makes to the Willamette Valley, we felt that it was an important topic to focus our wiki on, and ideal for helping students understand and connect to their local landscape. Environmentally, the Willamette Valley growing region has high agricultural diversity and accounts for more than 50 percent of the total annual agriculture production in the state (Oregon Department of Agriculture, "Growing Regions in Oregon"). At 12 percent of total jobs in 2009 (Oregon Department of Agriculture, "Oregon agriculture produces a large economic footprint"), agriculture employment in Oregon is significant. Culturally, a large portion of farm workers in Oregon are migrant and seasonal (approximately 99,923 people in 2001) with over half residing in the Willamette Valley (Larson 23).

Within the Willamette Valley and larger metropolitan areas such as Portland, there is an ever-increasing focus on the local food movement. Home to proclaimed "foodies," Portland is recognized for eateries that focus on local, sustainable sources of produce, meats, dairy, and grain products. The partnership of Portland's chefs and local farmers is ever visible. Within the last ten years, the number of farmers' markets in Oregon has more than doubled in the state (Kulongoski), with 57 located within the Willamette Valley (Oregon Farmers' Market Association). The retail sector has also responded to the demand for regional foods by sourcing and marketing commodities as "local" (Dunne et al. 5). L. Cole documents education efforts such as initiatives to purchase over 30 percent of food locally for school lunches and grants, enabling Portland Public Schools to increase spending for local foods. These business, education, and political initiatives symbolize the public support of local sustainable agriculture in the Willamette Valley. In this region the established sense of community and prior support of sustainable agriculture initiatives provided a great topic for wiki implementation.

The initiatives in the Willamette Valley are not unique but reflect national efforts to increase the consumption of local foods and help sustain communities. For example, since 1994, the number of farmers' markets in the United States has increased by nearly 3,000 (Shaffer and Cox). Educational institutions can play a particularly large role in shaping the nation's food system with their ability to provide opportunities for engagement with surrounding communities (Sacks). With a Willamette Valley agriculture wiki, we are able to provide opportunities for engagement through links between producers and consumers, and thus, as Feenstra (34) suggests, help sustain local communities. Our model of a Willamette Valley agriculture wiki is widely applicable to other communities throughout the US who are going through similar experiences in efforts to shape local agriculture and influence healthy eating choices. However, this wiki model does not have to be limited to agriculture but could be used on any central, driving, 'hot' sustainability topic in a region such as energy, pollution, immigration, climate change adaptation, or water.

Making Links: A Wiki in the Works

In order to enhance student-learning opportunities and facilitate capacity building within the academic and Willamette Valley communities, we collaborated to create a fully functional wiki, developed assignments for student contributions, and assessed impacts on students' learning experiences. The student collaborators were fully involved in each phase of the development of the wiki; Schlegel, in particular, took leadership on a number of the most significant tasks, with the remainder of the team working in consultation. The development of the wiki came to conclusion in three main phases: finding a site host; designing the layout; and developing pages and adding materials including text, maps, pictures, and figures.

In addition to creating the site, we wanted to increase accessibility to the wiki and develop interest. To achieve these objectives, we created community outreach materials (e-postcards and postcards), provided individual workshops, and facilitated university seminars to introduce faculty members and staff to the wiki and suggest possible uses. Our goal was to create opportunities for the wiki to be easily accessible to a broader audience. The following sections outline the steps taken in the development of our wiki and the methods used to assess the impact on students of contributing.

Developing the Wiki

In selecting a wiki host, we encountered problems when host sites charged fees for services (we had no budget to sustain the wiki), or were free but had limited capabilities such as storage space or a maximum number of users. Realizing not all wikis were equal and that our site had specific needs, we developed a list of preferences for our wiki that included cost, software requirements, user interface, available space, and ease of use. Using a search site called Wikimatrix (http://www.wikimatrix.org/) created by CosmoCod, we searched for host sites based on our three most important characteristics: a hosted site without software, free of charge, and with 1GB of storage space. There were no wikis that fit these qualifications. We lowered the storage space, created user accounts for the most applicable sites to gain an understanding of a wiki's abilities, and found a wiki provider, wikidot.com. With this wiki, we were unable to meet some of our original requirements such as storage space, language, and what-you-see-is-what-you-get (WYSIWYG) editing. However, we applied for and were granted education status on the site, allowing it to remain a free resource with 5GB of storage space.

The next phase was to design the wiki. Enlisting the help of on campus technological support, we created custom style sheets (CSS) in order to change the layout, colors, tabs, logo, title, and site map of our wiki. To design the site we obtained CSS files from other users of *Wikidot* that were modified to our preferences.

The third phase was to build the wiki. We based the wiki on a site map that consisted of tabs for the top of the wiki and a left-hand navigation panel. All tabs were included in English and Spanish to appeal to a broader audience reflective of the local agricultural community. For each of the headings and subheadings, we provided bilingual overviews of how the topic related to Willamette Valley agriculture, included references, links to other relevant web pages, and pictures. Previously gathered materials including student works from grant recipient materials, internship research, class assignments, and senior thesis papers were compiled and placed onto the wiki. By providing initial relevant material, we sought to enhance users' understanding of Willamette Valley agriculture, as well as provide examples of the type of information that could be contributed to the site.

In order to better market the wiki, we established a branding technique that included a logo and phrase that was displayed on our outreach materials: "*Share/ Compartir. Grow/Cultivar. Learn/Aprender.*" Outreach materials were distributed to local organizations. We conducted in-person visits with selected organizations to discuss how the site would be beneficial to them, obtained their input on linking the wiki to their organization, and in some cases created a wiki page on their behalf. To view the wiki go to: http://willamettevalleyagriculture.wikidot.com/.

Assessment of Educational Impact

In order to assess the impact of using the wiki on student learning experiences we designed two anonymous surveys that were administered in two different courses focused on sustainable agriculture. The first survey was administered the first day of each course (August 2010) before students were aware that they would be contributing to the wiki. Questions were structured to assess factors that may influence students' experiences contributing to the wiki, including personal data such as age, gender, education level, history of computer access/use, and previous experience with wikis. The second survey was administered at the end of the semester (December 2010) after students had contributed to the wiki. The personal data questions were repeated with new questions on ease and challenge of posting to the wiki and how students interpreted the experience. The questions asked were categorical.

The two classes surveyed were a freshmen level course, designed to introduce students to university learning, and an upper division, writing-intensive course in the sciences. Both courses had a strong, place-based component to enhance student learning by providing connections to the local landscape. The introductory course, titled *The*

Geography of Food, focused on writing, discussion, and critical reading. Composed of fourteen freshmen selected by the administration based on student preferences, the class represented a range of academic interests as well as socioeconomic and hometown geographic diversity; therefore, not all students necessarily identified closely with the topic. For their final papers, the students in this class were required to write about what it would be like to eat a local food diet in their hometown. Through this topic they defined "local" and developed arguments about the benefits and challenges of a local food diet. The students then uploaded their final documents to the wiki, in a section created in one of the tabs, titled *Eating Local/Comida Local* (http://willamettevalleyagriculture.wikidot.com/what-is-it-like-to-eat-local).

The upper division course was titled *Sustainable Agriculture in the 21ˢᵗ Century*. Course goals were similar to the class described above (writing, discussing, reading); however, the course is more content-focused. It contained sophomores, juniors, and seniors who represented a diversity of academic majors in the sciences, social sciences, and humanities. The final papers were group assignments that built on annotated bibliographies and individual research on agricultural sustainability. The sixteen students were divided into three groups for the final project, focused on economic, environmental, and social sustainability. Each group prepared a report on what agricultural sustainability in the Willamette Valley would look like, based on their group's perspective. These final papers were then added to the wiki in the *Willamette Valley/Valle de Willamette* section (http://willamettevalleyagriculture.wikidot.com/modeling-sustainable-agriculture-in-the-willamette-valley).

Wiki Benefits and Concerns

The survey results suggest that contributing to the wiki positively impacted students' learning experiences. In total, thirteen females and sixteen males (one student was absent on the final survey day) completed both surveys with twenty students in the age category of 15-19, eight in 20-24, and one in 30-34. Those surveyed included fourteen freshmen, seven sophomores, three juniors, and five seniors. The preliminary surveys suggested that students had extensive experience using computers and wikis, but had little exposure contributing to wikis or maintaining websites such as blogs. All but two students indicated that they owned their own computers (seventeen students had owned a computer for 0-4 years and ten for 5-9 years) and all but one answered 'yes' to the question 'do you like spending time on your computer?' In addition, seven students (including two freshmen) had taken a computer class related to designing web pages, blogs, or wikis. Ten students had created or maintained a web site, blog, or wiki: two for fun, one because of curiosity, three for work, and four for a school assignment. Two students had previously added information to wikis, neither for a classroom exercise. All except two students indicated that they had used wikis (like *Wikipedia*) to search for information. Based on these results, we anticipated that students might be more reluctant about contributing to the wiki as it would be a new experience and potentially result in challenges dealing with the wiki interface.

The second set of surveys, completed on the last day of classes after students had contributed to the wiki, revealed that they had encountered obstacles in contributing, but that they perceived a number of values in the experience. In the upper level course, one student from each of the three groups uploaded the final paper. Of the freshman that uploaded their own papers, and the three who uploaded the group papers in the upper division course, eight indicated that the instructions were not difficult to follow and nine stated that they were. Four of those who indicated the instructions were difficult to follow stated that 'yes' they missed/skipped a part of the instructions.

Students were also asked to respond (yes or no) to eight prompts in order to assess the personal impact of contributing to the wiki. The students' responses indicated that they widely viewed contributing to the wiki as a positive experience with a diversity of impacts. Out of the 29 completed surveys:

- 83 percent said they liked the opportunity to make their paper available to a wider audience;
- 79 percent said that posting their paper to the wiki made the assignment seem more relevant;
- 76 percent appreciated having their research available and hopefully useful to others;
- 69 percent indicated that posting their paper on the wiki provided an opportunity to feel more connected to the greater off-campus Willamette Valley community;
- 69 percent liked having their paper posted in a place that family, friends, and community members at home could access;
- 52 percent felt that posting their research on the wiki helped breakdown some of the divisions between university campuses and off-campus communities; and,
- 52 percent stated that posting their papers in a location where more people could read them inspired them to make it better.

These results indicate that a wiki has a diversity of possible applications to enhancing sustainability student-learning experiences. As one student interviewed for a campus publication summarized: "It helped develop my skills as a writer and gave me an educational tool for whenever I need to learn more about farming, gardening or local food" (Willamette University).

Our results are similar to Wheeler, Yeomans, and D. Wheeler, who found that wiki assignments encouraged students to be more thoughtful in their writing, due to the student awareness of an audience (993). However, it appears that even more than judgments of their work, students valued contributing to the wiki for the potential knowledge-sharing benefits, whether these were for family, friends, home communities, or the Willamette Valley community. This is highlighted by how many students indicated that a positive consequence of the wiki was being able to share the research that they had done, in the hopes that it may be useful to others. It is also significant to note that students valued the place-based /real-life nature of contributing to the wiki. These results illustrate how, by opening wikis to public access, instructors widen the audience for student works; wiki use diversifies the ways in which students connect to their assignments in the classroom, appealing to students that traditionally may not feel connected to their writing. Additionally, educational institutions can disseminate information beyond the walls of the classroom, helping to meet equity goals of sustainability.

While the wiki provides an easily accessible form of technology for educational enhancement and knowledge sharing, there are critiques of wikis. In presenting these concerns and the ways that we chose to address them, our intention is to invite further discussion of the effective use of wikis as a tool for sustainability education and for capacity building within and between communities and educational institutions.

One common criticism of wiki use is the concern over accuracy of information, as any user may edit the site (Lundin 434; Cobus 24). For small, enclosed, educational wikis, a facilitator or instructor often monitors the site for accuracy; in open forums, the information may be self-policing, particularly if there is a large user base that seeks to protect their common interests, which enables the site to provide accurate information (Lundin 434; Cobus 24). With a displayed history and ability to revert back to previous versions, maintaining the ability to change corrections provides a safety net for inaccurate editing.

Another concern with wiki use is intellectual property rights, as this may inhibit the motivation to participate in the site (Ras et. al. 399; Vickery and Wunsch-Vincent 12; Wheeler, Yeomans, and D. Wheeler 992; Kane and Fichman 3). By publishing on a wiki, an author relinquishes their right to have the information exactly as it was written. As a result, authors cannot own the page they created and this may inhibit some contributions to the site. Knobel and Lankshear describe a wiki that was used in education that allows specifically for pages to have the ability to be unedited (632). This allows for the author to maintain control over their publication. While this does not allow for community collaboration on the individual work, it does encourage those who have a vested interest in a particular piece of writing to contribute to the site. In order to provide an opportunity to protect the intellectual property of contributors, we took two approaches. First we allowed people to add files, such as PDFs, that remain free of edits. Other users can, however, post comments about the documents. Secondly, to protect the contributions to the Willamette Valley agricultural wiki, we employed a service called Creative Commons Attribution License (http://creativecommons. org/licenses/by/2.5/). The Creative Commons serves as an ethical code stating that information from the site may only be used with permission from the author or for appropriate uses.

Additional problems with wikis are, as Ras et al. addressed, the motivation of use by different parties; getting people to contribute to the site is necessary for its success (397). Motivation for wiki use within the classroom is different than motivation for use outside of the classroom. While instructors have facilitated wiki use in educational settings, their existence does not automatically elicit use and student behavior has been sometimes characterized as lurking with a reluctance to participate in open forums (Lundin 442; Wheeler, Yeomans, and D. Wheeler 992). Lundin acknowledged, however, that anonymity increased students' levels of contribution to the site (444). Additionally, education is based on self-promotion and reward, so there must be incentives for participation, such as a grade reward for individual contribution (M.

Cole 146). It is because of these behaviors that it is beneficial for instructors to facilitate use of the wiki, integrating it into preexisting educational standards and expectations of classroom participation (Lundin 444; M. Cole 146). A wiki does not replace an instructor, but rather can aid in the development of curriculum (Kane and Fichman 11). Instructors can facilitate contribution and use of a wiki through integration of the site into their curriculum, promoting an environment of critical thinking and collective knowledge. Our results from the student surveys highlight the potential for success of this technique.

Outside of the classroom, incentives to participate in the wiki are also needed because there is no instructor facilitating its use. Due to the vital role agriculture plays in the Willamette Valley, community members have an incentive to participate. For agricultural producers and related organizations, contribution to the site publicizes their causes and goals for free, increasing community awareness. For consumers of Willamette Valley agriculture, posing questions and information makes their desires more widely known by those who share common interests. Despite community outreach materials and instructions that incorporated these incentives, providing motivation for contributing to the wiki, contributions remain low. This could be because of the complexity in contributing to the wiki, as we were not able to get a site that had WYSIWYG editing. Instead, we created detailed instructions for editing each page. The lack of off-campus contributions could also partially be the result of a lack of awareness of the wiki's existence. However, we monitored usage statistics to assess the utilization of the site and according to Google Analytics (http://www.google.com/analytics), within the first six months, over 1800 visitors from 77 countries viewed the wiki. Within the first year, the number expanded to well over 100 countries and the monthly visits continued to remain high. Another possible reason for a lack of contributions may be understood through looking at Wikipedia. Although Wikipedia has millions of entries and is viewed widely on a daily basis, a survey by Wikimedia in collaboration with the joint center of the United Nations University and Maastricht University found that less than fifteen percent of the contributors are female and the average age of contributors was in the mid-20s (Cohen). The demographic that our wiki on Willamette Valley agriculture appeals to may be broader than those who are commonly contributing to wikis.

An associated problem with wikis is accessibility, due to its location on the Internet and employment of new technology (Chu 173). Katz, Rice, and Aspden profiled the typical Internet user in the United States, concluding that they are generally young males who are urban dwelling, affluent, better educated, and white (409). We targeted the population of the Willamette Valley that has specific ties to agriculture; thus, our wiki needed to appeal across gender, age, education, racial, and locational gaps. In Oregon, approximately 60 percent of all farms have access to the Internet, with residential access in the majority of Willamette Valley counties over 70 percent (United States Department of Agriculture: National Agriculture Statistics Service). This is a significant portion of farms in the Willamette Valley; however, the population is demographically different than the profiled Internet users. Farm workers, commonly migrant and Spanish-speaking in Oregon, may have less access than the statistics state. To address this concern and reach this population, we appealed directly to farm worker organizations that can increase access and aid in making resources available. We also worked to make a significant portion of pages of the wiki bilingual.

In addressing concerns with wikis in general, and the obstacles that we encountered in creating the Willamette Valley agriculture wiki, our goal was to provide further insights into the opportunity for this technology to be used as a way of linking educational institutions and local communities through collaborative knowledge. Although the technology is not without challenges, as our results indicate, the potential benefits to contribute to sustainability education are high and the compromises made are not substantial.

Conclusion: Food for Thought

Our research suggests that the benefits from developing open-access wikis and their use as a classroom tool for place-based learning have the potential to go beyond the wiki itself. The wiki increased the opportunity for place-based learning exercises and focused on a particular location and real world events, which increased students' interest and thus involvement in the learning process. Smith notes that an important component of place-based learning is that it allows for a strengthening of students' connections to others and the region where they live (593). Place-based learning assignments situated in the landscape that surrounds us, published on a wiki, add not only to the sense that what a student is doing is real, they also help a student establish a sense of place and understanding of where they live by strengthening their connections to others and to the region. Contributing to the wiki allowed for an opportunity to increase participants' sense of community—both virtual and physical.

By providing an inexpensive arena for publication of new and existing information, the role of knowledge distribution and acquisition in education is revised. With the introduction of the Willamette Valley agriculture wiki, opportunities were created for individuals to publish material online in both editable and non-changeable formats. As researchers have pointed out, students apply an increased level of critical thinking to their writing when they know there is an audience, such as the audience of an open access wiki site (Wheeler, Yeomans, and D. Wheeler 993; Camihort 30). While the wiki provides a place for publication, it also provides a location for knowledge acquisition. The goal of education, as M. Cole describes, is changing (141). Emphasis has previously been placed on the instructor to facilitate learning and impart wisdom to students, but the movement is now toward the student to be responsible for his or her learning (M. Cole 141). Rather than instructor-imparted learning, constructivist and collaborative methods of learning suggest that students can be creators of their own knowledge, and using a wiki can contribute to this process (M. Cole 142). Responding to this shift in an education paradigm, the wiki offers the ability for students to create and assemble their own knowledge.

Connecting educational institutions with the local community deconstructs some of the barriers to knowledge acquisition. As Sacks described, it is the role of the educational institution to reach out to the surrounding location; "at any institution of higher education—meaningful engagement with our surroundings enhances our institutional mission while serving the needs and interests of our community" (Sacks 31). Educational institutions, however, often keep their endeavors privy to their members or those of like institutions. Breaking down those walls allows a relationship to be born between educational knowledge and the knowledge of the community, enhancing academia and benefiting community.

The wiki allowed for capacity building through shared information. John and Melster described the process of gaining knowledge as a dichotomy of individual and group information that can be shared from peer to peer, group to peer, peer to group, or group to group (165). A wiki can allow for all of these avenues of information sharing to be provided in one location. Through interactions with a place- and topic-based wiki, and as a result of continual contributions and modifications of information, the comprehension of a subject, in this case Willamette Valley sustainable agriculture, can grow.

The creation of the Willamette Valley agricultural wiki serves the needs of the regional community by creating a collective knowledge base about a topic that is integral to the economic stability, cultural understanding, and overall sense of place for the region. With multiple educational institutions across the Willamette Valley, several of them liberal arts institutions, there is a desire and a need to give back to the surrounding community. Building upon the collective understanding of the importance of sustainable agriculture in this region, the wiki provides a source of community and capacity building for a wide audience from diverse backgrounds. This framework for integration of pedagogical processes with community knowledge provides a resource for adaptation of the technology to other subjects, to assimilate a collective base of information and to foster strong community ties, while meeting the needs of educational institutions in their desires to cultivate and develop engaged citizens.

Notes

1. The student collaborators for the wiki development and co-authors of this paper (Schlegel, Giombolini, and Dunne, sophomores at the time of this research) participated in all aspects of creating this site including content decisions, locating a host site, design, and writing pages. Schlegel, in particular, was the lead on many of the most important phases with decisions being made with the consensus of her peers.

2. Emerging from the discipline of ecology and counter culture movements in California, the goal of considering an area a bioregion is to establish a link between nature and culture, with an understanding that humans both influence and are influenced by their environment (Berg and Dasmann 399).

Works Cited

Berg, P., and R.F. Dasmann. "Reinhabiting California." *The Ecologist* 7 (1978): 399-401. Rpt. In *Reinterpreting a Separate Country: A Bioregional Anthology of Northern California.* Ed. P. Berg. San Francisco: Planet Drum, 1978. 217–220. Print.

Camihort, K.M. "Students as Creators of Knowledge: When Wikipedia is the Assignment." *Athletic Therapy Today* 14.2 (2009): 30-34. Print.

Chu, S.W.K. "Using Wikis in Academic Libraries." *Journal of Academic Librarianship* 35.2 (2009): 170-176. Print.

Cobus, L. "Using Blogs and Wikis in a Graduate Public Health Course." *Medical Reference Services Quarterly* 28.2 (2009): 22-32. Print.

Cohen, N. "Define Gender Gap? Look up Wikipedia's Contributor List." *The New York Times* 31 Jan. 2011: A1, A12. Print.

Cole, L. "Growing Lunch." *The Oregonian* 14 Oct. 2008. Web.

Cole, M. "Using Wiki technology to support student engagement: Lessons form the trenches." *Computers & Education* 52 (2009): 141-146. Print.

CosmoCod. *Wikimatrix.* June 2009. Web.

Creative Commons. *Creative Commons Attribute License.* June 2009. Web.

Dunne, J.B., K.J. Chambers, K.J. Giombolini, and S.A. Schlegel. "What does 'local' mean in the grocery store? Multiplicity in food retailers' perspectives on sourcing and marketing local foods." *Renewable Agriculture and Food Systems* 26.1 (2011): 46-59. Print.

Feenstra, G. "Local food systems and sustainable communities." *American Journal of Alternative Agriculture* 12.1 (1997): 28-36. Print.

Google. *Google Analytics.* July 2011. Web.

John, M., and R. Melster. "Knowledge Networks—Managing Collaborative Knowledge Spaces." *Advances in Learning Software Organizations Proceedings.* 2004. 165-171. Print.

Kane, G., and G. Fichman. "The Shoemaker's Children: Using Wikis for Information Systems Teaching, Research and Publication." *MIS Quarterly* 33.1 (2009): 1-17. Print.

Katz, J.E., R.E. Rice, and P. Aspden. "The Internet, 1995-2000—Access, Civic Involvement, and Social Interaction." *American Behavioral Scientist* 45.3 (2001): 405-419. Print.

Knobel, M., and C. Lankshear. "Wikis, Digital Literacies, and Professional Growth." *Journal of Adolescent & Adult Literacy.* 52.7 (2009): 631-634. Print.

Koehler, A., and F. Fuchs-Kittowski. "Integration of Communities into Process-Oriented Structures." *Journal of Universal Computer Science.* 11.3 (2005): 410-425. Print.

Kulongoski, T. *State of Oregon Proclamation.* Office of the Governor, 2008. Web.

Larson, A. *Migrant and Seasonal Farmworker Enumeration Profiles Study: Oregon.* National Center for Farmworker Health, 2002. Web.

Leuf, B., and W. Cunningham. *The Wiki Way: quick collaboration on the web.* New Jersey, NJ: Addison-Wesley, 2001. Print.

Lundin, R.L. "Teaching with Wikis: Toward a Networked Pedagogy." *Computers & Composition* 25 (2008): 432-448. Print.

Millard, D.E, C.E. Bailey, P. Boulain, S. Chennupati, H. Davis, Y. Howard, and G. Wills. "Semantics on demand: Can a Semantic Wiki Replace a Knowledge Base?" *New Review of Hypermedia and Multimedia* 14.1 (2008): 95-120. Print.

Noveck, B. *Wiki Government: How Technology Can Make Government Better, Democracy Stronger, and Citizens More Powerful.* Washington, DC: Brookings Institution Press, 2009. Print.

Oregon Department of Agriculture. "Growing Regions in Oregon." June 2009. Web.

Oregon Department of Agriculture. "Oregon agriculture produces a large economic footprint." Mar. 2011. Web.

Oregon Farmers' Market Association. *Oregon 2009 Farmers' Markets.* June 2009. Web.

Ras, E., G. Avram, P. Waterson, and S. Weibelzahl. "Using weblogs for knowledge sharing and learning in information spaces." *Journal of Universal Computer Science* 11.3 (2005): 394-309. Print.

Sacks, H. L. "We Learn What We Eat: Putting Local Food on the Table and In the Curriculum." *The Chronicle of Higher Education.* 55.13 (2008): A31-A32. Print.

Shaffer, J.B., and B. Cox. "Number of Farmers Markets Continues to Rise in the U.S." *United States Department of Agriculture.* Agriculture Marketing Services, 2008. Web.

Smith, G. "Place-based Education: Learning to Be Where We Are." *Phi Delta Kappan* 83.8 (2002): 584-594.

United States Department of Agriculture: National Agriculture Statistics Service. *The 2007 Census of Agriculture.* 2007. Web.

Vickery, G., and S. Wunsch-Vincent. *Participative Web and User-Created Content: Web 2.0, Wikis and Social Networking.* France: Organization for Economic Co-operation Development, 2007. Print.

Wheeler, S., P. Yeomans, and D. Wheeler. "The Good, the Bad and the Wiki: Evaluating Student-Generated Content for Collaborative Learning." *British Journal of Educational Technology.* 36.6 (2008): 987-995. Print.

Willamette University. "Professor and students create online resource for local agriculture." *Willamette University: People of Passion and Purpose* 15 Feb. 2011. Web.

Psychology, Sustainability, and Sense of Place

Milene Z. Morfei, Wells College

Abstract: Pedagogical techniques are described in two very different psychology courses. The first, Ecopsychology, is a seminar for first-year students and is part of the general education curriculum. The students learn about sustainability and sense of place through readings, films, guest speakers, and many outdoor activities. They reflect on their experiences in formal and informal writing assignments, class discussions, and portfolio presentations. The second course, Psychology of Environmental Sustainability, is an upper-level class that is also an elective in the Environmental Studies major. The students are assigned readings in psychology and related fields to learn about environmental problems and how to apply psychological research and concepts to change environmentally destructive behavior. They apply their knowledge in group service-learning projects targeted toward Wells College and the surrounding community. The groups present their projects to the Wells community at the end of the semester.

Milene Morfei, Ph.D., is Professor of Psychology and Ida Dorothea Atkinson Professor at Wells College in Aurora, NY. In addition to teaching her students about environmental sustainability, she has been actively involved in sustainability efforts at Wells College for the past several years. She is on the President's Climate Committee at Wells, and she regularly attends conferences and workshops sponsored by the Association for the Advancement of Sustainability in Higher Education (AASHE). Dr. Morfei has presented two recent papers, one on college sustainability efforts and one on teaching, at Greening of the Campus conferences in 2009 and 2012.

What does psychology have to do with sustainability? Ask yourself this: How can we possibly have any hope of changing environmental destruction caused by human activity without a good understanding of what motivates human behavior? For the past several years, it has been my privilege to teach an upper-level psychology course at Wells College that applies psychological concepts and research to real-world environmental problems. This essay will describe some of the pedagogical techniques I have used in the course, many of which could be adapted for use in other social science and humanities offerings.

I have also taught a very different course for first-year students as part of the general education curriculum. While developing an ecological sense of place at Wells College, students spend time connecting to the natural world and reflecting on their experiences through class discussions, formal and informal writing, and journaling. Much of what I have done in this course could easily be adapted to first-year seminars at other institutions.

Given the increasing urgency of climate change, helping students to understand, connect, and engage with the challenges we face is vital. The field of psychology provides the insights into human behavior that are needed in this endeavor. The subject matter easily lends itself to current trends in experiential and service learning, and the opportunities for development of students' critical-thinking skills are boundless. In both of the courses described below, students become actively engaged in ways that take them beyond the typical classroom experience.

Ecopsychology

As is the case at many colleges and universities, Wells College requires first-year students to enroll in seminars that are part of the general education curriculum. The seminars are taught by faculty members from many different disciplines, and each professor chooses the topic for her or his course. All sections address common goals and objectives (e.g. transition to college, writing skills, discussion skills, critical thinking, multiculturalism), and the various topics provide the content. This is the course description for my 15-student section:

> This course examines the relationship between humans and nature. Our increasing separateness from the natural world has negative repercussions for us and for the planet, and we will explore ways in which reconnecting with nature may impact psychological well-being and environmental sustainability. Through course readings, writing assignments, class discussions, and direct experience with the natural world, we will experience nature and relate our experience to the literature on ecopsychology.[1]

With the above course description in mind, the sub-headings below delineate the various assignments and activities I utilized to promote my students' connections to the natural world. I strive for a paperless class; all of the written assignments are submitted electronically.

Reading Assignments and Written Responses

We read two books during the course of the semester. We began with *A Reenchanted World: A Quest for a New Kinship with Nature*, by J. W. Gibson, followed by *Animal, Vegetable, Miracle: A Year of Food Life*, by Barbara Kingsolver. In addition to reading the material assigned for each class, students were required to submit a double-spaced reading response that indicated their thoughtful, critical analysis of a portion of the reading. The purpose was to enhance their critical-thinking skills. It was also a useful tool in promoting class discussion; each student was prepared to share her/his thoughts on some aspect of the reading. I would add, too, that the response assignment makes it more likely that students actually do the reading!

Journal Assignment

Each week, the students submitted a journal entry that addressed their personal reflections on their connections to the natural world. They could use the assigned reading as a springboard for their entries if they wished, but I encouraged them to be open to any sources or experiences that helped them reflect on their connections to nature. They could use past experience, class activities, class discussions, recent nature encounters, or anything else that helped them to articulate their feelings about the environment. This assignment provided an opportunity for students to personalize their relationship with the natural world in a way that helped them understand its importance to their own well-being. It was also another means of promoting fruitful class discussion.

Formal Writing Assignments

Students were required to write three papers during the semester. Each paper asked students to consider their connections with nature in different ways, and the paper instructions provided clearly articulated guidelines on how to do this. Students received extensive feedback on their first drafts and submitted second (and sometimes third) drafts for their final grades on the paper.

Paper 1: Your Natural History
Even students who grew up in metropolitan areas had some experience with nature. They might have spent vacations outside the city, or there may have been parks in their neighborhoods. Perhaps their family had a small garden (even a window herb garden). They may have had house plants or pets. The first paper asked them to reflect on one or two experiences that came to mind as they considered their "natural histories." They then had to analyze their experience(s) in a five- to seven-page paper. The paper instructions provided some questions to help them begin analyzing their experience.

Paper 2: A Sense of Place
This paper required students to take a few different perspectives in considering their sense of place in specific ways. With guidelines to help them formulate their thoughts, I first asked them to think about their connectedness to a bioregion in their formative years. For many, this was the area where they were raised; for some, it was a special vacation spot. Secondly, I asked them to reflect on whether they were beginning to feel connected to the natural environment at Wells College. We are situated on Cayuga Lake in the Finger Lakes Region of central New York State, and this exceptionally beautiful area lends itself to the kinds of connections that I was hoping to read about in my students' papers (and I was not disappointed). We also have wooded areas that students enjoy exploring. For a third, broader perspective, I showed the students a video clip of Carl Sagan's "Pale Blue Dot." I asked them to consider the planetary sense of place that Sagan describes so eloquently.

Paper 3: Helping Others Care and Connect
This was a research paper that required students to utilize outside sources to make a case that humans need to connect (or reconnect) with nature for our own health and well-being. They had to write an APA-formatted paper with a clearly defined thesis. I made two excellent books by Richard Louv available to them: *Last Child in the Woods* and *The Nature Principle*.

Final Presentation

In lieu of a final exam, students prepared a ten-minute PowerPoint presentation. They were given guidelines to help them convey their growth over the course of the semester. They were asked to think about where they were at the beginning of the semester in terms of their feelings of connectedness to the environment, and then think about whether they had a more profound connection at the end of the course. Their presentation could include any meaningful activities, discussions, papers, journals, etc., that helped illustrate their growth. Many of the students included pictures of the natural world—many of which were taken on the beautiful Wells campus.

Class Activities

The activities in which students engaged over the course of the semester were, perhaps, the most important part of their ecopsychological experience. We began the semester with a trip on the Floating Classroom, which is an educational tour boat that travels on Cayuga Lake. Students learn about the lake, collect water samples, and begin to develop their sense of place in our bioregion.

I occasionally showed nature films—the PBS "Nature" program was particularly suitable for my purposes. As mentioned above, I also showed the short video clip of Carl Sagan's "Pale Blue Dot." This clip is readily available on YouTube.

A local poet and friend, Howard Nelson, came as a guest to read nature poetry.

The first time I taught the class, he read from his book: *Earth, My Likeness: Nature Poetry of Walt Whitman*. This past semester, he read many of his own nature poems from *The Nap by the Waterfall*.

Finally, I cannot say enough about the value of the many outdoor experiences that provided the best and most obvious way for the students to develop their connections to the natural world. The fall of 2011 was uncommonly warm and beautiful—probably and ironically due, at least in part, to climate change. There were several days during the semester that I changed my game plan at the last minute and sent the students outside. I would usually give them some guidance and instructions in terms of walking alone, not talking with anyone, turning off phones, etc.

I would ask them to find a place to simply relax and feel nature. After they had spent at least 20 to 30 minutes outside, we would get back together for reflection on their experiences, either through free writing or discussion. I know from their journals that this was an extremely valuable and important activity. Many of them commented that they learned to spontaneously take a nature walk when the stresses of college life began to weigh on them.

The Psychology of Environmental Sustainability

This is a 300-level course that I have been teaching since 1999. The course was originally titled, "Environmental Problems and Human Behavior," and the title change coincided with a shift in pedagogical approach a few years ago. Although I always included a final project in the course requirements that provided students with an opportunity to apply their knowledge of psychology to real-world environmental problems, the course now has group service-learning projects that address local environmental issues. The course description is as follows:

> This course explores research and theory on the interactions between human behavior and the environment. The goal of the course is to examine ways in which increased understanding of human behavior may be the key to creating solutions to environmental problems. Students will be encouraged to think critically about the ways in which psychological perspectives may provide insights into creating a sustainable future for the planet and its inhabitants. Projects will focus on the Wells campus and surrounding community.

The sub-headings below indicate the various assignments and activities that I utilize in the course. Again, all of my classes are paperless; therefore, all assignments described below are submitted electronically.

Reading Assignments and Written Responses

I have used a number of different texts and readings during the years I have taught the course. One of the challenges is that most of the students in the class are psychology majors who may or may not fully understand the environmental problems we are facing. One of my first tasks is to bring them up to speed by providing at least some information about environmental issues. I have often used a very good text by

Gerald Gardner and Paul Stern, *Environmental Problems and Human Behavior*. It gives a good overview of environmental problems, and it also has a useful model for addressing solutions with psychological concepts and research. I have used a number of other books and readings, both in lieu of or in addition to the Gardner and Stern text. My planned books for this coming semester are *Eaarth: Making a Life on a Tough New Planet*, by Bill McKibben (misspelling of Earth is intentional); *Fostering Sustainable Behavior: An Introduction to Community-Based Social Marketing*, by McKenzie-Mohr; and *EcoMind: Changing the Way We Think to Create the World We Want*, by F. M. Lappé. There will also be additional readings from psychological journals. An excellent resource that I am considering for next year's iteration of the course is *Conservation Psychology: Understanding and Promoting Human Care for Nature*, by Susan Clayton and Gene Myers.

As is the case in most of my courses, students submit written responses based on their reading assignments. This is their opportunity to critically analyze and engage with the reading in a more in-depth way than simply reading the assignments. It provides fodder for class discussions and makes it less likely that students will skim through the material.

Discussion Facilitation

Students are required to facilitate discussion of one or two of the assigned readings during the semester. They prepare an outline and notes that are submitted to me electronically, and they use that material to promote discussion and critical analysis in class. This is an excellent tool for helping students develop communication and critical-thinking skills.

Group Service-Learning Projects

Early in the semester, the class decides what the service-learning projects will be. The projects are meant to address sustainability issues on the Wells campus or in the surrounding community. We brainstorm a list of possible projects, and then we vote to decide which ones to pursue. The class has 18 to 20 students, and we usually work on four different projects with four to five students in each group. After the projects have been determined, the students are randomly assigned to work on one of them.

In addition to promoting service learning and providing an opportunity for students to apply their knowledge to real-world problems, the group experience helps students learn to work in teams. This can be a challenge, particularly depending on the personalities, strengths, and weaknesses of the group members. I require them to appoint a coordinator in each group, and that person's task is to keep the project on track and communicate with me as necessary. I also ask the groups to assign particular tasks to each group member so that there is no confusion as to who is responsible for the identified duties.

I teach this class as a three-hour seminar that meets once a week. Given the challenge that students often have in finding meeting times that work for all group members, I provide some class time for them to meet. After the projects are underway, the groups meet for 20 to 30 minutes immediately following the seminar break. I have learned that it is wise to have them report back as to what they worked on during that time to ensure that they are, indeed, working.

The students' work is evaluated in a number of different ways:

Project Proposal
Even though we decide as a class which projects to pursue, each student is required to submit a proposal, in APA format, that includes a title page; abstract; general description of the group project; participants (people in the group); methods (description of how they plan to address the sustainability issue, including the tasks assigned to each group member); results (what they hope to achieve, and to whom their final presentations will be targeted); and discussion (at this point, what they hope their project will achieve and possible next steps). The purpose of the assignment, in addition to giving them practice with APA format, is to help them define the parameters of the project in a way that focuses their efforts.

Project Presentation
During the last class of the semester, each group presents its project to the Wells community. We advertise this as an event open to all, but each group also sends specific invitations to people whom we particularly hope will attend (e.g. the president, the chief financial officer, the head of buildings and grounds, the dean of students, etc.). Their presentations highlight the issue they are addressing, the barriers to solving them that they have identified, the ways in which they have applied psychological concepts in attempting to address the issue, and any other points the groups feel are important to share with the community. We do a "practice run" of the presentations in class the week before the groups present their work to the community, and I have found this to be invaluable. They do a remarkably more polished, professional job when they present to the public.

Final Paper
The final paper is an expansion and completion of the research proposal submitted earlier in the semester. I am particularly interested in how they applied psychological principles in their discussion of the project. This assignment also includes a separate document in which the students answer specific questions about their contributions and the contributions of the other members of the group. In most cases, the students in each group receive the same grade for the project (I give individual grades for the proposal and final paper), but exceptions can be made if someone is an obvious "slacker."

Although there are many pedagogical challenges in doing this sort of service-learning project, I have found it to be a very effective way to achieve several goals. The students learn to apply psychology to real-world issues on their own campus; they learn to work in teams; they improve their communication and presentation skills; the campus presentations bring more community awareness to sustainability issues; and the students' projects are often the impetus for positive change on the Wells campus.

Note

1.   Any course materials mentioned in this essay, including syllabi and writing assignments, can be obtained by contacting mzmorfei@wells.edu.

Works Cited

Clayton, Susan, and Gene Myers. *Conservation Psychology: Understanding and Promoting Human Care for Nature*. Oxford, UK: Wiley-Blackwell, 2009. Print.

Gardner, Gerald T., and Paul C. Stern. *Environmental Problems and Human Behavior*. Upper Saddle River, NJ: Pearson, 2002. Print.

Gibson, James W. *A Reenchanted World: The Quest for a New Kinship With Nature*. New York, NY: Metropolitan Books, 2009. Print.

Kingsolver, Barbara. *Animal, Vegetable, Miracle: A Year of Food Life*. New York, NY: Harper-Collins, 2007. Print.

Lappé, Frances Moore. *EcoMind: Changing the Way We Think to Create the World We Want*. New York, NY: Nation Books, 2011. Print.

McKenzie-Mohr, Doug. *Fostering Sustainable Behavior: An Introduction to Community-Based Social Marketing*. 3rd ed. Vancouver, BC: New Society Publishers, 2011. Print.

McKibben, Bill. *Eaarth: Making a Life on a Tough New Planet*. New York, NY: Times Books, 2010. Print.

Nelson, Howard. *Earth, My Likeness: Nature Poetry of Walt Whitman*. Berkeley, CA: North Atlantic Books, 2010. Print.

---. The Nap By the Waterfall. Fulton, MO: Timberline Press, 2009. Print.

reDesign Art for All: Creating an Interdisciplinary Program with Graphic Design, Sustainability, and Student Leadership

Jp Avila, Christine Cooley, and Lace Smith, Pacific Lutheran University

Abstract: William McDonough, co-author of *Cradle to Cradle*, says, "Design is the first signal of human intention." With design, a revolution can begin with a shared vision. To be inspiring, the vision is clear, easily understood and riddled with imagery that will enrapt anyone. And with Pacific Lutheran University's reDesign program, that is exactly what can be done. The reDesign project offers a vision for the beginning of a different way of thinking - the first of incremental steps to reveal the image of a sustainable society. Modern lifestyles contribute to environmental destruction at unimaginable levels, yet most consumers contribute unawarely. Corporate sustainability initiatives seem to act on the assumption that the problem lies with the environment. The root problem has never been with the natural world, but rather the human connection to it. The reDesign program focuses on leadership, social justice, and creative problem solving to address the societal motivations behind behavior. Students learn to analyze, based on a variety of environmental, social and fiscal frameworks, and are guided by the program's mission: "Compassionately Led, Sustainably Focused, Creatively Directed."

Jp Avila, MFA, is an Associate Professor at Pacific Lutheran University and chair of the Department of Art & Design, where he teaches graphic design. He has a master's degree in Visual Communications from The School of the Art Institute of Chicago. Jp has written, lectured, and presented work on design strategy, non-linear visual narratives, and usage of comics in academia. He has written articles on comics, holidays, and sustainable design within PLU. Jp's current work is focused on approaches of design through sustainable practice. He continues to explore work based on non-linear, narrative storytelling.

Christine Cooley, LEED AP and MBA, is the Sustainability Manager at Pacific Lutheran University. She currently leads a Sustainability Office of over twenty students and another full time staff member. Christine's past work focused on large group facilitation, energy reduction, and sustainability project management. She received a B.S. in Environmental Science from The Ohio State University, where she also worked as the university's first sustainability professional, in Business Operations. Christine was director of the record breaking 2008 Earth Day event in Columbus, OH and, as a student, was involved in passing a LEED building policy at OSU. She enjoys biking, organizing the Tacoma chapter of Green Drinks, and hiking Pacific Northwest mountains.

Lace M. Smith, MBA, is the Assistant Director of Student Involvement and Leadership for Technology and Social Media at Pacific Lutheran University. Serving eight years in the PLU's Division of Student Life, she has rich experience in student activities, university housing, global education, and leadership development. She received her B.A. in Studio Art from the University of Puget Sound and her Masters of Business Administration from Pacific Lutheran University. She has been a facilitator for the Student Social Justice Training Institute, multiple queer student leadership retreats, and has presented at the National Association of Student Personnel Administrators national conference and NASPAtech, the Student Affairs Technology Conference. When she is not using any variety of Apple products, she spends time drawing, taking hikes, and playing trivia at the local pub.

Introduction – the Value of Design Thinking

William McDonough, co-author of *Cradle to Cradle*, says, "Design is the first signal of human intention."[1] Creating vision is essential to any large-scale problem, and few problems are so urgent as the environmental collapse of the planet. Solutions will be of "game-changing" proportions and will thus require complete and absolute buy-in from society.

Revolutions can only begin with a shared vision, regardless of what the following steps may bring. To be inspiring, a vision must be clear, easily understood, and riddled with imagery. To date, very little exists in the vision of a new, worldwide sustainable paradigm. Adjectives used to paint an image of sustainability look to correcting our current way of life, rather than starting from a new beginning. Design thinking can create a shared vision, and that shared vision can bring about revolution.

Pacific Lutheran University (PLU) is attempting to use design thinking as a way to catalyze the shared vision that is needed to reach a sustainable society. While doing so, students have the opportunity to express their own vocations, and fulfill the Pacific Lutheran University mission statement: "to educate students for lives of thoughtful inquiry, service, leadership and care—for other persons, for their communities and for the earth."

Design Thinking + Sustainability

The reality of anthropogenic climate change is well agreed upon within the fields of science. Municipalities, businesses, and universities are all increasingly concerned about environmental impacts, and how they contribute. As a result, a groundswell of action has occurred in recent years. These acts, however well intentioned, are not directing their energy in efficient ways. Recent history shows that corporate social responsibility initiatives are gaining popularity; however, the initiatives boast progress in terms of "less bad" as opposed to fulfilling a vision of a truly better world and, in the worst cases, amount to blatant "greenwashing."

Headlines frame environmental achievements in terms of how much waste is reduced, kilowatts of energy are saved, or less materials are consumed in production. One has only to think of how strongly bottle water companies advertise the small amount of plastic in their inherently unnecessary product. Businesses operate along a status quo, missing out on tremendous cost-saving and value-adding alternative ways of operating.

In reality, the root problem never lies in either the natural world or the human spirit, but rather with the connection between the two. This is a subtle but important distinction that can allow for new approaches towards sustainability. The past centuries have severely strained this relationship and reckless use of technology has exponentially increased this disconnect. Evidence of this strained relationship has manifested in worldwide shortages of clean water, sprawling mis-development, and the widespread effects of global climate change.

Design thinking assists creative problem solving without the hindrance of traditional approaches. Individuals and organizations trained with these concepts can analyze processes that better articulate a balance between business practices, human needs, and the environment's health. Incorporating design thinkers into the product or service process can be seen as a first incremental step towards revealing the image of a sustainable society.

Enter reDesign

The Pacific Lutheran University "reDesign" program is an incubator for developing pathways to a more sustainable future with design. Based on a variety of disciplinary influences, reDesign takes a dynamic approach to helping students understand their environment, both tangible and social. In this program, students develop leadership competencies and an understanding of how they can fulfill the values of sustainability through better design. Progress can be quantified by increasing the triple bottom line of People, Planet, and Prosperity.

The redesign program doesn't stop at academics; it extends into the students' relationships with the university, the community, and themselves. reDesign illustrates the interconnectedness of academics with environmental preservation tools, social justice analysis, and leadership skills required to effect change. Students learn to analyze situations from multiple frameworks. As they evolve in the triple-bottom-line conversation, students will be able to learn and master core concepts around sustainable design thinking, involving a seamless integration of the curricular, co-curricular, and outside community.

What distinguishes PLU's philosophy of sustainability is an emphasis on navigating the human relationship with the natural world in a way that will move beyond "less bad" to an intentional good. To be replicable and sustainable itself, the program must rely on *processes* of change and focus less on the change itself or its end product.

In a society of design level thinking, corporate social responsibility would look much different. A more appropriate business approach would be to examine touch points between business and the natural world, and then seek out improvements in those interactions to balance human needs and the environment's health. This method can lead to a result greater than the sum of its parts.

One excellent example would be the carpeting company Interface, which for months attempted to reduce the harm of its glue, until discovering a natural adhesion system that no longer needed chemicals at all.[2] Once it broadened its outlook from simple reduction methods to truly rethinking the process, Interface came up with a solution that would have been unreachable with old ways of thinking. Design thinking takes traditional approaches to Corporate Social Responsibility (CSR) to a new level. Businesses that work towards a linear reduction in harm, solely to adhere to regulatory demands such as ISO 140000, neglect the part of sustainability that could add the most value. Consideration for the human element can open creativity and reduce costs.

reDesign Phase One :: The Project

Pacific Lutheran University is already well-known for its leadership in sustainability. Upper level administrators have been vital to the creation of national sustainability consortiums, and in 2007 PLU became a charter signatory of the American College and University Presidents Climate Commitment, thus placing us on a path to carbon neutrality by 2020. There is a long-standing sustainability committee that has helped to oversee this transition, as well as a system of green fees, habitat restoration projects, and the banning of bottled water on campus. PLU was the first university participating in AASHE's (Association for the Advancement of Sustainability in Higher Education) STARS program (Sustainability Tracking, Assessment and Rating System), and received a Silver rating in 2010.

Since the formation of the Sustainability Office, these projects have continued with a current staff of two professionals and over twenty students. As well as these nationally recognized components, the University has adopted its third long-range planning document, *PLU 2020: Affirming Our Commitments, Shaping Our Future*, which discusses the need for a diverse, just, and sustainable community. reDesign is the next step in PLU's progression. It is a program intended for expanding the university's commitment to and concept of sustainability in all aspects.

In order to uncover its needs, resources, and possibilities, reDesign needed to be about exploration. At first it was just a fragile idea, forged by Jp Avila, Associate Professor of Art + Design and Chrissy Cooley, PLU Sustainability Manager. Before the house or first group of students were established, these two began collaborating to improve sustainability outreach and help undergraduates design projects that could have positive real world impacts. They served together as mentors to the students working on projects, such as the South Sound Sustainability Summit and Expo, and unPLUg.

In each case, these were pre-existing programs put on by the PLU Sustainability Office that were dramatically improved by using elements of design. unPLUg, a campus wide energy reduction competition, suffered from an image problem where students distrusted the intentions of the University. A comical advertising campaign was able to shift the perception of campus residents from distrust and apathy to vigorously supporting unPLUg so much that there was an additional four percent reduction in electricity usage. Likewise, the South Sound Sustainability Summit benefited from an advertising campaign designed by PLU students, but the process went even further. A student designer was able to format an innovative folding nametag that eliminated the need for paper handouts and became the main topic of conversation at the introduction table. It was a clever design solution to a sustainability problem and encapsulated the strengths that the two disciplines (design and sustainability) had when combined.

Once it became obvious that there was a great enough need, Avila began working within the Department of Art + Design towards finding new opportunities to support student interests in this area. One aspect was the founding of what became the reDesign House. Another came to fruition with a course he would co-teach with Assistant Director of Student Involvement and Leadership, Lace Smith. The course, taught as a special topics seminar, was named "Design for Social Change." It was a pilot academic project for teaching the history, theory, and practice of design in publicly-engaged, community-based, and socially-active projects. This class was separate but concurrent with the house project; it served to test the academic waters and develop a curriculum for the field. Assessment from the class evaluations illustrated that students within Art + Design were ready for civic engagement. They felt it was an essential opportunity to grow within their vocational calling as designers.

In this early stage, reDesign was an ambition to discover how well the disciplines of sustainability and design could work together. The initial group of students that were involved in this embryonic stage received no course credit and were selected based upon personal interest. As such, within reDesign, these students learned to analyze situations using a variety of environmental, social, and fiscal frameworks. This was the first of many incremental steps towards revealing their image of a sustainable society. This pre-reDesign phase helped set the baseline for what would become the program. The program's current students are still guided by the motto developed for that initial group: "Compassionately Led, Sustainably Focused, Creatively Directed."

reDesign was always ambitious in its goals. The first step in the process was to determine what resources were available. For this step, the assessment scope was as wide as possible, including both liabilities and resources related to other purposes. For example, financial capital was limited, but this limitation created an opportunity to look elsewhere. By expanding exploration away from traditional funding sources within University academics, we were able to suggest that reDesign occupy an underutilized tenant property the University owned on the perimeter of campus. This provided us with a unique space to operate in for nearly no direct cost. It also created value for the university by improving a neglected space.. Dubbed the reDesign House by the pre-reDesign cohort, the house became an academic home and classroom/ meeting space for the students. Here they could learn while experimenting within the house as a living laboratory. The house became a practice not only in the empirical reduction of environmental harm, but also in the introduction of joy and beauty.

From these initial undertakings, the project concentrated on exposing students to other designers in their field working on similar projects. The CompostModern 2011 conference gave four students the perfect opportunity to do so. The mission of CompostModern is:

> ...to transform products, industries and lives through sustainable design choices. CompostModern engages designers, sustainability professionals, artists and entrepreneurs to collaborate in realizing a more environmentally, culturally and economically sustainable world.[3]

Not only did students learn much from the conference, but they also spent time at the California College of the Arts, touring its facilities and talking with Nathan Shedroff, chair of the Masters of Business Administration in Design Strategy and Debra Johnson of the Pratt Institute of New York. These two visits were useful in identifying obvious passion for sustainability and design and how each of these educators was able to translate that passion and drive to their students.

reDesign :: the Academic Program

Returning to Pacific Lutheran University, it was obvious that a like-minded program was doable and necessary. PLU design students who attended the conference were able to clearly articulate the process they wanted to see happen at the University to help create change in their community. The capabilities had been developed with the house and the class; both were proving viable.

With these new resources, reDesign explored the opportunity to move beyond special projects and collaborations and create a fully functional program, one that focused on providing support for vocations, connections to the community, and knowledge about social issues. With the Department of Art + Design as the backbone for program support, the learning objectives outlined for the BFA in Studio Arts provided a basis to enhance the quality of education reDesign students would receive. Art + Design's mission is broken down into: a) Learning Objectives, which are shared throughout all majors within the department; b) degree-specific objectives, which are unique to the concentration; c) skill-specific objectives, which are again focused on each concentration; and d) historical/theoretical-specific objectives.

From there, the reDesign program expanded to create more unique goals that support the Department and the University's Institutional Learning Objectives. For instance, the degree-specific objectives for the BFA in Studio Arts, with a concentration in Graphic Design, state that students will:

- Have the ability to solve visual communication problems, including the skills in research, analysis, generation of alternative solutions, testing, and presentations.

- The ability to orally defend and respond to client-based information.

- Ability to organize design problems and work productively as a member of a team.

A goal of reDesign was to both enhance those degree objectives and provide more opportunities for students to achieve broader department objectives. That goal led to the first official reDesign student cohort. Five students were identified who shared interests with the first group of students who worked with pre-reDesign. This cohort was recruited to enhance the individual perspectives in design thinking, with a focus on the interconnections between People, Planet, and Prosperity, the "triple bottom line" value shared by all three mentors.

reDesign :: the Co-Curricular Program

The co-curricular experience at PLU is a collection of intentional extensions to learning that offers students opportunities to practice critical thinking in experiences relevant to their lives. reDesign is a seedbed for students to engage in a unique layering of both the Art + Design curriculum and student leadership of co-curricular work. Each student is charged to enter into the community to find a problem that can be solved collaboratively, using principles of design and sustainability. These can address issues unique to the local Parkland/Tacoma community or of larger scope in our society, such as discrimination and racial stereotypes. reDesign students explored causes they are closely connected to and helped raise awareness and create solutions by applying their design skills and problem solving techniques.

By providing a bridge between learning within and beyond a student's course of study, reDesign creates a dynamic freedom of movement that attracts students to involvement and leadership, both at PLU and in the greater community. This ability to move and integrate students into this sustainability- and leadership-focused co-curricular program reinforces the lived effort and experience of creating a more just, diverse, sustainable, and verdant world.

reDesign Phase Two :: from Project to Program

The original reDesign cohort was given the task of developing a working knowledge of sustainability principles, such as Janine Benyus' theory of Biomimicry, the concept of waste equals food, the perils of greenwashing, as well as the principles of analytical design. They then applied this working knowledge to a single project of their choosing. Students worked out a series of goals, objectives, benchmarks and processes. They were introduced to these skills via a four-day workshop. This workshop of shared project building made this first-time group the core model that eventually became the premise for a degree in sustainable design.

Students continued to look for opportunities to express their scope of knowledge and expertise. What was most exciting was that students, when provided the opportunity to challenge themselves, exceeded conventional expectations. By providing a forum for the three advisors to listen to feedback from students, the reDesign program moved towards more cross-campus collaborations that framed a liberal-arts education, including design strategy skill-sets and a passion for social justice, within a new degree program.

The first cohort learned concepts and processes required to challenge users with well-visualized information pertinent to the client's objective. This is the technique used in the study of design, so we continued to apply the same methodology to their community-based work. The first student to do so, Siri Johnson, led a summer-long study with the mentors to explore working with the community. Her work with a local business prompted reDesign to explore questions regarding client-based requirements and socially-conscious economic repercussions. Her work helped to develop the basis for other student projects.

Based on the evaluations and interviews, it became clear students were hungry for more. They achieved the expectations placed before them and then added more; it was not uncommon to find others outside of the program hearing whispers of what the reDesign program was doing and wanting to know how to contribute.

Some projects from the first cohort consisted of drafting plans for an interactive outdoor learning space, which was developed and presented to several key University faculty and staff. Another group helped organize and maintain a SurPLUs store, consisting of materials gathered from around the University that were then sold and donated to the community. This increased access for reDesign's potential community collaborators, such as schools, small businesses, and nonprofits. The first official cohort has maintained these initiatives, as well as taken on the adventurous task of creating and maintaining a 20-foot, spray chalked, infographic of energy consumption in the resident halls throughout the month of October.

reDesign :: Next Phase

It was New York installation artist Vik Muniz who said,

> My experience with mixing art with social projects is that, that's the main thing. It's just like taking people away—even if it's for a few minutes—from where they are and showing them another world, another place, even if it's a place from which they can look at where they are. It changes everything. Wouldn't this be an experience in how art could change people? Can this be done? And what would be the effect of this?[4]

This quote serves as inspiration to reDesign because, if this is what happens when art and social projects are connected, imagine the possibilities if those concepts and ideas were introduced intentionally at the undergraduate level. Students would gain the ability to sustain these "few minutes" of another world where anything is possible. One of the program's goals is that any of the reDesign students will be well positioned to create this change when the opportunity comes. They will facilitate change using the tools that the program impresses upon its pupils: leadership, sustainability, and design.

Current recruitment for the program revolves around students majoring in a BFA in Studio Arts with a concentration in Graphic Design. Students are sought out for their prior interest in social issues. Since they are in a focused environment to enhance their portfolio for future career opportunities, the next logical step is to explore what fundamental requirements would be needed in a student's academic landscape to take these design practices, knowledge of social responsibilities, and leadership qualities into their careers. The answer, as the reDesign Program sees it, is a new Bachelor of Arts degree in the Art + Design program. To develop better relationships between design students and their vocational calling, it seems necessary to support the reDesign Program with a bachelor degree focused on sustainable design.

For this to occur, the University would need to fortify its existing foundations in sustainability. The existing Sustainability Office would need to transition into a formal center with the purpose of creating community-based education and dialogue, as well as a resource bank of sustainable practices. The center could operate out of the reDesign House, and be fortified by interweaving it with academic departments as well as student affairs, to create a better integrated, stronger, more dynamic effort. These efforts will help eliminate redundancies, open a path to a greatly expanded series of programs, and create a better defined process for staff and students to be involved in.

The development of the Center for Sustainability would prove to be a model which is grounded in the mission of the institution, that supports long term planning for a diverse, just, and sustainable community; supported with undergraduate research, projects, and studies; and places PLU as a leader in this type of multi-departmental thinking. When these efforts are given a structured environment to grow in, they will bear even more fruit. This will further express PLU's commitment to the American College and University Presidents Climate Commitment.

This Center is an important evolution at our university. Staff would exemplify the needs of the university, with both student affairs and operational professionals. Having such operational expertise housed within the Center opens doors to using the campus and surrounding community as a living laboratory. Thinking of the campus as a complex ecosystem, the Center could serve as a switchboard from student interest to actual campus cases. This maximizes students' education and portfolios, and allows the campus to capitalize on a free source of research and creativity.

Conclusion

Through observations of both reDesign and the programs that inspired it, it seems that any program of this nature needs to be specific to the local community. The three advisors who began reDesign have found a way to sustain individual energy by connecting with partners that span the campus. Every university unit is an integral partner to the sustainability movement. It is critical for universities and other institutions to find connections between campus groups in order to support efforts like sustainable practices. reDesign operates off the beaten path while following this call to action.

For reDesign, the pan-university connection has broken down the well-fortified barriers between academic departments and two different offices in two separate divisions of the institution. It is these new connections that assist in reaching more dynamic solutions for living and working more sustainably, and help to hold the interest of administrators, students, and potential donors. The world does not have clear-cut divisions and thus a student's education cannot either. Academia must continue to infuse design thinking and the theoretical models of social justice into all aspects of a student's life. Only then will reDesign achieve its goals in regards to the principles of the triple-bottom-line, equipping students to live their lives in ways that benefit People, the Planet, and Prosperity.

Works Cited

"CompostModern 2011." AIGA. San Francisco, CA: Herbst Theatre, 22-23 Jan. 2011.

McDonough, W. "Cradle to Cradle Design." Ted 2005. Monterey Conference Center, Monterey, CA. Feb. 2005. 23-26.

Muniz, Vik. *Waste Land*. Almega Projects, 2010. Film.

"Sustainability Innovations." Interface Global, n.p. 10 Feb. 2013. Web.

Contemplative Poetics and Pedagogy for Sustainability

Gurleen Grewal, University of South Florida

Abstract: Reading contemplative nature writing is an effective way to awaken the ecological imagination, as this literature facilitates an understanding of interconnectedness that belongs at the heart of sustainability. The most powerful way of absorbing the ecological sensibility of these texts is by incorporating contemplative pedagogy, so that the art of sensing, seeing and listening with relaxed awareness is also practiced by the students. The practice of silently witnessing contents of the mind (thoughts-feelings), while not engaging them, calms and quiets the mind, increasing clarity. However, the implications of cultivating silence/cultivating awareness are more radical, for in effect this practice of non-doing can be a powerful method of undoing the conditioned self. If the teaching of sustainability ought to include other ways of knowing and open up space for genuine self-inquiry, honoring both cognitive and affective registers, then contemplative pedagogy has much to offer. Modeled in each contemplative practice is the wisdom of slowing down and living mindfully in the present.

Gurleen Grewal is an Associate Professor of English at the University of South Florida, Tampa, where she has also taught in Women's Studies and served as founding director of the Center for India Studies. A scholar of American Literature and feminist postcolonial studies, her recent publications and teachings pertain to Toni Morrison, contemplative pedagogy, Toni Morrison, literature and the environment. She is currently editing a collection of essays on "Sustainability in Indian Thought and Tradition."

It is a century now since Darwin gave us the first glimpse of the origin of species. We know now what was unknown to all the preceding caravan of generations: that men are only fellow-voyagers with other creatures in the odyssey of evolution. This new knowledge should have given us, by this time, a sense of kinship with fellow creatures; a wish to live and let live; a sense of wonder over the magnitude and duration of the biotic enterprise...These things, I say, should have come to us. I fear they have not come to many.

- Aldo Leopold, "On a Monument to the Pigeon," *A Sand County Almanac*

Halfway through teaching his last undergraduate wildlife ecology course in the spring semester of 1947, Aldo Leopold formalized his teaching objectives in a two-page essay, "Wherefore Wildlife Ecology?" In it, he states his goal is "to teach [students] how to read land"—land being "soil, water, plants and animals"—so that they can respond to the call of conservation by "living it" rather than "turn[ing] it over to bureaus" (336-337). Holding modern science and culture responsible for the "fallacy in present-day conservation," that of privileging only the economic in "the human relation to land," he declares that "[i]t is, or should be, esthetic as well" (337).

The balance between the utilitarian and the aesthetic is a balance between what Pierre Hadot, in his reading of the idea of nature in Western thought over twenty-five centuries, calls the Promethean and the Orphic, "two fundamental attitudes" to nature (317). Prometheus "by devoting himself to the service of mankind, steals divine secrets by ruse or by violence" thereby "affirming mankind's right to dominate nature" (317). He governs science and technology, while Orpheus presides over "aesthetic perception," "a mode of understanding nature" through philosophical discourse, poetry, and art (211). The Orphic perception is more receptive to surmounting the troubling dichotomy of human and nature often present in the Promethean mode. To educate for sustainability, to revise and complicate the anthropocentric, utilitarian and alienated approach to self and nature ingrained in us, this essay favors combining contemplative environmental writing with contemplative pedagogy.

Literary environmental studies are well equipped to foster the aesthetic value of land as Leopold defines it. As Roger J. H. King notes, this "literary tradition ... re-introduces subjectivity and moral connectedness to the landscape missing in the natural sciences" (357). Environmental literature and ecocriticism have expanded across materialist, feminist, critical race and postcolonial studies to critique transnational issues of social injustice. While there is great value to studying texts that examine the unsustainable economic and social relations—the exploitative and the catastrophic in humanity's relationship with each other and the environment, studying literature that generates respect and receptivity toward the natural world can do much to create what Mark S. Cladis (in this volume) calls the "the culture of sustainability." Likewise, transforming the mindset of our students, so that they become more receptive and compassionate, ought to be an important goal of teaching (for) sustainability. Contemplative pedagogy, by cultivating awareness, offers a profoundly transformative mode of learning, since it affects our very ways of knowing and being.

Orphic Readings of the Land

Given the post-Enlightenment mindset of global capitalism, the questions at the heart of sustainability and environmental ethics are epistemological and concern our attitudes to both self and nature. As further noted by King, "The dominance of the natural scientific view of Nature as the site of merely physical relations and forces does not just advance a particular cognitive project. It also gives legitimacy to the economic and political interest of those engaged in commodity production under present conditions by undermining alternative construals of Nature which would invest it with moral aesthetic values capable of justifying a moral critique of the prevailing social system" (356).

A scientist whose appreciation of the wild reflected a contemplative, poetic sensibility, Leopold learned his love of nature by contemplating it early in his life; his most cherished adult routine was walking acres of land at daybreak with his dog and notebook. In *A Sand County Almanac,* this Leopold comes through as much as the scientist—perceptive, responsive, dwelling in early morning mists of silence, drawing connections, seeing interrelations; the contemplative and the scientific enquirer are seamless. We learn much from the Leopold who thrills to the bugle calls of sandhill cranes, who notices with tenderness the insignificant little plant draba, and who lets himself be taught by the "fierce green fire" dying in the wolf's eyes (130).

Let us note that the qualities Leopold wishes Darwin's findings had evoked in general public discourse—"a sense of kinship" and coexistence "with fellow creatures," "a sense of wonder over the magnitude and duration of the biotic enterprise"—belong to the poetic or Orphic imagination and have a decidedly contemplative dimension. Such wonder has been voiced across civilizations: in global indigenous conceptions of the natural world as sacred, in ancient and medieval Asian poetry (Indian, Chinese, and Japanese), in the writings influenced by Taoist and Buddhist perceptions, by British Romantic poets, and American poets from Ralph Waldo Emerson to Mary Oliver, and by literary naturalist writers from John Muir to Barry Lopez. The most eloquent writers do not simply speak to ideology—they express awe, reverence, and a sense of expanded consciousness in the presence of the nonhuman world.[2]

These authors' shared understanding of the natural world can best be summed up by Mary Oliver's statement in *Winter Hours*:

> When I write about nature directly, or refer to it, here are some things I don't mean, and a few I do. I don't mean nature as ornamental, however scalloped and glowing it may be. I don't mean nature as useful to man if that possibility or utility takes from an object its own inherent value. Or, even diminishes it. I don't mean nature as calamity, as vista, as vacation, or recreation. I don't mean landscapes in which we find rest and pleasure—although we do—so much as I mean landscapes in which we are reinforced in our sense of the world as a mystery, a mystery that entails other privileges besides our own— and also, therefore, a hierarchy of right and wrong behaviors pertaining to the mystery, diminishing or defending it. (101)

Unraveling the Conditioned Self

Many of the nature writers already mentioned experience and record a transpersonal dimension of the self in their writings. "It's well known that Henry David Thoreau invented the discipline of ecological writing, less well understood that the speculative equipment he took to the woods included a vision formed by Eastern and Western contemplative spiritualities," writes Mary O'Reilley. In practically all spiritual traditions, silence and solitude in nature is recommended as being conducive to the cultivation of wisdom. Why is this so? Firstly, let us recognize that the human is also part of the natural world and that our separation is the work of language and cultural episteme. For the restless, alienated mind, the value of the so-called non-human world lies in its being unconditioned by dualistic thought. It not only "disregards human approval" (as does the llama in Denise Levertov's poem, "Come Into Animal Presence"), it affords human consciousness a glimpse into the mystery of things by exerting its own vast silence upon the mind.

For writers after Thoreau, nature is often the site for the unraveling of the conditioned self and the attendant epiphanies of transpersonal consciousness. Alice Walker has this to say: "In the moment of direct perception of nature another order is glimpsed. This shift brings with it an intimation of the numinous, a moment of new perception which leaves a trace. It is as though the cells of the body develop a taste for more perceptions, more traces" (88). In the writings of Mary Oliver and Annie Dillard, such engagement with nature brings forth a connectedness that is spontaneous and prized by each writer. What each knows well in the silent act of perception is the "subject of the present moment" (Dillard 1974).

For Oliver, a poet of deep listening and seeing, the world of nature is both refuge and classroom because, being one with itself, it knows no separation. The grass is her prayer mat and the deer, heron, and iris are preachers, teachers of inwardness. When the centrality of the human world is displaced, nature is not an "environment"—it is the geography of the sacred: each bird, leaf, hoof print, and splash indicate a presence of the reality, now temporal, now eternal. Oliver combines imaginative vision with the attentive observations of a naturalist in which every living thing is simply itself and, in being so, becomes an epiphany. Called to experience presence in everything, Oliver asks in *Winter Hours*, "Just where does self-awareness begin and end?" Not only in the celebrated poem "Wild Geese," but also throughout her *oeuvre*, Oliver painstakingly shows how nature returns us to our "place/in the family of things" (14).

Oliver's statement regarding her poetry highlights her own departure from the anthropocentric model of environmental protection: "My work doesn't document any of the sane and learned arguments for saving, healing, and protecting the earth for our existence. What I write begins and ends with the act of noticing and cherishing, and it neither begins nor ends with the human world" (*Winter Hours* 99). If contemplative nature poetry runs the risk of dismissal for its apolitical or asocial content, Oliver's stance demonstrates *how* the contemplative and the transpersonal re-enter and transform the space of the social. Only in the vanishing or expanded boundaries of the separate self can one locate an agency where interconnectedness and interdependence guide thought and action, where doing arises from a cognizance of the profound relationality of being. Oliver seems to fit the definition of a transpersonal ecologist given by Warwick Fox—one who is "not interested in supporting approaches that serve to reinforce the primary reality of the narrow, atomistic, or particle-like volitional self":

> For transpersonal ecologists, given a deep enough understanding of the way things are, the response of being inclined to care for the unfolding of the world in all its aspects follows 'naturally'—not as a logical consequence but as a psychological consequence; as an expression of the spontaneous unfolding (development, maturing) of the self." (250)

Oliver's writing confirms the understanding of other ecopoets like Wendell Berry and W.S. Merwin that it is an attunement of love, humility, and awe for the natural world that is the abiding source of ecological sustainability. Can such attunement be taught? Contemplative pedagogy says it can be cultivated.

Contemplative Pedagogy

The most effective way of absorbing the ecological sensibility of these texts is by incorporating contemplative pedagogy, so that the art of sensing, seeing, and listening with relaxed awareness is also practiced by the students who read these texts. If the teaching of sustainability ought to include other ways of knowing and open up space for genuine self-inquiry, honoring both cognitive and affective registers, then contemplative pedagogy has much to offer. As such, *any* course on sustainability might incorporate in its pedagogy the mode of contemplative inquiry.

According to Hadot, the ancient Greek and Roman philosophers "strongly sensed the paradox and scandal of the human condition: man *lives in* the world without *perceiving* the world" (258). The "habitual utilitarian perception, necessary for life" requires us to "separate ourselves from the world qua world":

> In order to live, mankind must 'humanize' the world; in other words, transform it, by action as well as by his perception, into an ensemble of 'things' useful for life. Thus, we fabricate the objects of our worry, quarrels, social rituals, and conventional values. That is what *our* world is like; we no longer see the world qua world. (258)

Citing Bergson's "displacement of attention" and Merleau-Ponty's "phenomenological reduction," Hadot clarifies what is required for new perception to occur: "a radical rupture with regard to the state of unconsciousness in which man normally lives. . .Aesthetic and philosophical perceptions of the world are only possible by means of a complete transformation of our relationship to the world: we have to perceive it *for itself*, and no longer *for ourselves*" (254). Contemplative traditions across space and time have devised various exercises to cleanse habitual perception. And they advocate what the ancients knew: "We must separate ourselves from the world qua world in order to live our daily life, but we must separate ourselves from the "everyday" world in order to rediscover the world qua world" (258). The contemplative traditions of India (Hindu and Buddhist), for example, relied on the cultivation of silence, solitude and awareness of breath to anchor the mind to the present moment; freed from the fluctuations of past and future mentations, the mind could more readily come to perceive the nature of reality. Hadot's account of ancient Greco-Roman spirituality speaks to a similar engagement with the present: "the transformation of one's view of the world was intimately linked to exercises which involved concentrating one's mind on the present instant. (250)."

> In Stoicism as well as in Epicureanism, such exercises consisted in separating oneself from the future and past"…Such a technique gives the mind, freed from the burden and prejudices of the past, as well as from worry about the future, that inner detachment, freedom, and peace which are indispensable prerequisites for perceiving the world qua world. We have here, moreover, a kind of reciprocal causality: the mind acquires peace and serenity by becoming aware of its relationship with the world, to the extent that it re-places our existence within the cosmic perspective. (259)

Thus, for the ancients, eastern and western, the goal of life was to achieve the state of wisdom, "a way of life" that "brought peace of mind, " "inner freedom," and "a cosmic consciousness" (265).

Contemplative Theory

The theory and practice of contemplative pedagogy across the disciplines has developed over the last ten to fifteen years as various scholars-practitioners have tapped into the wisdom of contemplative traditions from a secular perspective. Recent interdisciplinary research in neurobiology, cognitive science, and philosophy supports the thesis that contemplation is good for individual and collective social health. Practices from various contemplative traditions have been found "to harness neurologic and immune improvements in the practitioners' lives" (Siegel 96). Besides improving students' attention, the contemplative mode introduces a self-reflexive capacity essential to solving life's problems. The demonstrated value of contemplative practice has led to the formation of the Association for the Contemplative Mind in Higher Education. Contemplative pedagogy intends to awaken the mind and heart to new learning possibilities and ways of being.

David Levy in his webinar "No Time To Think: The American University and its (Anti-)Contemplative Roots," critiques the West's drive to "more-faster-better" in the spheres of production and consumption that has led to a climate of information overload, fragmented attention, and busyness. I would agree with him that the culture of un-sustainability has infected the university: students' attention spans are shrinking as their levels of stress are increasing. How do we get these young anxious minds to find creative and thoughtful solutions for a sustainable world? We begin by slowing down the pace of things, by bringing silence into the classroom so that the cacophony of the restless mind is brought to each student's awareness. We give them the opportunity to glimpse the workings of the mind: its impersonal and universal tendency to oscillate between past (what is no longer here) and future (what is not yet here), so that the present is missed. Students can readily appreciate the fact that attention distracted by past or future mentation is a hindrance to learning.

Meditation, or the cultivation of silent witnessing of the mind/world, is at the heart of contemplative inquiry and pedagogy. In his study of mindfulness and neurobiology, *The Mindful Brain*, scientist Daniel Goleman writes "With mindful awareness the flow of energy and information that is our mind enters our conscious attention and we can both appreciate its contents and also come to regulate its flow in a new way" (Siegel 5). In the process, we come to understand something crucial about who we are. When we simply observe our thoughts, beliefs, emotions, and perceptions as they come and go, our detachment allows us to see that we are *not* identical with them; we see "the ebbs and flows of our own mind's activities as habits of mind, not the totality of who we are" (327). Freed from inner compulsivity, we are more present to our experience in the present moment; we are also less inclined to be reactive as past conditioning relaxes its grip on us. We become more 'centered': with practice, "the hub of the wheel of awareness can welcome anything from the rim—uncomfortable feelings and fear, memories or stories, social challenges or moments of isolation, with an approach of openness and equanimity" (223). In this sense, meditation is the art of welcoming all that arises in consciousness.

The Contemplative Classroom

In contemplative pedagogy, we invite our students to develop awareness as a "skill" by becoming more receptive, self-observant and reflexive, three qualities Siegel identifies as the hallmark of mindfulness (324). The intention to slow down and become aware guides each of the class activities. The instructor is a practitioner-guide who journeys alongside the beginner. The instructor need not be a "master." Here let's keep in mind the adage that we teach best what we most need to learn. In any case, it is a good practice in contemplative pedagogy to honor both the beginner and the teacher in ourselves and in our students. Every class meeting can become an opportunity to relate to the self via practices of attunement: we can begin the session by ringing a bell or gong and observing a few minutes of deep listening as the sound fades away taking us into the silence. We may lead guided sitting meditations that include slow deep breathing to still the mind and/or silent walking meditations in and out of the classroom. Instructions for walking meditation, mindfulness meditation, and many other contemplative practices can be found on the website of the Center for Contemplative Mind in Society. "Stopping, Calming, Resting, Healing," an excerpt from Thich Nhat Hanh's book on the Buddha's teachings, is a fine, short introduction to Buddhist meditation that can be shared with students. Hanh's *The Miracle of Mindfulness: An Introduction to the Practice of Meditation* is also a good resource for the class; it includes a reflection on interdependence, what he also calls *interbeing*, "to see one in all and all in one" (48).

In discussing articles or literary texts, the practice of slow reading of key passages, adapted from the *lectio divina,* a Catholic practice of scriptural reading, can be an effective way of deepening one's understanding of the material. In *lectio,* a slow reading aloud of the text several times is followed by silent rumination on the text until an insight develops. As Maria Lichtmann notes, "the practice of *lectio divina* can enable the objective to become subjective and thereby transformative, to enter our being and become part of us, without losing its objective status" (11-12). In this adaptation, which may also be done in small groups, or in one large circle, a student is asked to read a passage slowly. Another student or two reads the same passage again, slowly. The group or class is asked to simply listen without analysis. Then students ponder the text silently, each picking out a phrase or word that is meaningful to them. This word or phrase may then be shared aloud with the group without commentary. In this way, each student contributes to an engagement with the text, which is then open for discussion.

Arthur Zajonce correctly points out that "an ethics governing humanity's relationship to the Earth cannot be the outcome of a rational cost-benefit analysis merely, but must be predicated on a lived spiritual relationship to her" (118). Spending some quiet time outdoors, attuning to the natural environment, is a meaningful practice in itself. David Abram underscores the value of attuning to the physical terrain, of connecting our senses to "local sounds" and "seasonal scents":

> Transfixed by our technologies, we short-circuit the sensorial reciprocity between our breathing bodies and the bodily terrain. Human awareness folds in upon itself, and the senses—once the crucial site of our engagement with the wild and animate earth—become mere adjuncts of an isolate and abstract mind bent on overcoming an organic reality that now seems disturbingly aloof and arbitrary. (Abram 267)

Awareness of the reciprocity between "our breathing bodies and the bodily terrain" may be cultivated by an assignment that requires that every week students spend at least thirty minutes quietly in a natural environment and, after that, write on the subject of the present moment. These jottings can later be crafted into poems or prose pieces. The instructions for the assignment are as follows:

> "Walk slowly, mindfully, aware of all that you encounter. When you have walked enough, settle down on a spot that calls you to do so. Sit silently, aware of your breathing, and let your gaze take in the scene before you. 'Listen' with your whole body. Take all the time you need. Then write in your notebook, following the prompts adapted from Mary Oliver's poem, "Gratitude": *What did you notice? What did you hear? What did you admire? What astonished you? What was most wonderful? What did you think was happening?*"

Epistemic shifts can take place in these silent contemplative moments. Mark Coleman's *Awake in the Wild: Mindfulness in Nature as a Path of Self-Discovery* offers many nature-based meditation practices that can be suggested as "outdoor" assignments. Stephanie Kaza's *Mindfully Green: A Personal and Spiritual Guide to Whole Earth Thinking* is a wonderful text for any course on sustainability as it addresses mindful ecological living as a path of practice.

Conclusion

As Lawrence Buell notes, "issues of vision, value, culture, and imagination are keys to today's environmental crises at least as fundamental as scientific research, technological know-how, and legislative regulation" (5). Literary imagination has often been the vehicle of a profoundly ecological understanding. As Mark Long notes, a poem becomes "a space in which we might learn to construct alternative ways of thinking and acting in the world" (59). Quietly observing, quietly undoing the dualisms that support alienation from and indifference to the nonhuman world, these solitary ruminations return us to ourselves, revealing to us an amplitude of being that is necessary for sustaining diversity, equality, peace—life itself. Examining the sensibility of contemplative environmental writing can facilitate an ecological-philosophical understanding of interconnectedness that needs to be at the heart of sustainability education.

Contemplative pedagogy, by cultivating awareness, offers a transformative mode of learning since it affects our very ways of knowing and being. The contemplative practice of silently witnessing the contents of the mind (thoughts-feelings), while not engaging them, calms and quiets the mind, increasing clarity and wellbeing. Transforming the mindset of our students so that they become more receptive and compassionate ought to be an important goal of teaching (for) sustainability. Contemplative pedagogy signals that practical and balanced care of the self is as important as anything else the class may teach—an important lesson in sustainability. However, the implications of cultivating silence/awareness reach further, for in effect this practice of non-doing can be a powerful method of revising the conditioned self that is home to unsustainable, over-consumptive habits.

Notes

1. The mode of perception Hadot calls Orphic is also found in the philosophic discourse and poetry of ancient India, China and Japan. Perhaps the world's oldest ecological philosophy of nature is found in the Vedas, India's Sanskrit texts of 1500 BCE. For Taoist, Chan and Zen Buddhist poetry of Asia, see anthologies such as *Mountain Home: The Wilderness Poetry of Ancient China,* tr. David Hinton, (New York, NY: New Directions, 2002) and *The Poetry of Zen*, eds. Sam Hamill and J.P. Seaton, (Boston, MA: Shambhala, 2004).

2. Among the many American nonfiction works that can be assigned (excerpted or in their entirety) are H.D. Thoreau's *Walden*, Aldo Leopold's *A Sand County Almanac*, Mary Austin, *The Land of Little Rain*, Edward Abbey's *Desert Solitaire*, Barry Lopez's *Arctic Dreams*, and Annie Dillard's *Pilgrim at Tinker Creek*. For contemporary American nature poets, see selected poems by A.R. Ammons, W.S. Merwin, Denise Levertov, Gary Snyder, Wendell Berry, and Mary Oliver's collection of poetry and prose, such as *Winter Hours* or *What Do We Know*?

Works Cited

Berry, Wendell. *A Timbered Choir: The Sabbath Poems 1979-1997*. Berkeley, CA: Counterpoint Press, 1999.

Bryson, J. Scott, ed. *Ecopoetry: A Critical Introduction.* University of Utah Press, 2002.

Coleman, Mark. *Awake in the Wild: Mindfulness in Nature as a Path of Self-Discovery.* Novato, CA: New World Library, 2006.

Dillard, Annie. *Pilgrim at Tinker Creek.* N.Y., NY: Harper Perennial Modern Classics, 1998.

Fox, Warwick. "Transpersonal Ecology." *Environmental Ethics: The Big Questions.* Ed. David R. Keller. Oxford, U.K.: Wiley-Blackwell, 2010. 245-251.

Glazer, Steven, ed. *The Heart of Learning: Spirituality in Education.* New York: Jeremy P. Tarcher/Putnam, 1999.

Hadot, Pierre. *Philosophy as a Way of Life.* Oxford, UK: Wiley-Blackwell, 1995.

Hamill, Sam and J.P. Seaton, eds. *The Poetry of Zen.* Boston, MA: Shambhala, 2004.

Hogan, Linda. Dwellings: *A Spiritual History of the Living World.* New York: Touchstone, 1996.

King, Roger J. H. "How to Construe Nature: Environmental Ethics and the Interpretation of Nature." *Environmental Ethics: The Big Questions.* Ed. David R. Keller. Oxford, U.K.: Wiley-Blackwell, 2010. 352-359.

Leopold, Aldo. *A Sand County Almanac and Sketches Here and There.* New York: Oxford University Press, 1968.

Levertov, Denise. "Come into Animal Presence." *Selected Poems.* New York: New Directions, 2002. 19.

Levy, David M. "No Time To Think: The American University and its (Anti-)Contemplative Roots." A Center for Contemplative Mind Webinar. May 19, 2010.

Lichtmann, Maria. *The Teacher's Way: Teaching and the Contemplative Life.* Mahwah, N.J: Paulist Press, 2005.

Lopez, Barry. *Arctic Dreams.* New York: Vintage, 2001.

Nhat Hanh, Thich. "Stopping, Calming, Resting, Healing." *The Heart of the Buddha's Teachings: Transforming Suffering into Peace, Joy, and Liberation.* New York: Broadway Books, 1999. 24-27.

Oliver, Mary. *Winter Hours: Prose, Prose Poems, and Poems.* New York: Mariner Books, 1999.

--- "Gratitude." *What Do We Know?: Poems and Prose Poems.* Cambridge, MA: Da Capo Press, 2002. 40-41.

--- "Wild Geese." *Dream Work.* New York: The Atlantic Monthly Press, 1986. 14.

O'Reilley, Mary. Online Syllabus on "A Contemplative Spirituality of Environmental Writing." *The Center for Contemplative Mind in Society.*

Scigaj, Leonard M. *Sustainable Poetry: Four American Ecopoets*. Lexington, KY: University of Kentucky Press, 1999.

Siegel, Daniel L. *The Mindful Brain: Reflection and Attunement in the Cultivation of Well-Being*. New York: W.W. Norton, 2007.

Thoreau, Henry David. *Thoreau on Water: Reflecting Heaven*. Ed. Robert Lawrence France. Boston, MA: Houghton Mifflin, 2001.

Walker, Alice. "A Bird Discovers the Sky: A Review of Joanna Field." *A Life of One's Own*. Los Angeles: Tarcher, 1981. In *Material for Thought*, no.14. Far West Editions. San Francisco, CA. 1995.

Zajonc, Arthur. *Meditation as Contemplative Inquiry: When Knowing Becomes Love*. Great Barrington, MA: Lindisfarne Books, 2009.

Using Geography to Address Sustainability in an Online 4-8th Grade Teacher Certification Program

William Forbes, D. Michelle Williams, Tiffany Ingram
Stephen F. Austin State University

Abstract: Sustainability has recently emphasized an interdisciplinary "triple bottom line" based on mutually reinforcing economic, environmental, and social foundations of quality of life. Among the social sciences, geography is uniquely suited to address interdisciplinary sustainability due to its tradition of researching interaction of economies and societies with natural habitats.. The online 4-8th grade teacher certification program at our university provides an opportunity to "train the trainer," instilling sustainability concepts into course material that links directly with state K-12 standards. The paper addresses sustainability content within the program's three geography courses and how that content can be reapplied in the K-12 context, emphasizing student engagement, problem-based learning, and use of geographic technology.

Dr. William Forbes is an Associate Professor of Geography and Director of the Center for a Livable World at Stephen F. Austin State University. He teaches classes in world regional geography, biogeography, economic geography, physical geography, political geography, and study abroad. Dr. Forbes received his Ph.D., M.S., and M.A. from the University of North Texas and a B.S. and B.A. from Humboldt State University. His dissertation revisited Mexico's Rio Gavilan, where "perfect" land health was noted by conservationist Aldo Leopold in the 1930s. Dr. Forbes publishes research on historical-environmental geography and environmental ethics. The Center for a Livable World is a new research center on humanities and social science aspects of sustainability, so far producing two anthologies and an interdisciplinary pilot project that examined livability of a small East Texas city.

Dr. Dawn Michelle Williams taught special education for 20 years, served 10 years as a middle and high school administrator in Kansas and Texas, and is currently employed as an assistant professor and coordinator of the middle level grade online completer program at Stephen F. Austin State University in the Department of Elementary Education. She holds Masters Degrees in Special Education and Educational Administration, and completed her Doctorate in Educational Leadership at Stephen F. Austin State University.

Tiffany Ingram received her degree from the University of Texas at Austin in Geography and the Environment. She is currently seeking her Master's in Education from Stephen F. Austin State University.

Introduction

This essay is unique from other contributions to this volume, in that it addresses incorporation of sustainability into online education. The essay also emphasizes special capabilities of one of the social sciences, geography, to help pre-service teachers integrate sustainability's "triple bottom line" of economy, environment, and society. The essay also covers processes in sustainability, geography, and teaching that foster higher order thinking and opportunities for service learning through the online format.

Such linkages between K-12 and higher education help address another key theme of sustainability, concern for future generations. Another important linkage is that between education and surrounding communities. Universities and K-12 schools offer a wealth of talent that, when applied to the local economy, environment, and society, can foster broader thinking about future development and quality of life. Ideally, such linkages bridge collaborative thinking and implementation, leading to actions that best fit needs of human and natural communities. Online geography courses for pre-service teachers act as first steps across that bridge.

Middle Level Grades Online Completer Program

Stephen F. Austin State University's Middle Level Grades (MLG) Online Completer program provides an opportunity for nontraditional students across the state of Texas who have completed at least 45 hours at a Texas Community College to complete a teaching degree online. Interested students are required to live sixty or more miles from campus, be employed full time in a school as a paraprofessional, have other full time employment, or be unable to attend classes on campus due to other extenuating circumstances.

Candidates are also required to have a 3.0 or higher GPA, prior online coursework, and experience working with children. Research shows that programs with stringent requirements are more successful (Denton et al.; Rotherham & Mead; Schweizer, Hayslett, & Chaplock). Students are also required to visit campus for a two-day workshop each semester. The agenda includes advising, test preparation, and observation in the University's charter school and local middle schools. Teacher candidates also complete two practicum experiences in their local schools and one semester of student teaching at an approved SFASU site.

Smith et al. stressed the importance of learner to learner, learner to instructor, and learner to content interaction within the online course. The University's Office of Instructional Technology provides intensive training for faculty in developing web-based courses and teaching online. In the MLG program, quality student/teacher interaction occurs through video conferencing, discussion boards, chats, e-mail, and/or instant messaging.

Online teacher education programs are becoming more popular. For many participants, this program is the only option for completing a teaching degree. The online format also reduces environmental impacts of commuting.

Sustainability Processes

The term sustainable development originated with the 1987 book *Our Common Future*. Efforts tried to address cultural and environmental impacts resulting from a singular focus on economic development. While highlighting an interdisciplinary approach since its beginning, sustainability more recently emphasizes a "triple bottom line," based on mutually reinforcing economic, environmental, and social foundations of development.

Other essays in this volume attest to sustainability's holistic emphasis on entire systems, rather than on separate aspects of the triple bottom line (see Avila, El-Mogazi, Gould, Paehlke, Stephens). Temporal thinking is also important in sustainability. Rates of change from globalization call us to action. Processes to analyze can range in scale from an individual lifestyle to a household, campus or neighborhood, to entire cities, states, nations, or global networks.

Examples of such processes can include: a neighborhood's ability to reduce its energy use and carbon emissions (Berton; London Sustainability Exchange); a city's capability to provide alternative transportation routes to school and work (Goodyear, "Bike maps;" "Commute by bicycle"); the ability of a nation such as the UK to reduce its consumption levels or "ecological footprint" (Goodall; Pearce); and the ability of a corporation such as Wal-Mart to rethink its entire global production system to reduce packaging, sell organic clothing and produce, and require suppliers to increase worker safety (Clifford; Humes).

Examination of such integrated processes can reveal surprising overlaps of benefits. A recent Danish study indicated biking or walking to school increases student concentration for up to four hours, adding educational benefits (Goodyear, "Bike/Walk to school"). Many sustainability (or livability) enhancement measures implemented by cities, corporations, and schools offer economic benefits, including reduced costs in energy, packaging, traffic or, in the case of greenways, flood control and pollution filtering. Flood control by urban green space often provides the largest dollar values in "ecosystem services."

Geographic Processes

Among the social sciences, geography is uniquely suited to address interdisciplinary aspects of sustainability due to its focus on mixing the social sciences (human geography) and natural sciences (physical geography). *Human-environment relationships* are often covered under regional geography.

Geography has a long tradition of research and teaching that addresses interaction of societies with natural habitats to form culture regions. This topic is addressed in two of the three required geography courses in the SFASU Middle Level Grade program - World Regional Geography and Historical Geography of the US. Physical Geography, the third required geography course, directly addresses ecosystem processes and environmental issues as a natural science. Geography also looks at spatial (locational) aspects of other subjects, through its sub-disciplines within physical geography (such as biogeography and climatology), human geography (such as demography and economic geography), and regional geography. Although geographers should be adept at both natural and social science, certain sub-disciplines emphasize the mix (these include historical geography and cultural and political ecology).

Thus, interdisciplinary foundations of economy, environment, and society are already included within geographic studies. Adding themes in sustainability that are strongly tied to spatial (locational) thinking —such as alternative energy sources and transportation modes, environmental justice, globalization, greenways, local food systems, and "smart" growth—presents a natural link between the discipline and current events.

State standards (Texas Essential Knowledge and Skills, or TEKS) include geography elements in every K-12 grade, even though there is only one required course named geography—world geography, most often taught in ninth grade. Teachers of other social science courses tend to mix required elements of various subjects (geography, economics, history, mathematics, or natural science) into one lesson for efficiency. State standards (TEKS) also indicate teachers *should* "facilitate classroom and outdoor investigations for at least 50% of instructional time."

A number of organizations and websites provide practical ideas for K-12 teachers to use in the classroom and field as they teach geography (for examples, see National Council for Geographic Education, National Geographic Education, and individual state geography alliance websites). Many activities provide an opportunity for students to think critically about environmental, economic, and social issues related to sustainability.

Teaching Processes

Transitioning to a more sustainable and livable world, whether in the K-12 or adult-community context, can require active learning and collaborative problem-solving. Freire, Matthews, and Noddings all agree that dialogue and problem solving are imperative if we expect to sustain a democratic and civil society. Dewey (*Democracy in education*) referred to education as the means to the social continuity of life. Therefore, teacher candidates are trained to promote an educational climate that includes meaningful and robust communication.

Freire refers to "problem posing," a method in direct contrast to the traditional dispensing of information into the minds of students. Dewey (*Democracy in education*) outlines five steps in this problem-discovery process (examples of sustainability applications are added in parentheses):

1. *Continuous activity for which one is interested* (for instance, letting students choose from a selection of sustainability topics, such as renewable energy, alternative transportation, recycling, or greenways);
2. *A problem involved in the interest that stimulates thought* (such as how to create bicycle or walking routes to school);
3. *Ability to make observations concerning the problem* (such as ability to field review safe bike and walk routes with little traffic and obstacles);
4. *Suggesting and developing solutions* (such as mapping best bike routes);
5. *Opportunity to apply and test the solutions* (for example, a field test ride or survey of teachers and students on interest in using proposed routes).

Many state K-12 standards, such as the Texas Essential Knowledge and Skills (TEKS) for Social Studies, also emphasize critical thinking and problem-solving. At each grade level (6-8) there is a TEKS element for social studies skills stating "The student applies critical-thinking skills to organize and use information" (TEA). Another TEKS element states, "The student uses problem-solving and decision-making skills, working independently and with others, in a variety of settings."

Another important teaching process to promote sustainability is service learning. It helps extend the realm of concern beyond the individual and family, a necessity when expanding focus from only economic development to an equally integrated economy, environment, and society.

Dewey (*School and Society*, 27-28) wrote of saturating students with a spirit of service and stated it was the "best guaranty of a larger society which is worthy, lovely, and harmonious." Additionally, Noddings (94) discussed the importance of teaching children to "care for other human beings, and all must find an ultimate concern in center of self, for intimate others, for associates/acquaintances, for distant others, for animals, for plants and the physical environment, for objects and instruments, and for ideas."

Aldo Leopold saw a land ethic as part of the natural evolution of ethics, over time expanding concern from the individual to family to community to nation and, now, to the biotic community: "The land ethic simply enlarges the boundaries of the community to include soils, waters, plants, and animals, or collectively: the land" (202-203). Leopold's land ethic is not only included in online versions of geography classes - students are also referred to the Leopold Education Project, which promotes K-12 engagement with Leopold's field work.

Teaching classes online does not exclude opportunities for service-learning. An online class in sustainability recently required local service-learning activities or an alternative assignment. Most students chose the service-learning activity. A student located five hours away organized an after-school sustainability club, engaging parents and children in self-directed activities such as recycling and alternative transportation. Another remote student set up a community garden at a military base.

In summary, the most effective teaching processes involve students in cooperative learning activities and thus create a capacity for associative living. Students learn to listen, respect others, express themselves, resolve conflict, and solve problems, skills which all increase the likelihood of innovation for a more sustainable future. These teaching processes are modeled in the online courses so they can be replicated at the K-12 level.

Sustainability content in three geography courses

Sample content follows, illustrating key processes of sustainability, geography, and teaching within three online geography courses.

Course 1 - Physical Geography

Physical Geography (GEO 130) provides a systematic examination of the physical environment with primary emphasis upon nature, location, and general patterns of landforms, climate, vegetation, and soils. It describes processes that shape earth surfaces at global, regional, and local scales. Physical geography provides understanding of the natural science template upon which human activity plays out, both temporally and spatially.. Key sub-topics relating to sustainability include the geologic time scale, biogeography, climate, and soils.

Geologic time scale

The geologic time scale is particularly useful in illustrating the present rate of extinction which, at 1,000 times the natural background rate, is considered by many to be the most critical environmental issue on the planet (Wilson). Surprisingly few people are aware of the extent of this process going on today.

Five mass extinctions are evident in the geologic time scale, at approximately 440 million, 370 million, 250 million, 210 million, and 65 million years ago. Leakey and Lewin suggest we are in the midst of the sixth mass extinction in the planet's history—yet the first to be caused by a biological agent (humans). This process sets up critical thinking, posed as online discussion points—what is our role as humans? Do we have a responsibility to other species? When does it eclipse economic development, when it interferes with human basic needs or with merely human desires that could be altered?

Biogeography

Biogeography covers the distribution of plants and animals. Students are quizzed on a module related to Texas ecological regions, most of which have been greatly altered since the 1800s by grazing, fire suppression, urbanization, and agriculture. Just one example is the coastal prairie region. The population of Attwater's Prairie Chicken, dependent on open prairie that frequently burned over to keep brush down, once numbered one million. Due to alteration processes above, *less than one percent* of the coastal prairie remains. Attwater's Prairie Chicken now numbers less than 100 individuals.

Problem posing and problem solving related continue in an online discussion format. How much of the pre-modern landscape has been altered by humans? What is the best way to preserve a species relying on now fragmented habitats? Is zoo preservation enough? Where is extinction occurring most? Do its main causes vary by location? Habitats like coastal prairie surround Houston, the fourth largest city in the US, allowing field trips or service learning.

Biogeography modules also address another critical habitat, bottomland forest, which provides the best habitat (food, water, cover) for the most species of any habitat in Texas. This forest also provides significant ecosystem services for humans through flood control and pollution filtering. Two-thirds to three-fourths of such forest are gone in Texas. Bottomland forest is much like the tropical rainforest in its importance for species and ecosystem processes.

This "rainforest" analogy is used in online discussion and in field settings surrounding Dallas, Houston, or other Texas cities. Several entities involve students in bottomland forest outdoor activities. An example is Groundwork Dallas, a non-profit organization that engages underprivileged students in south Dallas with the nearby Great Trinity Forest. Service-learning activities can include restoration through planting of mast (food)–producing tree species (oak, pecan) and installation of duck nest boxes to replicate missing tree nesting cavities. Student engagement in restoration may be more beneficial than the change in habitat (Maiteny).

The Physical Geography text, *Elemental Geosystems* (Christopherson), also includes the geologic time scale, biogeography, extinction, and critical thinking questions. Another two key processes it addresses are climate change and soil erosion. Both of these processes, as with extinction rates and extent of landscape change, are not well understood by the general public.

Climate change

The text and online modules emphasize natural glacial (cooling) and interglacial (warming) periods during the Quaternary Period (encompassing the Pleistocene and present Holocene). This temporal scale helps illustrate that, although we are in an interglacial (warming) period, it is the *rate* of warming that is of great concern. This is illustrated by datelines placed on an image of Gangotri Glacier in the Himalayas, showing that the rate of glacial retreat is far more pronounced since the Industrial Revolution.

The text and modules also cite other supporting data from ice cores, tree rings, and phenology. The latter involves recording of the timing of biological events, with many processes (such as first spring tree buds and first spring sightings of migratory birds) showing up earlier on the calendar as the planet warms. Phenology presents an opportunity for students to record their own sightings at their hometown, backyard, or school. Significant outdoor experiences can be important in fostering sustainable behavior later in life (Maiteny).

Another teaching point of global warming is the value of long-term data. Phenology is most useful when it is compared to records kept over long time frames. Henry David Thoreau noted bud breaks and neo-tropical migratory birds coming later in the spring to his cabin at Walden Pond in Concord, Massachusetts, illustrating a cooler climate in the mid-1800s. Linking to a related *New York Times* article to generate discussion provides a break from the typical module format.

Complementary information for climate change discussions can include a graph of long term temperature data. This becomes relevant during an especially cold winter when climate change critics (often students) are prone to voice skepticism.

Students can see periodic dips in temperature in certain years, but an overall rise in temperature over decades. Climate change can also show multiple benefits from resolutions, such as development of renewable, non-fossil fuel energy sources that not only reduce carbon emissions but also foster US energy independence, international competitiveness, and new jobs.

Soil erosion

Soil erosion is also addressed in the text and online module. This is another critical, unsustainable process that typically flies "under the radar" of the public. *Elemental Geosystems* illustrates a global *rate* of soil erosion that far exceeds the soil building process, along with the startling fact that humans move more earth globally than do natural processes such as river deposition, floods, and wind.

The online Physical Geography course currently requires a short research paper. Education majors in the class are to explore a topic through literature review, then answer a research question: how would you teach this topic to a certain grade level? New citations on teaching geography provide the foundation for the results section of the paper.

The paper assignment offers an opportunity for pre-service teachers to design outdoor learning. For example, pre-service teachers can conduct literature reviews on basics of urban and rural soil erosion. They can then design lessons based around online teaching resources and human interaction with soil. They can take students outside to show results of recent rain, and question them on what happens to soil impacted by the power of water.

Teachers can foster higher-order thinking skills, asking what impact humans have by covering soil with concrete (hastens runoff and erosion rates), leaving forested stream buffers (captures runoff from farms and urbanization), or plowing fields along the contour of the slope (reduces rill and gully erosion).

Teachers can also guide students to think temporally by looking at soil horizons in a road cut and inquire—what horizon is most fertile? How long does it take for soil horizons to develop? This exercise illustrates how societies interact with and adapt to natural landscapes.

Course 2 - World Regional Geography

World Regional Geography (GEO 131) not only fills a requirement for pre-service teachers, but is an elective within the University core curriculum under the category of social sciences. The course provides a broad investigation of the world's culture regions. It covers basic cultural, demographic, economic, political, and physical patterns, with current events highlighted. World Regional Geography also covers processes of globalization, including consumption patterns, expanded measures of well-being, reductions in cultural diversity, trends in population, and adaptability to economic and environmental change.

Consumption patterns

An especially valuable sustainability concept to kick off problem posing and problem solving is that the US, with approximately 5 percent of the world's population, participates in about 25-30 percent of the world's resource consumption. Is this consumption rate sustainable? Is it fair to other nations? Do other nations have adequate environmental or worker safety precautions? Should other nations develop as we did? Can Fair Trade products "scale up" to adequately address the issue? What processes could reduce our consumption? Can we replicate the UK's reduction in consumption? (Goodall; Pearce)

Measures of well-being

Another key process addressed in World Regional Geography is the increasing expansion of measures of well-being. The main textbook used is *World Regional Geography: Global Patterns, Local Lives* (Pulsipher). The text addresses measures of well-being beyond Gross Domestic Product (GDP), including the United Nations Human Development Index (HDI), which adds important health and education data to GDP.

This can be complemented by recent, more extensive indices, many available on the internet, that include gender empowerment, happiness surveys, and environmental impacts of citizens. The Happy Planet Index is most related to sustainability, as it combines many of these categories, with the highest weighted factor being ecological footprint. It is also interactive - students not only see how nations are rated (Costa Rica is often highest) but obtain their own score based on their personal lifestyle.

The Happy Planet Index helps illustrate that happiness does not rise proportionally with income, once households get above a base level to meet their needs (about $10,000/year in developing nations and $70,000/year in the US). This concept can help students think critically about the true value of highly-consumptive lifestyles (New Economics Foundation).

Cultural diversity

Sustainability is also about reducing rates of cultural change from globalization. Similar to biodiversity loss, elimination of working languages and cultures reduces diversity. In some cases a hybrid of local and global culture forms, where some elements of the older culture remain (Haraway).

World Regional Geography online includes student to student interaction, commenting to each other on loss of languages around the world. This loss often occurs at nearly the same rate and in the same locations where biodiversity loss is greatest—the tropics. Students also comment on examples of people gifted at learning languages, as a counter to limited linguistic abilities of most US citizens.

Population

Another exercise engages students with the demographic transition model, which illustrates changing birth and death rates as nations develop over time. Students visualize the US as a developing nation by noting higher birth and death rates of the 1800s, when the nation was more rural. Students can find evidence in local, historic cemeteries. Older sections typically have more small graves, indicating child mortality rates that exist today in less developed nations.

Students can also visualize the demographic transition by thinking about numbers of siblings they have, their parents had, and that their grandparents had. Families typically get larger as you go back generations to a more rural, less developed nation. Urbanization tends to lower birth rates around the globe.

Critical thinking asks: How exceptional is the US? Was it once a developing nation? What is the effect of population on the environment? Is it linear—do more people bring an equal increase in degradation? Or does impact vary by nation? Does an urban citizen in China or India have the same impact as an urban citizen in the US? How do ecological footprints of US citizens compare to that of European or Japanese citizens? These are important questions to answer.

Adaptability

State and national K-12 standards include how societies adapt to landscapes. A complementary text is Jared Diamond's *Collapse*. The international, historical examples of successful and failed cultures help students think in longer time frames about sustainability, through dominance of individual nations, stability of economic systems, and (perhaps most importantly) rate of adaptation to economic and environmental change by modern societies.

Course 3 - Historical Geography of the US

Historical Geography of the US (GEO 344) addresses both spatial and temporal thinking, focusing on *human-environment interactions*. The course covers historical and spatial interpretation of growth and development of the United States, human activities that shaped landscapes, and environmental and *cultural landscape* changes and patterns.

Cultural landscapes

Layers of landscape (housing, commercial buildings, agricultural styles, transportation networks, and other visual signs of culture) are "peeled back" to reveal earlier natural conditions and later impacts and modifications, each of which contributes to the present landscape. The main textbook is *The Making of the American Landscape*, edited by University of Chicago geographer Michael Conzen. The text nicely augments modules and is particularly good at illustrating social adaptations to physical landscapes.

The massive influence of the Industrial Revolution becomes evident in the US, through exponential population growth of Eastern US cities, westward expansion via railroads and highways, and dominance of extractive industries.

A nice complementary text is *Contemporary Ethnic Geographies in America* (Miyares and Airriess), which covers immigration and subsequent acculturation, assimilation, and migration within the US by various ethnic groups. Students can trace their own group and think critically about not only varied group experiences but also variations of experiences *within groups* that help avoid stereotypes.

Rate of change

Space-time compression (rate of travel over a certain distance) is illustrated by increasingly more efficient transportation networks such as waterways, railroads, high-tech export centers, and interstate highways. Students can find local examples near their hometowns to illustrate a globalization process first-hand. For example, a prominent local historical marker indicates a trip from East Texas (Nacogdoches) to Central Texas (Waco) once took three *days* by stagecoach. It now takes three *hours* by auto.

In summary, Historical Geography relates to sustainability through study of changing landscapes over time. Key sustainability questions arise: what cultural landscape will we leave for future generations? At the current *rate* of change, will we include the present diversity of life forms and cultures?

Conclusion

Geography has a long tradition of global and interdisciplinary thinking, offering special capability within the social sciences to address sustainability. It holistically integrates economic, environmental, and societal processes. When combined with key education processes, classes challenge many students' perception of geography as place name memorization. Geography can engage students in problem posing and problem solving, fostering higher-order skills related to sustainability.

Such engagement with pre-service teachers in an online setting provides a unique opportunity to "train the trainer" in concepts of sustainability. The key statement of sustainable development asks us to avoid compromising the needs of future generations. Engaging pre-service teachers with geography can help promote sustainability in multiple generations who otherwise might not encounter this enduring blend of economy, environment, and society.

Works Cited

Berton, B. "How Fort Collins Created America's First Zero-Energy District." *Atlantic Cities* 22 Feb. 2013. Web.

Christopherson, Robert W. *Elemental Geosystems.* Upper Saddle River, N.J: Pearson Education, 2005. Print.

Clifford, S. "Walmart Plans to Buy American More Often." *New York Times* 15 Jan. 2013. Web.

Conzen, Michael, ed. *The Making of the American Landscape.* Oxford, UK: Routledge, 2010. Print.

Denton, J. J., Davis, T.J., Capraro, R. M., Smith, B. L., Beason, L., Graham, B. D., and Strader A. R. "Examining applicants for admission and completion of an online teacher certification program." *Educational Technology & Society* 12.1 (2009): 214-229. Print.

Dewey, John. *School and Society*. Chicago, IL: The University of Chicago Press, 1900. Print.

Dewey, John. *Democracy in Education: An Introduction to the Philosophy of Education*. New York, NY: McMillan, 1916. Print.

Diamond, Jared. *Collapse: How Societies Choose to Fail or Succeed*. New York, NY: Penguin Books, 2005. Print.

Freire, Paolo. *Pedagogy of the oppressed: 30th anniversary edition*. New York, NY: Continuum, 2007. Print.

Goodall, Chris. "Peak Stuff: Did the UK Reach a Maximum Use of Material Resources in the Early Part of the Last Decade?" 2011. Web.

Goodyear, Sarah. "Bike maps that give riders the info that they actually need." *Atlantic Cities* 15 Feb. 2013. Web.

---. "You don't have to be superhuman to commute by bicycle." *Atlantic Cities* 28 Jan. 2013. Web.

---. "The Link Between Kids Who Walk or Bike to School and Concentration." *Atlantic Cities* 5 Feb. 2013. Web.

Haraway, Donna. "Situated Knowledges: The Science Question in Feminism and the Privilege of Partial Perspective." *Feminist Studies* 14.3 (1988): 575-599.

Hume, Edward. *Force of Nature: The Unlikely Story of Wal-Mart's Green Revolution*. New York, NY: Harper Collins, 2011. Print.

Leakey, Richard, R. Lewin. *The Sixth Extinction*. New York, NY: Doubleday, 1995. Print.

Leopold, Aldo "The Land Ethic." In, *A Sand County Almanac and Sketches Here and There*. New York, NY: Oxford University Press, 1949. Print.

"Sustainable Merton." London Sustainability Exchange, Energise Merton Action Plan. Web. 23 June, 2012.

Maiteny, Paul T. "Mind in the Gap: Summary of Research Exploring 'Inner' Influences on Pro-Sustainability Learning and Behaviour." *Environmental Education Research* 8.3 (2002): 299-306.

Matthews, D. "Afterthoughts." *Kettering Review* Fall 1998: 74-76.

Miyares, Ines M., and Christopher A. Airriess, eds. *Contemporary Ethnic Geographies in America*. Boulder, Colorado: Rowman and Littlefield Publishers, 2007. Print.

New Economics Foundation. "The Happy Planet Index." 2013. Web.

Noddings, N. "What does it mean to educate the whole child?" *Educational Leadership* 63.1 (2005): 8-13.

Pearce, Fred. "The New Story of Stuff: Can We Consume Less?" *Yale Environment 360* 28 Nov. 2011. Web.

Pulsipher, Lydia, and Alex Pulsipher. *World Regional Geography: Global Patterns, Local Lives*. New York: W. H. Freeman, 2006. Print.

Rotherham, A.J., and Mead, S. "Teacher Quality Beyond No Child Left Behind: A Response to

Kaplan and Owings (2002)." *National Association of Secondary Principals Bulletin* 87.635 (2003): 65-76. Print.

Schweizer, H., Hayslett, C.,& Chaplock, S. "Student Satisfaction and Performance in an Online Teaching Certification Program." *The Journal of Continuing Higher Education* 56.2 (2008): 12-15. Print.

Smith Canter, L. L., Voytecki, K. S., and Rodriquez, D. "Increasing Online Interaction in Rural Special Education Teacher Preparation Programs." *Rural Special Education* 26.1 (2007): 23-27. Print.

Wilson, Edward O., ed. *Biodiversity.* Washington: National Academy Press, 1988. Print.

World Commission on Environment and Development. *Our Common Future.* Oxford, UK: Oxford University Press, 1987. Print.

Promoting Sustainability Through Enhancing Resilience: Transdisciplinary Teaching and Learning in the Cross Cultural Context of ESAVANA

Suzanne Walther, Utah Valley University; Loren Intolubbe-Chmil, Robert Swap, University of Virginia

Abstract: Beginning over a decade ago, an international network of transformative educational experiences has evolved as the Eastern-Southern Africa and Virginia Networks and Associations (ESAVANA), catalyzed through the collective engagement between partner universities in ESAVANA regions. Central to this network is the practice of multi-disciplinary collaboration that transcends the traditional classroom through innovative pedagogy as well as experiential teaching and learning. ESAVANA reflects a model for research, education, and engagement that is grounded in the tenets of relationship, respect, and reciprocity. Thus, the ESAVANA framework represents a context for 'catalyzing engagement', primarily through regional community-university partnerships. Through sustained iterative feedback, ESAVANA network participants engage in teaching and learning intended to: leverage partnerships and existing social capital between higher education and communities on the ground for the enhancement of regional well-being; disseminate innovative approaches for the education of tomorrow's leaders; and cooperatively develop sustainable approaches to real world concerns, with an emphasis on the southern and eastern Africa regions. Grown out of the educational experiences are student-led collaborative projects that have three aims: 1) to provide students with an experiential educational environment; 2) to address challenges to sustainability with the communities in the places where ESAVANA students learn; and 3) to increase the resilience of those communities and the environments where the projects are situated. It is our experience that in meeting these three aims, the international and cross-cultural relationships of ESAVANA become self-sustaining. This essay will offer an overview of the coursework as well as representative case studies of community-based projects that reflect these aims.

Dr. Suzanne Walther is an Assistant Professor in Earth Science at Utah Valley University, where she teaches a variety of Geography, Geology, and GIS courses. She is a fluvial geomorphologist, whose research investigates human-environment interactions, sediment mobility, and dam impacts. Her work utilizes remote sensing and geographic information system (GIS) methods to study the riverscape for use in environmental management. Dr. Walther's current projects include river assesment in Oregon; the Jordan River, lower Provo River, and Capitol Reef National Park in Utah; and using GIS to map potential for water-based service learning projects in Mexico. She has also been involved in research and study abroad in southern Africa through the University of Virginia.

Loren Intolubbe-Chmil is a Teaching & Research Associate at the University of Virginia and Adjunct Faculty at Piedmont Virginia Community College in Charlottesville, whose work centers on education for change and transformative teaching & learning that centers on social justice and civic engagement. Loren has been working with the ESAVANA-related January term course and study abroad course since 2009, in addition to advising on several field-based research experiences in a variety of settings as engaged scholarship initiatives.

Dr. Robert Swap is a Research Professor of Environmental Sciences at the University of Virginia, focusing on issues faced by coupled human – natural systems in developing countries. He was named the 2012 Virginia Professor of the Year by the Carnegie Foundation for the Advancement of Teaching and the Council for the Advancement and Support of Education. Over the past 13 years he has leveraged his 25 years of collaborative international research and education experience into the development of an international network, the Eastern/Southern Africa Virginia Networks and Associations (ESAVANA) program, that focuses on addressing real world issues that developing regions face through education, research and outreach. He has collaborated with faculty from UVa's Schools of Architecture, Business, Commerce, Education, Engineering, Nursing, and Medicine to create a form of transdisciplinary, globally engaged scholarship to address the needs of his colleagues and their communities. As part of this work, he has created a series of innovative courses to provide a continuum of learning for both undergraduate and graduate students. These include: an interdisciplinary summer study abroad program in South Africa; an intensive January Term course on the ethics, protocols and practice of international research; a series of Global Development Studies courses (both introductory and practice based) and also supervises students engaged in international service learning and community engagement projects. He believes that now, more than ever, these types of educational experiences have emerged to be an essential component of a comprehensive University education.

Introduction

Study abroad and cultural exchange programs represent an increasing trend in higher education, whereby "over the past thirty years, educators throughout the world have tried to help students understand...interconnectedness and to help weave a garment of global awareness and mutuality by building international bridges of understanding through the promotion of study abroad" (Lutterman-Aguilar and Gingrich 45). In concert with the growing emphasis on study abroad is an effort to provide coursework that is intended to catalyze the transformative power of interdisciplinary collaborations.[1] This essay offers a narrative case of the intersection of study abroad and interdisciplinary teaching and learning, as an approach to: a) promoting sustainability grounded in resilience; and b) expanding possibilities for transdisciplinary pedagogy.[2] Where many study abroad programs still tend to emphasize language competency or context-specific knowledge, this study abroad program and the larger network of which it is a part is designed to cultivate transferable skills, through experience in multiple disciplinary and community-based settings.

Beginning over a decade ago, an international network of transformative educational experiences has evolved as the Eastern-Southern Africa and Virginia Networks and Associations (ESAVANA), catalyzed through the collective engagement between partner universities in ESAVANA regions. Central to this network is the practice of multi-disciplinary collaboration that transcends the traditional classroom through innovative pedagogy, as well as experiential teaching and learning. ESAVANA reflects a model for research, education, and engagement that is grounded in the tenets of relationship, respect, and reciprocity. Thus, the ESAVANA framework represents a context for 'catalyzing engagement,' primarily through regional community-university partnerships. Behind this existing framework lies the original study abroad course (2002) as a main driving force. Exposure and education through experiencing people and place, in this case in southern Africa, often provides motivation for students to pursue further learning and build on relationships formed through their membership in the larger ESAVANA network to which they have been introduced.[3] Through sustained iterative feedback, ESAVANA network participants engage in teaching and learning intended to: leverage partnerships and existing social capital between higher education and communities on the ground for the enhancement of regional well-being; disseminate innovative approaches for the education of tomorrow's leaders; and cooperatively develop sustainable approaches to real world concerns, with an emphasis on the southern and eastern Africa regions.

A logical extension of the collaborative, educational experiences are student-led collaborative projects that have three aims: 1) to provide students with an experiential educational environment; 2) to address challenges to sustainability with the communities in the places where ESAVANA students learn; and 3) to increase the resilience of those communities and the environments where the projects are situated. It is our experience that, in meeting these three aims, the international and cross-cultural relationships of ESAVANA become self-sustaining. This essay will offer an overview of the coursework, as well as highlight a representative case of a community-based project that reflects these aims.

ESAVANA as a Transdisciplinary Context

ESAVANA is an international, collaborative academic and research network which emphasizes study abroad and cross-cultural exchange as primary modes for engagement. There are two foundational courses within ESAVANA; one is a summer study abroad course entitled *People, Culture, and the Environment of Southern Africa* and the other is a January intersession course entitled *Ethics, Practices, and Protocols of International Research.* Additional courses that are part of the consortium include *Useful Knowledge and Its Role in the Local and Global Community* and *Development on the Ground.* These courses are taught collaboratively by faculty whose disciplinary interests include fields in physical and social sciences, and are offered through the University of Virginia, which is one of the charter institutions of the ESAVANA network.

There are a few key ways in which the ESAVANA coursework and community-based field experiences are unique. The first is in the disciplinary background and interests of the undergraduate students; undergraduate participants have represented majors such as Political & Social Thought, Global Development Studies, Anthropology, Civil Engineering, Nursing, and African Studies. An additional dimension to the community of undergraduates lies in the intentional and significant participation of international students, who are recruited from partner universities in eastern and southern Africa. The third way in which the coursework and community-based experiences are unique is involvement of key in-region faculty and community partners in planning of courses.

One of the main driving forces for development of different pedagogical approaches within ESAVANA has been the surge in undergraduate and graduate students seeking international experiential learning activities. Long-term, established relationships between regional partners and course faculty have resulted in a mutually beneficial strategy to advise, mentor, and prepare U.S. undergraduate students to: a) work collaboratively with eastern and southern Africa colleagues; and b) develop responsible and respectful community engagement projects, many of which are focused on increasing community resilience and sustainability. Accordingly, both courses, as part of the ESAVANA network, seek to cultivate transdisciplinary interactions, reflecting an abiding commitment to the development of an international intellectual community. This commitment signals a shift over time towards a useful balance between the physical and social sciences.

Thus, importantly, the ESAVANA coursework places a strong and sustained emphasis on experiential learning, with students from the U.S. and Africa jointly involved in learning through less traditional and informal means. As a result, contextual learning may occur through intentional or serendipitous encounters; within communities or workplaces; through shared travel and living experiences of U.S. and African students; and/or from community scholars, practitioners, and local community members. This allows students to learn from one another and, through a range of expertise, navigate the dissonance created by different knowledge authorities, rather than simply from faculty as more discipline-bound 'experts.'

Summer Study Abroad: People, Culture & the Environment of Southern Africa

The summer study abroad component of ESAVANA, *"People, Culture & the Environment of Southern Africa* (PCESA), is designed as an experiential learning-based course which focuses on community engagement and the complexity of interrelationships through multiple lenses. It was developed as an intensive introduction to the complexity of coupled human-natural systems of southern Africa. Beginning in 2002, the course brings approximately fifteen U.S. and five regional southern African students through urban and rural settings in South Africa and Mozambique each year. The course experience includes formal lectures, site-visits, reflective exercises, and cultural encounters with community members in their everyday social and work environments.

The PCESA coursework centers on four modules, reflecting a scaffold model that emphasizes interdependence, community engagement, and social responsibility through transdisciplinary pedagogy. The four modules are placed within the geographical context of a large river basin in southern Africa and are designed to capture much of the complexity of the people, their culture, and their interactions with the environments found within this region. Module I introduces the social, political, historical, economic, and environmental complexity of the southern African region; Module II emphasizes understanding the role of community engagement, cooperative/collective entrepreneurship, indigenous knowledge, and sustainable utilization of natural resources; Module III further explores issues of environment and sustainability, participatory and justice-oriented approaches, community engagement, and international collaboration; and Module IV examines how participatory approaches focused on the environment, education, microenterprise, and health are working towards sustainable responses.

January Term: Ethics, Practices & Protocols of International Research

The January Term (Jterm) course was developed in 2006 as a preparatory course for undergraduates seeking international research and service learning experiences. What is unique is that from the outset, the course purposefully incorporates space for the presence of our international colleagues in the classroom as colleagues and regional knowledge authorities. As members of the ESAVANA network, international students and faculty are invited and supported as participants in the course in their roles as lecturers, facilitators, and local experts, thereby balancing exchanges between the northern and southern hemispheres and promoting collaborative learning experiences.[4] These international colleagues share expectations about engaged scholarship and community-based inquiry, mentoring students through the development of project proposals.

Emphasis is placed on the ethics and protocols of engaging communities in international settings, especially in rural and urban Africa. During the first week, students engage in readings that center on deconstructing common notions of service learning, research, and development. These readings are coupled with lectures given by scholars and faculty who share their experiences and perspectives from the field, and presentations from undergraduate researchers who have participated in ESAVANA coursework and field experiences. All activities are bolstered through small group activities which build relationships and help jointly process the breadth of the content, in preparation for the group project development phase.

The group project component is intended to support undergraduates in internalizing ethical habits and approaches in the conception, development, and implementation of conducting research in international settings. Students select project groups based on interest. Each student group is facilitated by the visiting international scholars, who place a particular emphasis on the cultural and global competencies they believe to be essential to the ethical practice of conducting research.

Transdisciplinary Pedagogy & Practice

The transdisciplinary nature of ESAVANA allows for faculty, graduate students, undergraduates, and community partners, who represent a range of disciplinary interests, to come together in a way that catalyzes the potential of perspectives, approaching sustainability and resilience from an asset orientation. From the start, ESAVANA has demonstrated interest in coupled human-natural systems with foundational faculty from the fields of environmental science and anthropology. Over time, the coursework has been infused with literature and emphasis on education as a field, as well as on political and social thought. A number of student projects from the course have come to fruition beyond the classroom. These projects have varied between activities that are more environmental or more people focused, while being increasingly representative of student interest, in-region need, and community support. The current iteration of the ESAVANA coursework has been strongly influenced by physical and social scientists committed to the development of engaged scholarship that contributes to more sustainable practice and, ultimately, more resilient coupled human-natural systems.

In addition, graduate student and undergraduate participation in ESAVANA-related coursework and community-based projects consistently reflect a mission of working across academic programs and departments, with a philosophy of inter/transdisciplinarity as an asset to engaged scholarship and community-university partnerships. The emphasis here is on recognition of the value of diverse lenses for critical thinking and creative problem-solving, the realization that there is significant knowledge residing outside of the Academy, and development of the mindset that seemingly divergent perspectives and dissonance are fertile ground for creation of *sustainability* and *resilience*.

Student-Led, Community-Based Projects

There are numerous examples of undergraduate, student-led, community-based projects which have been designed as a result of participation in ESAVANA coursework. These include work in regions of the world such as Mongolia, Nicaragua, South Africa, Zambia, and the U.S. In many cases, faculty and students have participated in more than one project, which has allowed for synergy of ideas, a continuum of expertise, and approaches from an abundance of disciplinary perspectives. The foci of these community-based initiatives have ranged from methane biodigestors, to slow sand water filters, to cooperative markets, to community-led sanitation, to energy efficient stoves.

Here, we offer one particular case, the energy efficient wood stove project, as an example of student-led, community driven projects. The much needed expansion of cook stove technology into rural areas of South Africa requires a non-traditional approach that differs from the more familiar top-down corporate model to ensure community buy-in and long term sustainability. The student momentum for this evolving effort originated from their participation in one or more courses focused on community engagement, development on the ground, and the ethics, protocols, and practice of international research. The courses students participated in were comprised of varied experiences: semester long (Engineering in Community Settings; Useful Knowledge; Development on the Ground), intensive intersession (Jterm), and collaboratively taught immersive study abroad (PCESA).

Originally an in-class project, the rocket stove design and implementation of energy efficient wood stoves evolved as a transdisciplinary, community-centered endeavor that is highly representative of sustainability, resilience, and transferability. The faculty members who contributed to this project are from the disciplines of Environmental Science, Education, Engineering, and Anthropology; the graduate student mentors from Education and Engineering; and the undergraduate participants from Global Development Studies, Engineering, and Economics. In addition, the original design and curriculum were jointly developed with the participation of stakeholders in South Africa, including student leaders from the University of Venda's Global Sustainability Club, and piloted in a U.S.-based elementary school before in-region activities commenced.[5]

Rocket Stoves

Relationships of more than a decade, between U.S.-based faculty and their southern Africa colleagues, helped contribute to the development of this student project. These relationships allowed students from both the U.S. and South Africa to come together around the expressed need[6] of improving stove efficiency, so as to produce less smoky conditions around rural primary schools, as well as to reduce consumption of firewood by these schools. Extensive dialogue and preparation using an asset-based approach[7] led to development of a modified Rocket Stove (a high efficiency, masonry, wood-burning stove) within the South African provinces of Limpopo and Mpumalanga since 2009. The prototype was constructed in 2010 at a primary school in the Vhembe district of Limpopo, one of the poorest and most underserved provinces in South Africa. Given the success and local interest generated in the efficient stoves, a local craftsman constructed four additional stoves at a nearby primary school, using the same Rocket Stove design a year later. In 2012, the second iteration of the Rocket Stove design was introduced at three additional schools and at a regional university-sponsored science education center. There are now a total of thirteen stoves between the Limpopo and Mpumalanga provinces.

The goal is that this technology will continue to spread through the initiative of local communities because of the benefits they provide: preliminary quantitative findings indicate a significant reduction (of at least fifty percent) in the use of firewood, cooking time (upwards of sixty percent), and incidence of burns. Anecdotal evidence suggests an improved ambient air quality compared to traditional open fires (de Chastonay, et. al.). With these reported improvements associated with the construction of the modified Rocket Stoves, school administrators have stated that they now purchase less wood, freeing financial resources to be directed towards other needs. In one school, the money saved was used to create an expansive garden, which has provided nutritious vegetables to supplement student meals and also generated additional school revenue.

Perhaps one of the most important benefits of this student-initiated Rocket Stove project, which extends beyond the environmental, financial, and health impacts mentioned above, is that local experts are now constructing these improved stoves with existing assets and knowledge, *without* a dependency on outsiders for their construction. This may be the strongest evidence for not only receptivity by communities in the Vhembe district of South Africa's Limpopo Province, but for the sustainability of the effort. Schools engaged in this project to date have indicated a sense of increased organizational resilience through: reduced use of environmental capital (consumption of firewood); improved use of human capital (school cooking and cleaning staff do not have to arrive as early to cook and have more time at school available for cleaning and gardening); and redistribution of financial capital (school administrators can now reallocate funds dedicated to firewood to other existing priorities).

The project extends lessons learned from the experiential approaches instilled during Jterm and PCESA related coursework. It has been our experience that practical methods and hands-on implementation result in noticeable and immediate benefits. These benefits have caused a natural spread of this technology through the region by word of mouth. The success of this project and the interest it has generated, both in-region and back in the U.S., point to the need for more rigorous, mixed methods research to address questions that evolved during field experience. The relationships that ESAVANA faculty and students helped create continue to expand with incorporation of new units to the ESAVANA network, such as the Sustainable Energy Technology and Research Centre (SeTAR) at the University of Johannesburg, South Africa. Evolving relationships and expanding base of knowledge and expertise are making it possible to develop testing methodology to optimize the cost and efficiency of institutional-sized Rocket Stoves.

Institutions such as schools are the perfect place to spread cook stove technology. Hundreds of children create new knowledge systems by transferring information they have garnered on cooking efficiency and environmental conservation from school to their homes. Thus, all stakeholders are in a position to work collaboratively in determining the efficacy of stove implementation in an integral accounting fashion.

Final Thoughts

A saying from the African tradition posits that "to go fast, you walk alone; to go far, you walk with many." ESAVANA embodies this philosophy in many ways, approaching engagement with a mindset of intention and inclusion, while enhancing resilience through an asset-oriented lens.

Of course, context matters,[8] and rocket stoves are just one example of a collaborative response to a locally identified issue that has transformed into a locally sustainable approach. Further, this case represents the shift from context-specific initiatives to those which are intended for the transferability of skills and replicability of design.

Through the ESAVANA network and its suite of collaboratively designed coursework, sustainability is promoted with an emphasis on engagement and community resilience. We believe that such an approach is only possible when all stakeholders, students, faculty, partners, and communities come together within the facilitative and enabling environment of trust, created through the transdisciplinary teaching, learning, and community-engaged initiatives described above.

Notes

1. See Conrad & Gunter 2000 for a more complete discussion on the intersection of transformative learning and interdisciplinary teaching and learning.
2. Max-Neef 2005 provides a comprehensive framework on transdisciplinarity and the critical shift to recognizing the value of the cogeneration of knowledge.
3. This has been presented and discussed in Swap, et al. 2007 and Intolubbe-Chmil, et al. 2012.
4. See Barkley et al. 2005 for a discussion on collaborative learning techniques.
5. The authors would like here to acknowledge the valuable contributions of numerous regional community partners, international collaborative faculty, graduate students, and undergraduate students who represent a transdisciplinary network which has promoted sustainability and the critical component of hand-off. For a more complete description of this case and of the many participants involved please see: http://news.virginia.edu/content/uva-south-african-collaboration-produces-clean-burning-efficient-cook-stoves-and-much-more; and Mason, et al., 2011.
6. Hunter 2006 has shown that responding to locally expressed needs encourages participation and long term success in programs aimed at mitigating local environmental problems.
7. This approach is described in detail in Kretzmann & Knight 1996.
8. Hunter, et. al. 2010 offer relevant insight into the tension between approaches to identified concerns and the feasibility of these approaches in context.

Works Cited

Barkley, Elizabeth F., Patricia K. Cross, and Claire Howell Major. *Collaborative Learning Techniques*. San Francisco, CA: Jossey-Bass, 2005. Print.

Conrad, Clifton F., and Ramona Gunter. "To Be More Useful: Embracing Interdisciplinary Scholarship and Dialogue." *New Directions for Higher Education* 110 (2000): 49-62. Print.

De Chastonay, Anne, Michael Bugas, Shreya Soni, and Robert Swap. "Community Driven Development of Rocket Stoves in Rural South Africa." *International Journal for Service Learning in Engineering* 7.2 (2012): 49-68. Print.

Hunter, Lori M. "Household Strategies in the Face of Resource Scarcity in Coastal Ghana: Are They Associated with Development Priorities?" *Population Research and Policy Review* 25 (2006): 157-174. Print.

Hunter, Lori M., Susie Strife, and Wayne Twine. "Environmental Perceptions of Rural South African Residents: The Complex Nature of Environmental Concern." *Society and Natural Resources* 23 (2010): 525-541. Print.

Intolubbe-Chmil, Loren, Carol Anne Spreen, and Robert J. Swap. "Transformative learning: Participant Perspectives on International Experiential Education." *Journal of Research in International Education* 11.2 (2012): 165-180. Print.

Kelly, Jane. "U.Va.-South African Collaboration Produces Clean-Burning, Efficient Cook Stoves, and Much More." *UVA Today* 5 Sept. 2012. Web.

Kretzmann, John, and John P. McKnight. "Assets-Based Community Development." *National Critic Review* 85 (1996): 23-29. Print.

Lutterman-Aguilar, Ann, and Orval Gingerich. "Experiential Pedagogy for Study Abroad: Educating for Global Citizenship." *Frontiers: The Interdisciplinary Journal of Study Abroad* 8 (2002): 41-82. Print.

Mason, Katelyn, Anne de Chastonay, Anne Rasmussen, Matthew Baer, Jessica Rothbart, Deanna Vogt, and Carol Anne Spreen. "Active engagement: Building sustainable stoves and relationships in Mashamba, South Africa." *The Jefferson Public Citizens Journal*. 2011. 87-94. Web.

Max-Neef, Manfred A. "Foundations of Transdisciplinarity." *Ecological Economics* 53.1 (2005): 5-16. Print.

Swap, Robert J., Suzanne C. Walther, Hanan Sabea, and Clare Terni. "Interdisciplinary Experiential Learning in the Form of Summer Study Abroad and the Longer Term Influences on Participants." *Association of American Geographers Annual Meeting*. San Francisco, CA. 2007.

III. THE CAMPUS AS SITE FOR PLACE-BASED LEARNING

A Decade of Lessons from Connecting Campus Greening with the Classroom at Rice University

Richard R. Johnson and Elizabeth Long, Rice University

Abstract: At Rice University in Houston, Texas, campus greening efforts have been linked to the classroom since the late 1990s, with a single class serving as a primary driver for environmental change on campus. The class—"Environmental Issues: Rice into the Future," cross-listed between the Sociology and Environmental Studies programs—allows students to engage in campus environmental issues and solutions in a tangible way through experiential learning. Students begin the semester as observers of the campus sustainability movement; then, through a group project, students become both observers of and participants in campus environmental change, as they use the campus as a laboratory for learning about sustainability and social movements. This paper explores the key lessons from a decade of student group projects, and the conditions that enable the projects and the class to be successful.

Richard Johnson is a Professor in the Practice of Environmental Studies in Sociology at Rice University, and serves as the Director of the Administrative Center for Sustainability and Energy Management for Rice. Prof. Johnson co-teaches courses in sociology, environmental studies, and chemical engineering, where he seeks to use the campus as a laboratory for learning about sustainability. His work in sustainability in higher education encompasses many spheres of the campus, from academics to operations to administration to research to student life. An urban planner by training, Prof. Johnson engages in consulting work that models the economic and environmental benefits of "green" infrastructure, such as urban greenways and trail systems. Prof. Johnson is also a research affiliate of the Kinder Institute for Urban Research, the Associate Director of the Center for the Study of Environment and Society, and is the former President of the Board of the Houston Farmers' Market.

Elizabeth Long is Professor of Sociology at Rice University, and serves as Chair of the Sociology Department. Trained as a cultural sociologist, she has taught cultural sociology, gender, theory, and a course on The Environmental Movement, as well as the course she co-teaches with Professor Johnson. She has served as the President of the Culture Section of the American Sociological Association. At Rice, she has participated in a variety of interdisciplinary initiatives, including service on Steering Committees for the Center for the Study of Women, Gender, and Sexuality as well as for the Center for the Study of Environment and Society. She is also involved with the Cultures of Energy Center. Her most recent book is *Book Clubs: Women and the Uses of Reading in Everyday Life*, and she is now researching the anti-fracking movement.

Introduction

Rice University, like many other colleges and universities across the United States, has created a robust sustainability program over the past decade, as the campus sustainability movement has swept across higher education. What makes the Rice story somewhat unique is that many of the university's sustainability initiatives originated, at least in part, with a single course, "Environmental Issues: Rice into the Future," which is presently cross-listed between the Environmental Studies (ENST 302) and Sociology (SOCI 304) programs. This paper explores the key lessons from a decade of student group projects in that course and its predecessor variants, and the conditions that enable the projects and the class to be successful.

Rice University is situated on a leafy 295-acre urban campus, the entirety of which is designated as the Lynn R. Lowrey Arboretum, located about three miles south of downtown Houston, Texas. The Rice campus consists of almost six million gross square feet of buildings. Rice's first class matriculated in 1912. For the 2011-2012 academic year, Rice enrolled approximately 3,700 undergraduate students and 2,400 graduate students, and boasted a faculty-to-student ratio of less than six-to-one.

A Movement Creates a Class, and a Class Creates a Movement

In the spring of 1990, Oberlin College professor and noted environmental educator David W. Orr launched a movement. Students graduating that year from historic Arkansas College (now Lyon College) may never know that their commencement speaker delivered an address that literally changed higher education. Dr. Orr, in posing the provocative question, "What is Education For?" issued an assignment for the university to:

> ...examine resource flows on this campus: food, energy, water, materials, and waste. Faculty and students should together study the wells, mines, farms, feedlots, and forests that supply the campus as well as the dumps where you send your waste. Collectively... support better alternatives that do less environmental damage, lower carbon dioxide emissions, reduce use of toxic substances, promote energy efficiency and the use of solar energy, help to build a sustainable regional economy, cut long-term costs, and provide an example to other institutions. The results of these studies should be woven into the curriculum as interdisciplinary courses, seminars, lectures, and research. No student should graduate without understanding how to analyze resource flows and without the opportunity to participate in the creation of real solutions to real problems. (Orr)

This challenge arguably marked the beginning of the modern era of the campus sustainability movement. Within just a few years, leaders at the University of Texas Health Science Center in Houston—inspired by Dr. Orr—created one of the first campus sustainability officer positions in higher education. The emerging focus on campus sustainability at that institution, with buildings as close as one block away from Rice, spilled across Main Street and inspired interest amongst a group of Rice faculty to "do something" regarding environmental issues at Rice. Their act was to create Rice's first campus sustainability course, "Understanding Environmental Systems," in the spring of 1998, which followed David Orr's challenge and studied the university as an environmental system embedded within a broader system of resource flows. The course also featured a field trip to the famed Earth systems science research facility Biosphere 2, located near Tucson, Arizona.

By the spring of 1999, "Understanding Environmental Systems," co-taught by the interdisciplinary team of Professor Paul Harcombe of the Ecology and Evolutionary Biology Department and Professor Don Ostdiek of the Policy Studies program, tightened their focus to the specific issue identified by the previous year's class as Rice's largest source of environmental impact: the University's contribution to global warming. That semester, students were organized into teams to quantify and project different aspects of Rice's carbon emissions, the results of which were assembled into Rice's first greenhouse gas inventory. Their study also included recommendations for reducing future emissions, much like a Climate Action Plan produced many years later by signatories of the American College and University Presidents Climate Commitment (ACUPCC). The students submitted their study to senior university administrators, with the perhaps naïve expectation that Rice would recognize the importance of global climate change and act upon their recommendations. Instead, they received no response.

The following year, the faculty and students recognized that their challenge was not necessarily just about finding technical solutions for reducing Rice's greenhouse gas emissions. Indeed, as the students wrote in their final report, "it quickly became apparent that in order to propose ideas that realistically could be implemented, we would need to understand the management systems and procedures at Rice" (University 303 Class Report). As such, they devoted considerable attention to exploring the organizational challenges to environmental change at Rice, along with possible solutions to overcome those challenges.

One key problem that they identified was the lack of a person with the appropriate authority to speak solely for environmental issues in decision-making. To remedy this, they proposed the creation of a university position, reporting directly to the President, with the power to impact budget and policy decisions in a pro-environmental manner. Another problem that they identified was that, while the university had signed the Talloires Declaration in 1996, it was not actively working towards implementing the ten commitments contained within that pro-environmental agreement. As a remedy, the students proposed that Rice develop and implement a campus-wide environmental policy. These steps, they believed, would position Rice as an organization to be better equipped to implement positive environmental change (University 303 Class Report).

After a one year sabbatical, the class resumed in 2002, and students studied the emerging sustainability programs of other universities, and in particular the environmental and sustainability policies of those universities. They drafted a sustainability policy for Rice, which included a recommendation to hire a sustainability coordinator to implement the policy. In a class meeting with then-University

President Malcolm Gillis, he reviewed their draft policy and raised concerns about its "vague" wording. The following year, with Professor Paul Harcombe serving as the sole instructor, the students persisted with their proposed policy, engaging the student government to help build political support amongst the student body for the policy. By late 2003 and early 2004, the student government president worked with the university president on further drafts of the policy, the final version of which was officially adopted by the Board of Trustees during their March 2004 meeting. The policy itself, drawing heavily from David Orr, calls for engaging students, faculty, and staff in environmental issues, and working with campus environmental centers and student environmental organizations to mitigate the university's environmental impact. The policy closes with perhaps Rice's strongest official position on environmental education by stating that "The University believes that students who graduate from Rice need to understand the concepts of sustainability and possess a sense of responsibility for the future" (Sustainability Policies). Later that year, Rice hired its first sustainability officer, Richard Johnson, to help implement the policy and to foster a culture of sustainability on the Rice campus (Evans).

Be the Change

From the onset, the focus of the class was on studying Rice as an environmental system and proposing measures to improve the University's environmental performance. In 2002 and 2003, the class evolved from merely conducting studies and suggesting improvements to actually working with the University community and especially senior administrators in enacting change—a shift to experiential learning. In 2003, the project experience decentralized from having the class work collectively on a single issue or two to a model in which teams of students pursue multiple projects. This model remains the heart of the course today.

In its current incarnation, the students in the class are introduced broadly to the concept of sustainability and to a general framework for understanding the impact of humans on the environment. They are also introduced to the concept of social movements, the environmental movement as a subset of social movements, and more specifically to the campus sustainability movement. As a class, they are also introduced to the staff members most closely concerned with the campus as a physical plant, such as the Buildings and Grounds staff, and those from Housing and Dining. They pick projects to work on from a list of ideas generated both in class, and by staff members who want to explore sustainable alternatives to varied ways "things get done" at Rice. Once they pick a project and divide up into smaller teams of four to five students, each team member must research the way one aspect of their project is handled by other universities. As they research other campuses and discuss how they can intervene by making a change and monitoring its effect on systems such as recycling, handling food waste, transportation, or lighting and heating, they "become the change." In other words, students become observers and participants in the campus sustainability movement through learning how to plan, implement, and assess the effectiveness of environmental change via the group project experience, using the Rice campus and its community as their laboratory (see Appendix B for the 2012 course syllabus). In doing so, they study sustainability measures at other universities related to their group project to identify key lessons and ideas for implementation at Rice.

Key lessons from a decade of course projects are as follows:[1]

- *Never underestimate the ability of a student project team to effect real change.* In the spring of 2006, three students began with a narrowly-scoped and well-defined project: to provide recommendations to "green" a dorm restroom sink renovation project that also met defined performance and budget requirements. As the students learned about the benefits of green building and the US Green Building Council's then-emergent Leadership in Energy and Environmental Design (LEED) program, their enthusiasm soared, and they developed a presentation about green building that they started showing to friends. Next, they showed the presentation to the elected presidents of many of Rice's residential colleges, as well as the faculty masters of several residential colleges.

  By the time the course faculty learned what they were up to, the students were already on the agenda to make a presentation to all of the faculty masters of residential colleges at Rice. The university at that time was in the early stages of planning two new residential colleges totaling nearly 650 new beds, and the faculty college masters—who are important stakeholders in any expansion to the residential college system—adopted a resolution following the students' presentation, advising the university that the future residential colleges should be LEED-certified buildings (there were no LEED-certified buildings at Rice at that time).

  At the conclusion of the students' final class presentation, the Vice President of Administration and the Associate Vice President for Facilities Engineering and Planning, who were in attendance, announced that all future new construction on the Rice campus would be built to meet, at minimum, the level of LEED Certified, where applicable. What began as a simple restroom renovation advisory project ended with a new policy that would forever change all future Rice building projects. And, in fact, the two new residential college buildings were completed in 2009 and certified as LEED-Gold buildings, and, as of May 2012, a total of eight buildings were certified at the LEED-Silver or LEED-Gold level, with two more certifications pending.

- *Access is critical.* A hallmark of the course is that students have direct access to many key university staff members, including senior administrators. The sustainability policy came about in part because the University president and other members of his leadership team visited the course. The commitment to LEED for new construction arose from a Vice President of Administration and an Associate Vice President for Facilities Engineering and Planning, who took time from their schedules to attend the student group presentations. Each year, the leadership team of Housing and Dining and the Custodial and Grounds department provide lectures and otherwise participate in the course. Other staff guests and partners include arborists, chefs, custodians, nutritionists, housing operations managers, and facilities personnel. Starting in the spring of 2005, the university's sustainability officer—a position created in part by the class—became a class co-instructor, further strengthening the ability of the class to connect with key administrators.

- *Trust is also critical*—and works hand-in-hand with access. Over the years, staff members have come to trust student project teams from the class, along with the oversight and guidance that the instructors provide, to the point that they will propose project ideas for the class. For example, in the summer of 2008, the Associate Vice President for Housing and Dining reported to the university's sustainability officer that several universities were experimenting with removing trays from campus dining halls ("trayless dining") in an effort to reduce food waste. He suggested that he would support a trayless dining pilot project if a student team from the course wanted to take that on as their project. In the fall, a team of students worked directly with dining staff on the pilot project, and found that plate waste dropped thirty percent and the use of energy, water, and cleaning chemicals to wash plates and trays dropped by about ten percent on each pilot day. The team collected student feedback from the pilot test, which positioned Housing and Dining to enact a campus-wide trayless dining program supported by the student government the following spring.

- *"Failed" projects can be successful.* In addition to having access to senior administrators, students in the course work directly with staff at all levels, who often prove to be key decision-makers. In the spring of 2005, two students attempted to develop a matrix showing the environmental benefits and pitfalls of common institutional flooring materials. The task of developing a methodology and conducting an assessment proved to be overwhelming, and the extensive amount of "greenwashing" in the flooring products industry made the task even more challenging. As a result, they were never quite able to arrive at a clear way to express how to make the most sustainable choices regarding flooring materials. However, during their project, they interacted frequently with a project manager in the Facilities Engineering and Planning (FE&P) department, whose job included overseeing many of the flooring projects on campus. Their interest spurred his interest in the environmental impact of his decisions and, as a result, he began including environmental considerations in some of his projects, such as specifying a carpet tile for installation in the student center that was designed to be infinitely recyclable into new carpet tile. While the students did not achieve their intended outcome, the project process itself proved quite influential to a key staff stakeholder.

    Four years later, a student team sought to provide design guidance for a vegetated "green" roof that would soon be constructed atop the kitchen of a residential college. They found, to their frustration, that the design and project management team was less open to the students' input than initially thought, and that many of the their recommendations, including providing easy roof access for maintenance and an irrigation system to keep plants alive during drought conditions, did not come to fruition (though in retrospect, the students' ideas proved to be prescient). Shifting gears, the students regrouped and determined that, in the remaining time that they had left, they could at least develop a series of recommendations to guide future green roof decisions on campus.

During the process of this research, the students met with a civil engineering professor to discuss the stormwater runoff benefit of green roofs. Intrigued by the question, the professor launched a research initiative and hired a member of the class to help study the effect of vegetated green roof systems on quantity and quality of stormwater runoff. This effort led to a grant and a partnership with the City of Houston. The results of the study enabled the university to understand the precise stormwater retention benefit of vegetated roof tray systems.

Further, the civil engineering professor has pressed more into low-impact development research, received additional grants, and is now helping to shape university planning decisions as a result of this research. Although the students were disappointed that they were not able to implement or make a visible change, these outcomes would have been far less likely had the student project team not pursued this project and encountered the resistance that they did. In fact, their project continues to yield benefits precisely because they did not achieve their initial desired outcome.

- *Students are resourceful.* Students often lack access to sizable budgets and "tools of the trade," and therefore must think in resourceful and creative ways to implement their projects. For example, prior to 2004, the recycling of plastics (#1 and #2) at Rice was handled informally by student volunteers, but in the fall of 2004 a student project team from the class proposed to institutionalize plastics recycling, which would require the purchase of a $6,900 plastics baler. Rice's Facilities Engineering and Planning (FE&P) department was unwilling to pay the full amount for the baler, so the students cobbled together funding from 13 sources, ranging from a $25 pledge from the Environmental Club to a $2,500 grant from the Leadership Rice program. Ultimately, FE&P contributed $1,250. Arguably, university staff would never have thought or bothered to pursue funding from so many different sources, but students are well connected to pursue and bundle small pools of money on campus to implement a project.

Similarly, students don't always have access to the standard tools and instruments that are used by facilities personnel to make measurements. In 2007, a student project team wanted to calculate the economic payback of installing motion sensors in an indoor common area with 24-hour lighting. Lacking the standard data loggers and monitoring equipment that would be used by a facilities electrical shop to determine the viability of the project, they resorted to using tools that they knew how to use. The project team set up a webcam inside the commons area programmed to take pictures at two minute intervals, which were then stored on a laptop. The students then developed a MATLAB program that automatically compared adjacent images in the sequence to determine whether there had been movement within the space.

Using these tools, they concluded that motion sensors would save approximately ten hours of lighting per day, which at that time equated to $2,000 in annual energy savings. Lacking the standard tools of the trade enabled the students to be resourceful and to think through the process of what data points they truly needed and how they might be able to collect that data using technologies that they understood and had readily available for use.

- *Engage constantly with project teams.* Throughout the course, the instructors constantly engage with the project teams to prevent procrastination, to provide guidance, and to help solve problems as they arise. The teams are formed at the end of the third week of the fifteen-week semester, and starting with the fourth week, the instructors meet directly with the project teams for 15-20 minute consultations roughly every two weeks. The teams are required by the end of the sixth week to submit a detailed prospectus describing what they intend to do, how they intend to do it, and a timeline for accomplishing their work. Around that time, each team assigns a reading for the rest of the class describing the broader environmental and social context for the issue that they are tackling, and they lead a class discussion about that reading. During week twelve, the teams are required to provide a status presentation to the entire class, which helps them to prepare their final end-of-class presentation. At the end of week thirteen, the teams submit a first draft of their final paper, which enables the instructors to identify potential issues with presentation of data, format of discussion, and introductory justification for why the project is worth doing.

  The multiple touch-points with the project teams are necessary because in a fifteen week semester, time is the enemy. This is particularly true if a project team requires frequent interaction with university staff who operate on a completely different timeline and with a different sense of urgency than the students. While the constant engagement results in a higher quality final project, it is very time intensive for the instructors. For this reason, enrollment for the course is capped at twenty, and while sometimes a few additional students are admitted, the class size never exceeds 25 because the instructors cannot effectively manage more than five project teams, which ideally have four or five students per team.

- *Sometimes project momentum is more important than project completion.* Given the short timeline of the semester, sometimes setting a project in motion is actually more important than completing it. For example, in the spring of 2007, a student project team wanted to find opportunities to recycle demolition waste from building renovations, and they discovered that the University intended to demolish several old apartment buildings near the campus that semester, to make way for a new graduate housing complex.

Prior to the demolition they tried to serve as advisors, to identify recyclable or salvageable materials to be removed in piecemeal fashion by individual contractors, but due to the tight construction timeline they were unable to be effective.

However, during the process they interacted with numerous salvage operations, contractors, and similar organizations, and developed a detailed list for key university staff regarding who could take what materials, and what the cost impact might be. That list was crucial months later in enabling three homes to be partially deconstructed, instead of demolished, to make way for a new off-campus university child care center. In fact, 10,000 bricks salvaged from the old homes were incorporated into the façade of the child care center, and many materials, such as mantles and hardwood floors, were salvaged from the homes. The success of the partial deconstruction, in combination with the University's LEED commitment, led to a university decision that all construction and renovation projects would be expected to recycle or otherwise divert at least fifty percent of construction and demolition debris from the waste stream.

While the students were not able to change the outcome of the particular demolition project that they began with, they set in motion a dialogue about the broader issue of construction and demolition waste, and they provided timely information to key stakeholders about viability and cost. By the time the semester ended, the discussion had enough momentum with university staff that it continued without the students' involvement, ending with a dramatic and positive change in operating practices. Incidentally, one of the student team members, who earned a degree in English, went on to a career as a waste reduction and recycling consultant.

- *Sometimes the end is not the end (or is but shouldn't be).* While some projects take on their own momentum beyond the course, the intent is for projects to reach a stopping point at the end of the semester. This presents several challenges. For example, sometimes the projects are experiments that prove to be viable, yet finding a champion to implement the project once the student team has disbanded can prove difficult. At times, the project is so compelling that staff members implement the project on their own, such as with trayless dining or construction waste recycling. But in the absence of a ready project champion on staff, options for continuing a project include future class project teams, as well as project-oriented student environmental organizations.

  Another challenge arises when students assume that a staff member will implement their project after the course. In the fall of 2010, a project team sought to improve communications about campus sustainability during the freshman orientation week by developing a brief video entitled "A Sustainable Day at Rice," to be shown to the incoming students. In their final report, the team made several references to staff members that they planned to speak with, who manage the orientation week process, to include the video on the orientation week agenda. The students had not taken the time to develop a staff project champion during the semester with a commitment to implementing the project and, as such, their vision for transforming the orientation week went unfulfilled.

- *Success breeds success.* Projects do not exist in a vacuum. To the contrary, they build on each other, and benefit not only from the maturation of the University's sustainability program, but also from the growth of sustainability initiatives at other schools as well. A key component of each project team report is to identify what other universities are doing to solve the sustainability issue at question, and to capture the lessons learned from those examples to develop a Rice-specific solution.

  During the fall 2011 semester, a student project team sought to reduce bottled water consumption on campus. As they researched bottled water initiatives and campaigns at other universities, they concluded that Rice had already taken several meaningful steps to reduce bottled water consumption, including eliminating bottled water sales from the student dining areas and providing filtered water machines on the serving lines and hydration stations in student commons areas instead. The students' solution, in part, was to expand hydration stations beyond the student dining areas to heavily trafficked areas of the campus frequented by all members of the Rice community.

  However, to actually install a hydration station, they needed $3,000. Thankfully, in spring 2010, Rice students voted to self-levy a fee to create the Rice Endowment for Sustainable Energy Technology (RESET), a committee that funds energy and sustainability projects initiated by members of the university community, especially students. The bottled water team applied for and received a grant of $3,000 for the purchase and installation of a reusable bottle filling station in Rice's student center and, within a few weeks of the end of the semester, the fixture had been installed. While this project would certainly have been possible without RESET, the presence of RESET made it much easier. Furthermore, learning from the success of other universities enabled the project team to quickly benchmark Rice's performance and focus on developing solutions.

  Another example illustrating that "success breeds success" comes from the fall 2010 class. A student project team studying the issue of food waste hoped to identify opportunities for diverting wasted food scraps from the landfill, potentially via composting. They learned that a farmer who sold produce at Rice's farmers' market (established in 2007) had recently begun supplying produce to the kitchen of Rice's Baker College. During a class brainstorming session, one of their classmates asked the team, "Don't farmers want food waste to make compost?" At that moment, the idea was clear: collect food waste from the kitchen, and give it to the farmer when he made his deliveries, so that he could use it on his farm as compost. This project would not have been possible a few years earlier but, thanks to an active, year-round farmers' market and a farmer making deliveries directly to a campus kitchen, the opportunity became available.

Conclusion

The "Rice into the Future" course has not only been a primary driver of environmental change on campus, it has connected students, faculty, and staff in a different way than is typical of other courses, readily placing students in the position of active problem-solvers working closely with other members of the campus community. As Johnson concluded in 2007, "while such classes are certainly not necessary for a campus to implement a successful campus sustainability program, the experience at Rice suggests that they can play a central and pivotal role, under the right circumstances" (Johnson).

The students even play an active role in shaping the future of the course itself. Each year, an entire class session is devoted to gathering feedback from the students about the project experience and the assigned materials, and the faculty will often adjust the syllabus and project work accordingly for the following year's course. Students in the fall 2010 class suggested holding a class outside of the classroom so, the following year, one of Rice's arborists met with the students outdoors and showed them how to care for trees. The following year, the class also went on a campus biodiversity walk led by an instructor from the Ecology and Evolutionary Biology Department, as part of a broader unit on biophilia and the ecology of place. At the end of the fall 2012 semester, students expressed interest in moving a panel discussion on the campus food system—which includes a local farmer, a Rice chef, the campus farmers' market manager, and Rice's dining director—from the classroom to a campus kitchen, so that they could better understand the cooking operations at Rice. This idea will be implemented for the fall 2013 course. Those same students also suggested creating an optional one credit hour immersive lab that includes field trips, expanded readings and discussions, and potentially project leadership training. The faculty are strongly considering implementing some variation of this proposal to provide a deeper experience for those who are truly passionate about the subject matter.

Students seem to appreciate this democratic approach to designing the course. However, some on occasion also seem to expect a course that fits neatly into a topical silo, which this course does not. Fortunately, both faculty members are from disciplines that are interdisciplinary by nature and training (sociology, environmental studies, and urban planning), and both are in a position (as a tenured departmental chair and as a campus sustainability officer) to ignore topical silos without repercussions. The nature of the syllabus has shifted considerably as this partnership has developed. Indeed, while the class has helped create and broaden the campus sustainability movement at Rice, that movement has also shaped the syllabus and evolution of the course. The interdisciplinary character of the course makes it broadly accessible to all Rice students, regardless of major or year of study. Many students who enroll in the course with no prior sustainability background decide after the course to join campus environmental organizations, pursue campus greening projects, take additional environmental classes, and even seek careers related to sustainability. As one student wrote in the anonymous 2011 course evaluations, "this is an incredibly unique course that offers students a chance to directly influence the University's environmental impact. Few other courses are capable of this and most cannot boast of even a fraction of that import. This is why I signed-up for the course: the ability to effect change, rather than merely hope for it."

Acknowledgements

The authors wish to thank Professor Emeritus Paul Harcombe, who led the class from its creation until his retirement in spring 2007. The authors also wish to acknowledge the hard work of the students of ENST 302/SOCI 304 and its predecessor classes. They have collectively left a positive legacy that continues to inspire. Finally, the authors wish to thank the faculty and staff who have participated in the course, whether as guest lecturers or as project partners, especially frequent participants Mark Ditman, Eusebio Franco, and David McDonald. The ongoing contributions, ideas, energy, and patience of these partners are greatly appreciated.

Notes

1.   An earlier form of this list was published in Johnson, Richard R. "Connecting Campus Sustainability with the Classroom." *Greening of the Campus VII Conference Proceedings*. Greening of the Campus VII, Ball State University, Muncie, IN. Ed. Robert J. Koester. Muncie, IN: Ball State University, 2007. 251-255. Print.

See Appendix B for the 2012 course syllabus of
SOCI 304/ENST 302: Environmental Issues—Rice into the Future.

Works Cited

A Sustainable Day at Rice University. Dir. Elizabeth Corkett, Kendra Erskine, Alex Honold, and Jasmine Pierreauguste. YouTube, 28 Nov. 2010. Web.

Course Evaluations for ENST 302 / SOCI 304. Houston, TX: Rice University, 2011.

Evans, Jennifer. "Johnson is an Advocate for Future Owls as Rice's First Sustainability Planner." *Rice News*. 13 Jan. 2005. Web.

Johnson, Richard R. "Connecting Campus Sustainability with the Classroom." *Greening of the Campus VII Conference Proceedings*. Greening of the Campus VII, Ball State University, Muncie, IN. Ed. Robert J. Koester. Muncie, IN: Ball State University, 2007. 251-255. Print.

Orr, David. "What is Education for?" In Context Winter 1991: 52-55. Web.

"Sustainability Policies." *Sustainability at Rice*. Rice University, n.d. Web.

University 303 Class Report. Rice University. May 2000. Web.

Integrating Sustainability Theory and Practice: Liberal Education and Effective Practice (LEEP™) at Clark University

Jennie C. Stephens, Clark University

Abstract: One approach to integrating theory and practice of sustainability in a liberal arts curriculum involves community-engaged coursework focused on combining practical experience with theoretical interrogation of the role of the university in promoting sustainability. Such a course, called "The Sustainable University," has been taught for the past seven years at Clark University, a small research university whose undergraduate curriculum is based on an emerging model that integrates Liberal Education and Effective Practice, i.e. LEEP™. This chapter describes how a course with guided engagement of semester-long, campus-based team projects facilitates student learning about the challenges and opportunities of sustainability through their own experiences. Coupling this experiential learning with theoretical inquiry based on reading, writing, and discussion-based assignments provides a way for students to juxtapose sustainable visions from multiple disciplines and perspectives with their own perceptions and experiences.

Jennie C. Stephens is an Associate Professor of Environmental Science and Policy at Clark University in Worcester, Massachusetts. Stephens' teaching, research, and community engagement focuses on socio-political aspects of energy technology innovation, renewable energy, and climate change education/awareness. Her work also explores stakeholder engagement in sustainable innovation and communication among different actors including "experts" and the public. Stephens received her Ph.D. (2002) and M.S. (1998) at the California Institute of Technology in Environmental Science and Engineering and her B.A. (1997) from Harvard in Environmental Science and Public Policy. Before joining the faculty of Clark University, she did postdoctoral research at Harvard's Kennedy School and she taught courses at Tufts, Boston University, and MIT.

Introduction

Educational institutions around the world have begun to respond to the emerging sustainability challenges of the 21st century in multiple ways (Stephens et al.; Vezzoli et al.; Graham and Stephens). Changes include adapting campus operations to demonstrate more sustainable practices (Sharp; Breen; Rappaport), supporting more socially engaged sustainability-related research (Stauffacher et al.; Kajikawa; Kates et al.; Crow), engaging more directly with non-academic communities to facilitate connections between knowledge and action (Coalition of Urban Serving Universities; Maurasse; Boyle, Ross, and Stephens), and adapting curriculum and pedagogical approaches to integrate sustainability in teaching and coursework (Tamura and Uegaki; O'Brien and Sarkis). One valuable approach to integrating sustainability theory and practice into the curriculum involves offering courses that combine practical experience with theoretical interrogation of the role, potential, and challenges of the university in promoting sustainability in society.

Integrating such sustainability coursework into liberal arts education provides particularly valuable opportunities because the practicality of a liberal arts education is being increasingly questioned in the current era of competitive job markets and rising costs of higher education (Labaree; Martin; Arum and Roksa). Responding to critical assessments of the learning and skills acquired in higher education (Arum and Roksa), universities and colleges are adapting in multiple ways. Many institutions offering liberal arts degrees are finding themselves striving to enhance curriculum relevance, salience, and practicability (Budwig et al.; Clark University *Liberal Education and Effective Practice: A Plan for the 21st Century*), while also promoting the power of a "grounded curriculum" in which the physical campus and surrounding community is critical to learning (Lang). Recent characterizations of high-impact learning experiences within liberal arts education have emphasized the value of pedagogical approaches that develop ethical and civic preparation, personal growth, and self direction (Kuh). Innovative courses that integrate theory and practice related to sustainability within the context of the university provide valuable opportunities to respond to the dynamic expectations of a liberal arts education in a rapidly changing social context.

This essay explores the value of designing sustainability coursework focused on the university by describing a course called "The Sustainable University" taught at Clark University. This institution is a small, liberal arts-based research university in Worcester, Massachusetts whose undergraduate curriculum is based on an emerging model that integrates Liberal Education and Effective Practice, i.e. LEEP™. The essay first explains the design of the course, its structure and objectives, and then describes the integration of the theoretical component with the practical engagement of semester-long, campus-based team projects. The essay concludes by describing how guided engagement of semester-long team projects facilitates student learning about the challenges and opportunities of sustainability. When this practical, experiential learning is coupled with theoretical inquiry based on reading, writing and presentation-based assignments, students are required to juxtapose visions of sustainability from multiple disciplines and perspectives with their own perceptions and experiences. This approach could be readily adapted at any university, college, or other educational organization.

An Innovative Course: "The Sustainable University"

A unique, community-engaged undergraduate course, "The Sustainable University" has been offered at Clark University since 2005. This course is designed to integrate both theory and practice of sustainability by examining the role of higher education in promoting change toward sustainability. Building on Clark's long-standing tradition of integrating campus projects in coursework, faculty in the Environmental Science and Policy program in the department of International Development, Community and Environment (IDCE) have integrated theoretical exploration of the notions of sustainability, sustainable development, and organizational and behavioral change within semester-long team projects focused on contributing to existing campus sustainability organizations or initiatives.

The course focus on the campus community provides a powerful opportunity for students to consider the practical challenges and opportunities of defining, designing and implementing so-called "sustainability" initiatives. The focus on higher education also provides students with the opportunity to appreciate that the societal role of higher education involves more than providing formal course instruction for enrolled students. Although the course itself conforms to this conventional aspect of higher education, students recognize other societal roles of universities and colleges, including being critical places of discovery and innovation, centers for political discourse, and catalysts for political action and social change. The course explores the unique potential that institutions of higher education have to contribute to transitions toward a more sustainable society and provides a context for considering the broad role of education in sustainable development.

The focus of this course on higher education also provides a lens for students to examine how organizations with complex structures make a myriad of decisions with environmental consequences. While universities are unique societal organizations in some respects, with their educational missions and prioritization of academic and intellectual pursuits, they are also faced with many challenges and limitations similar to those faced by other organizations, including balancing their budgets, sustaining their reputations, and attracting and retaining skilled professionals.

Perhaps the most powerful advantage of the focus on the university is that the course provides a framework and perspective with direct and personal connections for students to consider the challenges of promoting sustainability. This course, therefore, is an example of one approach to contributing to a "grounded curriculum" in which the physical campus and surrounding community is critical to learning (Lang). During this course, students learn to question, analyze, and reconsider everything around them, as they are encouraged to constantly ask themselves whether, how, and in what ways are their experiences in higher education contributing to or detracting from the sustainability challenges of the 21st century.

Course Structure and Goals: Integrating Theory and Practice

Although many details of the course have evolved over the seven years that it has been offered, the learning goals and basic structure of the course have remained constant. The goals of the course are for students to: 1) understand and experience the complex organizational and individual challenges and opportunities associated with socio-technical change toward sustainability; 2) explore the concept and application of sustainability and sustainable development; 3) gain skills, insights, confidence, and capacity to act as change agents; 4) contribute to ongoing sustainability efforts within the Clark and surrounding communities; and 5) develop oral and written communication skills as well as collaboration skills.

To achieve these goals, the course is structured around weekly reading and writing assignments coupled with a semester-long team project that contributes to ongoing campus sustainability initiatives. Participation, attendance and engagement in class sessions are critical, because the majority of in-class time is spent in discussion or dialogue about the required course readings or with student team presentations or team work. The weekly reading and writing assignments expose students to multiple, different theoretical and disciplinary perspectives related to the concept of sustainability and the role of higher education in society. The semester-long team projects provide practical experience in which students learn first-hand the challenges and opportunities of attempting to facilitate change toward a more sustainable community.

In addition to integrating a diversity of perspectives and scales, the course intentionally enrolls students with a broad range of experiences within the university, including first-year students as well as juniors and seniors who have been campus activists for several years. A graduate level section of the course was created in 2010 in response to graduate student interest; so, for the past three years, five Masters-level students have also registered for and contributed to the course.

A Diversity of Theoretical Perspectives

A diversity of theoretical perspectives on sustainability and higher education has been integrated into this course. The course presents a socio-technical systems perspective, encouraging students to recognize the inseparable connections between social change and technical change (Geels). This perspective is valuable because it requires consideration of the intertwined relationships between environmental mitigation initiatives aimed at behavioral change (e.g. encouraging individuals to take shorter showers or turn off the lights) and those targeting technical change (e.g.. installing low-flow shower heads or motion detectors to turn off lights).

To encourage students to question critically the very notion of sustainability and sustainable development, various readings provide different perspectives on these concepts (Filho; Leiserowitz, Kates, and Parris; Marshall and Toffel). With regard to considering how educational systems contribute to sustainability and human-environment connections, students read the work of David Orr and other critiques of how traditional higher education perpetuates unsustainable trajectories (Orr; Breen). Students are also required to read research and strategies on fostering behavior change toward sustainability (McKenzie-Mohr), university policies including the Clark University Climate Action Plan (Clark University *The Clark University Climate Action Plan*), and nation-wide initiatives to support institutional commitments of different kinds, including the American College and University Presidents Climate Commitment (ACUPCC) and the LEED certification program (Leadership in Environmental Excellence and Design). Various readings have been selected to integrate a global perspective on education and its role in sustainable development, including a review of worldwide trends in how universities are integrating climate change education (Filho, "Climate Change at Universities").

To complement the reading assignments and to promote engagement with the theoretical perspectives, students are required to write weekly reading response papers that are posted on the online course management system, so that the instructor and other students can read the assignments. In addition to posting a reading response, students are required each week to read at least two of their peers' assignments and provide feedback to their peers. This assignment, to write a reading response and critique other students' responses, is required before the class session during which the readings will be discussed. The timing of this assignment, the requirement that students read each others' responses and actively engage with the theoretical concepts before the full class discussion, facilitates a lively group discussion in class. In the weekly reading response papers, students are asked to accomplish four things: 1) critically discuss or reflect on specific themes, concepts or proposals presented in the readings; 2) demonstrate integrated thinking on the different readings, i.e. include some comparative assessment or identify connections among each of the different readings; 3) include at least one thoughtful discussion question; and 4) make an explicit connection between the concepts presented in the readings and their own experience working on the semester-long team projects within the course. These reading response assignments and the in-class discussion that follows also provide opportunities for students to question assumptions of the authors they have read, as well as question assumptions of their peers (other students in the course).

The Practical Experience: Semester-long Team Projects

The reading and writing assignments are coupled with semester-long team projects in which students are actively contributing to social, technical or organizational change on campus or in the local community. Students who register for this course understand that the practical experience associated with these team projects is a critical part of this course. These projects enable students to engage directly with the challenges associated with promoting sustainable behavior and fostering institutional and social change within their community. The projects require teams of students to work directly with a specific organization or existing initiative on campus, or within the Worcester community, to contribute in some substantive way to ongoing campus efforts. The student teams work in conjunction with the campus sustainability office, the Clark University Environmental Sustainability Taskforce, the Physical Plant

Department, or the Clark Sustainability Collaborative (a student group). Contributing to ongoing sustainability organizations in this way provides students with practical experience and unique perspective on the challenges, opportunities, and complexities of advancing sustainability initiatives.

Another critical aspect of the semester-long projects is experience students gain from working as a team. The teamwork required in this course provides students with opportunities to practice skills of cooperation, coordination, collaboration, contribution, communication, and complementarity (the six Cs of teamwork). Throughout the semester, students develop and demonstrate these skills within their team projects. They reflect on their learning in these areas through reflection integrated into the weekly reading response papers, as well as through a couple of other short, targeted team project reflection assignments that are read by the instructor and the peer learning assistant.

A set of potential team projects are predefined by the faculty instructor in conjunction with the Campus Sustainability Coordinator before the semester begins. Examples of recent projects include: 1) working with the Clark University Environmental Sustainability Taskforce to assess implementation options for addressing transportation within Clark's Climate Action Plan; 2) designing, fundraising and coordinating with the Campus Grounds Crew the installation of a Rain Garden on campus; 3) promoting awareness among faculty, staff, and students about the University's off-campus arboretum; 4) working with the student campus garden club and the sustainability food group to support the continued development of growing food in the garden behind the President's house; and, 5) in conjunction with the university sustainability office, maintaining and expanding the utility and awareness of a campus-wide inventory of all sustainability projects. Other projects in the past few years have included: 6) reviewing renewable energy options for the campus; 7) promoting behavior change in the residence halls through a sustainability competition; 8) helping to coordinate the Massachusetts Climate Action Network Annual conference, which was held on campus in the fall of 2010; and 9) exploring the potential of setting up a sustainability fund on campus to support new initiatives.

At the very beginning of the semester, after the students are introduced to a varied set of potential team projects, each student submits an application (including a resume and cover letter) to the instructor to apply for the team project options on which they would prefer to work. The instructor then interviews and evaluates each applicant and creates the teams. The teams begin intensively working together by the second or third week of the semester. Then each team presents a mid-semester presentation to the class, and at the end of the semester, the students design, coordinate, and implement a final public presentation and a final report that communicates the details of all that the student teams have accomplished throughout the semester. The final team presentation is in lieu of a final exam, and the final team report is the final written assignment for the course.

The semester-long team projects provide students with challenges that they are generally not accustomed to encountering in their college-level course work. In particular, the collaboration that is required in the teamwork is a unique experience for all of the students. Throughout the semester, they are required to practice and refine their skills of cooperation, coordination, collaboration, contribution, communication, and complementarity (the six Cs of teamwork).

The Teaching Team

Teaching this course provides some pedagogical challenges and requires a different set of skills than teaching a more conventional lecture-exam based course. One challenge of incorporating a major community-engaged project assignment into a course is the additional attention, support, and guidance that the student teams need to successfully develop and implement their projects. Within the community, the students become representatives of the program and the university, so emphasizing professional, respectful, and courteous behavior in all of their interactions is critical. To help with the support of the community-engaged team work, the teaching team for this course includes a peer learning assistant (PLA) in addition to the primary faculty instructor (a faculty member in the Environmental Science and Policy program). At Clark University, the PLA position provides opportunities for faculty to work closely with an advanced undergraduate student who has previously taken a given course and has some skills to assist in teaching the course. Unlike a teaching assistant, PLAs are not permitted to be involved in "grading" their peers, but they can play critical roles in facilitating class discussion and providing students enrolled in the course with extra help or attention. Given the intensity of needs associated with the semester-long team projects, in this course the PLA serves an important team-project facilitator role, involving regular check-ups with each of the teams and frequent communication with the instructor to consider how best to support each team.

In addition to the faculty instructor and the Peer Learning Assistant, students in the course benefit greatly from engagement and interactions with multiple individuals throughout the university community. Clark's Sustainability Coordinator, a staff member in the University's Physical Plant department, has been an integral part of the course, particularly in helping guide and direct each of the student team projects. The Sustainability Coordinator has also been an active and engaged member of the course, regularly attending class sessions and contributing throughout the semester in multiple, valuable ways. This collaborative relationship has enabled productive synergies between the students in the course and the initiatives and responsibilities of the Campus Sustainability Office. The Sustainability Coordinator has been extremely effective, dedicated, and efficient in communicating, responding and helping with many aspects of the course.

Institutional Context and Support:
Liberal Education and Effective Practice™ at Clark

This course has been well supported at Clark, as this pedagogical approach of integrating theory and practice is representative of the University's emerging curricular model, which focuses on integrating "effective practice" into a liberal arts education. Clark University's recently redefined undergraduate curriculum known as LEEP (Liberal Education and Effective Practice™) is currently emerging in response to changing expectations and competitiveness among colleges and universities offering a liberal arts education (Clark University, *Liberal Education and Effective Practice: A Plan for the 21st Century;* Budwig et al.).

The LEEP curriculum at Clark is enhanced by building on many of Clark University's strengths, including rigorous student engagement in academics, the linking of curricular and co-curricular experiences, the frequent traversing of disciplinary boundaries, and community engaged research and learning (Clark University *Liberal Education and Effective Practice: A Plan for the 21st Century*). This new and emerging model of liberal education at Clark integrates the existing wealth of intellectual and academic resources with learning of skills and capacities that are increasingly needed in the 21st century, i.e. preparing students to be effective, engaged citizens in a more dynamic world that requires innovation, creativity, and resilience (Budwig et al.).

The Sustainable University course described in this essay is among a range of courses at Clark that have contributed to the iterative process of defining and refining the university's emerging LEEP curricular model. The development of Clark's evolving LEEP curriculum involves extensive institutional commitment and faculty collaborative work on integrating effective practice through workshops and departmental retreats, revisioning of majors, and enhancing internship opportunities and alumni engagement to support academically connected, co-curricular, high-impact learning experiences for all students. The Sustainable University course provides a valuable example of the effectiveness of curricular change that integrates practical and collaborative experiences into a liberal arts education.

The value of a shift toward more integration of practical experiences in liberal arts higher education is widely recognized. In this volume, Gould describes movement from the metaphor of schools as "production lines" to one of schools as "seedbeds." This, coupled with the need for campuses to justify the need for physical presence beyond the virtual online classroom, provides compelling advocacy for a more "grounded curriculum" where student learning and engagement in the campus community is critical (Lang).

Conclusions

This example of the integration of theory and practice of sustainability in a liberal arts curriculum could be readily adapted at any university, college, or other educational organization. The community-engaged coursework, focused on combining practical experience through team projects with theoretical interrogation of the role of the university in promoting sustainability, provides a way for students to juxtapose sustainable visions from multiple disciplines and perspectives with their own perceptions and experiences.

This approach not only challenges notions of sustainability and how to work toward transitioning to a more sustainable society, but also encourages students to appreciate the role of universities in society. Students acknowledge and experience that universities provide more than formal course instruction for enrolled students; universities can also be critical places of discovery and innovation, centers for political discourse, and catalysts for political action and social change.

Guided engagement of semester-long, campus-based team projects facilitates student learning about the challenges and opportunities of sustainability through direct experience. Many students are humbled by these experiences, as their initial idealistic expectations of what they hope to accomplish change throughout the semester as new and unexpected challenges emerge. Many of the teams become disappointed when they realize that they are unable to accomplish as much as they had initially hoped within the timeframe of the semester. While this disappointment can be challenging, students also learn to realize how common this is in many "real-world" experiences. The complexities of engaging with and contributing to the team projects invariably ends up being greater than what the students initially anticipated. And through this perspective, the students learn to appreciate the practical skills of perseverance and navigating social and technical complexity.

Teaching a "grounded" course like this requires a different type of responsiveness and engagement with students and other community members than is typical of other courses. Effective integration of learning from the campus-based team projects and the theoretical course content requires creative attentiveness to connections between the students' experiences and the course readings. The structure of the course described here has evolved throughout the seven years that this course has been taught. The course has been continuously improved through ongoing re-assessment and reflection, including soliciting feedback from students, the teaching staff, and community actors who engage with students in the class. An additional dynamic element of teaching this course relates to the changing sustainability landscape and the evolving types of sustainability initiatives that the course must engage with. As societal awareness of the sustainability challenges facing the world increases, the scale and scope of sustainability initiatives is constantly changing.

One of the most rewarding aspects of teaching this course is recognizing the impact that this course can have on students' lives and their commitment to their community after the semester ends. While the team projects are officially completed at the end of the semester, many of the students continue to work on their sustainability initiatives beyond the semester, which suggests powerful, engaged learning that compels students to continue and expand their commitments after the course is over.

Works Cited

ACUPCC. *American College and University Presidents Climate Commitment.* 2009. Print.

Arum, Richard, and Josipa Roksa. *Academically Adrift: Limited Learning on College Campuses.* Chicago, IL: University of Chicago Press, 2011. Print.

Boyle, Mary-Ellen, Laurie Ross, and Jennie C. Stephens. "Who Has a Stake? How Stakeholder Processes Influence Partnership Sustainability." *Gateways: International Journal of Community Research and Engagement* 4 (2011): 100-18. Print.

Breen, Sheryl D. "The Mixed Political Blessing of Campus Sustainability." *PS: Political Science and Politics* 43.4 (2010): 685-90. Print.

Budwig, N., et al. *Liberal Education and Effective Practice: Clark Leep Working Document*

#1. Worcester, MA: Clark University, 2011. Print.

Clark University. *The Clark University Climate Action Plan*. Worcester, Mass. 2009. Print.

---. *Liberal Education and Effective Practice: A Plan for the 21st Century*. Worcester, MA: Clark University Task Force on Undergraduate Education, 2009. Print.

Coalition of Urban Serving Universities. *Urban Universities: Anchors Generating Prosperity for America's Cities*. 2010. Print.

Crow, Michael M. "Hope, Change, and Affirmation: New Values to Guide Institutional Innovation in American Higher Education." Speech, College Board Forum. Houston, TX. 6 Nov. 2008. Print.

Filho, Walter Leal. "Climate Change at Universities: Results of a World Survey." *Universities and Climate Change – Introducing Climate Change at University Programmes*. Ed. Walter Leal Filho. Berlin, Germany: Springer, 2010. Print.

---. "Dealing with Misconceptions on the Concept of Sustainability." *International Journal of Sustainability in Higher Education* 1.1 (2000): 9. Print.

Geels, F.W. "The Dynamics of Transitions in Socio-Technical Systems: A Multi-Level Analysis of the Transition Pathway from Horse-Drawn Carriages to Automobiles (1860-1930)." *Technology Analysis and Strategic Management* 17.4 (2005): 445-76. Print.

Graham, A.C., and J.C. Stephens. "Exploring Change toward Sustainability in Universities by Applying and Adapting Transition Management Theory." *A New Knowledge Culture, Universities Facing Global Changes for Sustainability*. 2008. Print.

Kajikawa, Yuya. "Research Core and Framework of Sustainability Science." *Sustainability Science*. 2008. Print.

Kates, R. W., et al. "Sustainability Science." *Science* 292.5517 (2001): 641-42. Print.

Kuh, G. D. *High-Impact Educational Practices: What They Are, Who Has Access to Them, and Why They Matter*. Washington, DC: Association of American Colleges and Universities, 2008. Print.

Labaree, David F. "Mutual Subversion: A Short History of the Liberal and the Professional in American Higher Education." *History of Education Quarterly* 46.1 (2006): 1-15. Print.

Lang, James M. "The Grounded Curriculum: How Can Our Courses and Teaching Capitalize on the Benefits of a Physical Campus?" *The Chronicle of Higher Education* 3 July 2012. Print.

Leiserowitz, A. A., R. W. Kates, and T. M. Parris. "Sustainability Values, Attitudes, and Behaviors: A Review of Multinational and Global Trends." *Annual Review of Environment and Resources* 31 (2006): 413-44. Print.

Marshall, J.D., and M.W. Toffel. "Framing the Elusive Concept of Sustainability: A Sustainability Hierarchy." *Environmental Science & Technology* 39.3 (2005): 673-82. Print.

Martin, Robert E. *The College Cost Disease: Higher Cost and Lower Quality*. Northampton, MA & Cheltenham, UK: Edward Elgar Publishing Limited, 2011. Print.

Maurasse, D. *Beyond the Campus: How Colleges and Universities Form Partnerships with Their Communities*. New York, NY: Routledge, 2001. Print.

McKenzie-Mohr, Doug. "Fostering Sustainable Behavior: Beyond Brochures." *IJSC* 3 (2008): 108-18. Print.

O'Brien, W., and J. Sarkis. *Sustainability Consulting Projects and High Impact Educational Learning*. Marsh Institute Working Paper 2012-23. Worcester, MA: Clark University, 2012. Print.

Orr, David. *Earth in Mind, on Education, Environment, and the Human Prospect*. Washington, DC: Island Press, 1994. Print.

Rappaport, Ann. "Campus Greening, Behind the Headlines." *Environment, Science and Policy for Sustainable Development* 50.1 (2008): 6-16. Print.

Sharp, Leith. "Higher Education: The Quest for the Sustainbility Campus." *Sustainability: Science, Practice, and Policy* 5.1 (2009): 1-8. Print.

Stauffacher, M., et al. "Learning to Research Environmental Problems from a Functional Socio-Cultural Constructivism Perspective, the Transdisciplinary Case Study Approach." *International Journal of Sustainability in Higher Education* 7.3 (2006): 252-75. Print.

Stephens, J.C., et al. "Higher Education as a Change Agent for Sustainability in Different Cultures and Contexts." *International Journal of Sustainability in Higher Education* 9.3 (2008): 317-38. Print.

Tamura, Makoto, and Takahide Uegaki. "Development of an Educational Model for Sustainability Science: Challenges in the Mind-Skills-Knowledge Education at Ibaraki University." *Sustainability Science* 7.2 (2012): 253-65. Print.

Vezzoli, Carlo, et al. "Why Have "Sustainable Product-Service Systems" Not Been Widely Implemented? Meeting New Design Challenges to Acheive Societal Sustainability." *Journal of Cleaner Production* 1.3 (2012). Print.

The Campus and Community as a Learning Laboratory: Possibilities and Limitations

Jay Roberts, Earlham College

Abstract: This chapter will examine the growing trend of "learning laboratories"—using college and university campuses and the local community for experiential sustainability education. Three learning laboratory vignettes will be highlighted: a collaborative faculty-student energy dashboard project, an interdisciplinary student sustainability seminar centered around completing a national sustainability assessment (STARS), and a senior environmental studies integrated research project on community mapping. Critical reflection on these three learning laboratory projects will reveal both the possibilities and the limitations of extending sustainability education in the humanities and social sciences beyond the four-walled classroom, as well as the broader pedagogical implications of the approach for higher education.

Dr. Jay Roberts is an Associate Vice President for Academic Affairs and Director of the Center for Integrated Learning at Earlham College in Richmond, Indiana. He teaches courses in both education and environmental studies and serves as a Teagle Pedagogy Fellow for the Great Lakes College Association. He also serves on the editorial board for the *Journal of Experiential Education*. Prior to his work at Earlham, Dr. Roberts was the Director of the Poplar Ridge Experiential Learning Center at the University of Virginia. Jay's research interests include the theory and practice of experiential education, place-based education, and education for sustainability. He recently published *Beyond Learning By Doing: Theoretical Currents in Experiential Education* with Routledge Press in 2011. His Ph.D. is in Curriculum Theory from Miami University.

Introduction: The Uneven Terrain of Higher Education

For a variety of complex and interdependent reasons, the ground beneath U.S. colleges and universities is shifting dramatically. Distance learning, video conferencing, crowd sourcing, and the extreme individualization and portability of learning have created aftershocks throughout K-12 and higher education. The recent "edX" initiative at MIT and Harvard is just one example of the wide-ranging impacts technology will have in the future of the Academy.[1] The flattening of information and knowledge resulting from our century's "Gutenburg Press Moment"—the Internet and rise in technological innovation—is well documented in the popular academic press (Darling-Hammond; Friedman).

The economic realities of the 2008 recession have led to serious and sustained questions regarding the value of traditional, residential four-year degree programs in general, and the less "applied" fields in the humanities and social sciences in particular. While fears of lack of career readiness are certainly nothing new in the discourse of U.S. educational reform, the combined load of low employment and rising student loan debt has made this historical moment particularly unnerving. Further, recent critiques of higher education question its value and purpose and call for radical reform. In 2011, the Association of American Colleges and Universities (AAC&U) published *A Crucible Moment: College Learning and Democracy's Future*, which slammed U.S. colleges and universities for failing at the fundamental task of fostering a sense of civic engagement and responsibility amongst students, faculty, and staff. Finally, as Andrew Delbanco states in *College: What It Was, and Should Be:*

> the role of faculty is changing everywhere, and no college is impervious to the larger forces that, depending on one's point of view, promise to transform, or threaten to undermine, it. As these forces bear down on us, neither lamentation nor celebration will do. Instead, they seem to me to compel us to confront some basic questions about the purposes and possibilities of college education. (6)

During this same historical moment, higher education has simultaneously witnessed a dramatic rise in sustainability initiatives on college and university campuses in the United States. Across the country, in community colleges, small liberal arts colleges, and major research universities, we find students, faculty, and staff engaging in various forms of "deep play" in relation to sustainability. Dorm energy competitions, college gardens, faculty-student collaborative sustainability research, community eco-justice related projects, interdisciplinary thematic coursework, and a host of other initiatives have emerged that point to new and innovative forms of teaching and learning. Early sustainability efforts concentrated on college and university physical plants and establishing degree programs. LEED certified buildings, green retrofits of existing facilities, environmental studies majors, and waste minimization schemes became part of a "first wave" of sustainability initiatives in the early 1990s. While this work is ongoing, a second wave of attention is emerging that focuses predominantly on the intersections between the curriculum and co-curriculum and extending sustainability beyond the classroom and campus boundaries into various communities of interest.

All of the activity surrounding sustainability leads to a central question: why is it, during a time of great turmoil and existential questioning of the value and purposes of higher education, that we see such growth, energy, and vitality in the area of sustainability? While the post-*Inconvenient Truth* era and the realities of climate change certainly have much to do with it, there is a deeper pedagogical force at play here. Projects of these sorts have real impact not only on bottom line sustainability measures but on how students, faculty, and staff co-create what John Dewey termed "educative experience." While some see these initiatives and activities as faddish, their popularity and success point to new forms of teaching and learning—forms that are more active, relevant, problem-based, collaborative, complex, and interdisciplinary.[2] This chapter will explore one specific pedagogical model of this emerging approach to sustainability education: the learning laboratory.

While laboratories have always been used in the natural sciences as a way for students, alongside their professors and teaching assistants, to test out classroom concepts, ideas, and theories, this notion has not been employed in the social sciences and humanities until relatively recently. But the basic idea of a learning laboratory— to consciously utilize and incorporate projects, problems, issues, and/or ideas from the campus or local community into the formal curriculum—can be used effectively in social science and humanities-focused courses. Importantly, learning laboratories are not "simulations" or contrived problem-solving initiatives. Typically, students and faculty are involved in a project organized around relevant and authentic problems or questions on campus or in the community with a strong emphasis on collaborative, experiential learning and "just in time" instruction from the professor. What follow are three vignettes—examples of learning laboratories initiated at Earlham College, a residential liberal arts school located in Richmond, Indiana.[3] Each vignette reveals both the possibilities and limitations of the learning laboratory approach in sustainability education. They also invite a broader discussion as to the pedagogical challenges and opportunities brought about by the seismic shifts in the landscape of higher education noted above.

Vignette #1

Bedazzling the University: Energy Dashboards and Sustainability Education

In considering the campus as a learning laboratory, one needs to look no further than the physical plant itself as a context for meaningful teaching and learning. As David Orr notes, although there has been little discussion of the educative value of the physical spaces of college campuses, they hold enormous potential: "The design of buildings and landscape is thought to have little to nothing to do with the process of learning or the quality of scholarship that occurs in a particular place. But, in fact, buildings and landscape reflect a hidden curriculum that powerfully influences the learning process" (128). One increasingly popular initiative to address the potential of the built environment is the use of energy dashboard systems. Typically, campuses contract with a provider to tap into buildings' energy metering system and display the energy use over a given period of time. These units are often quite impressive, involving large flat screen monitors, colorful displays, and interactive touch screen elements. The design notion here is to present real-time energy data to residents of, say, a dormitory, in order to motivate them toward energy conservation. This is a good and worthy goal.

However, one wonders if the educative potential of such installations is being fully utilized. In some respects, the proliferation of these sorts of systems smacks of a certain kind of sustainability "bedazzlement" of the college campus. It is relatively easy for a college or university to spend lots of money on a glitzy energy dashboard system; it may even lead to reduced energy consumption and heightened awareness of the importance of conservation, and it certainly looks good for admissions tours. But an opportunity may be lost when we plan, purchase, and implement things on *behalf* of students as opposed to *involving them* in the real work of practical, locally contextualized sustainability problem solving. This is where the concept of a learning laboratory can be of some use.

At Earlham College, the energy dashboard system is an ongoing learning laboratory project jointly coordinated between the Sustainability Office, the Green Science Group (a collaborative interdisciplinary student-faculty research team within the Computer Science and Environmental Science programs), and the Environmental Studies program. Rather than purchase an energy dashboard system through an external provider, the Green Science Group went about designing it from the ground up. This required complex computer programming, along with technical know-how, to tap into the campus' sub-metering system. Students and faculty spent countless hours working with the electricians from our maintenance department to troubleshoot problems and install monitors. Students collaborated with faculty from the Math department to design statistical models for presenting the data in accurate and visually appealing ways. Faculty, staff, and students from the Sustainability Office and the Environmental Studies program designed a dorm competition to highlight the new system and encourage traffic to the new website.

The end result is a rather modest visual display that works (for the most part). And yes, we even show it off on admissions tours. But most importantly, the students learned a great deal in the process. They learned very specific and practical knowledge in their respective fields (computer science, environmental science, and environmental studies). They also gained important co-curricular skills such as electrical work, social marketing, and interdisciplinary collaboration and teamwork. These are skills you cannot buy from an external vendor. They can only be earned through hard work and experience. As Dewey once noted, "There is no discipline in the world so severe as the discipline of experience subjected to the tests of intelligent development and direction" (90).

However, there are limitations to this sort of approach. The dashboard system crashes from time to time. It is difficult (but not impossible) to sustain the various maintenance requirements when you have high turnover of students on a college campus and no main figurehead coordinating the endeavor. The end result, while functional, is by no means "glitzy." This sort of effort also takes much more time and effort for all involved (Earlham's ongoing project has been three years in the making). It may even be, in the end, less effective as an energy conservation initiative than if we were to go all-in on a campus-wide energy dashboard system from a reputable vendor.

Yet, if the main focus of sustainability education on our campuses is student *learning*, laboratories such as these far outweigh more "bedazzled" sustainability installations that run the risk of treating students as passive consumers rather than as active citizens. One of the main lessons of our energy dashboard learning laboratory was how incredibly important the educational outcomes were for the students involved. Many listed their involvement as a signature highlight of their Earlham career. It is equally clear that each of the students will have a set of highly marketable and employable skills upon graduation. Most importantly, students, faculty, and staff involved in the project had the opportunity to discover deep connections between theory and practice, to see how knowledge can be put to use to make the world a better place, and to experience the critical importance of collaboration.

Vignette #2

We Are All Crew, Not Passengers: A Student-Led STARS Initiative

The Sustainability Tracking Assessment and Rating System (STARS) has become the de facto assessment mechanism for sustainability on college and university campuses in the United States over the last several years. The system involves a comprehensive inventory of on-campus sustainability initiatives and metrics that participating institutions must research and then self-report via a public, online rating system. Based upon the scoring system, an institution may earn a bronze, silver, gold, or platinum rating, which they can then proudly display as a sign of their commitment to sustainability. As colleges and universities across the country become more attuned to the importance of visible progress on sustainability efforts, STARS has become enormously popular, with over 210 participating institutions nationwide.

Here again, as with the energy dashboard system, a choice presents itself. Many universities have simply farmed the research and self-reporting functions of STARS to sustainability directors or coordinators on campus with little to no student involvement. Others may involve students in helping with elements of the research, but mostly in co-curricular arrangements, such as work-study, internships, or volunteer roles within a sustainability office. There is nothing inherently wrong with such approaches. But, as with the energy dashboard vignette, real curricular opportunities may be lost when we unnecessarily divide "school life" and "work life" in these ways.

Using the pedagogical framework of the learning laboratory, STARS presents an excellent opportunity for students in the natural sciences, social sciences, and humanities to put theory to practice in real, tangible ways. Educator and founder of Outward Bound, Kurt Hahn, once famously quipped in his Seven Laws of Salem: "You are all crew; not passengers. Let the responsible boys and girls shoulder burdens big enough, if negligently performed, to wreck the State" (Miner and Boldt 372). Students learn the responsibility that comes with knowledge by acting out in the democratic field of play—not by spectating from the sidelines. How do we expect students to gain the critical skills of civic engagement, of testing values against material constraints, of collaboration and consultation, if they have no such opportunities during their time at school? Hahn's notion of "crew" argues that students must do real work for them to truly understand citizenship in their communities of interest. Perhaps more provocatively, Hahn suggests that their burdens ought to matter—they ought to be big enough to feel a true sense of responsibility. Simulations, minor clerical tasks, or contrived role-playing initiatives simply won't do. So how might one go about living this out in a learning laboratory approach?

In 2009, the Environmental Studies program at Earlham assigned the Environmental Colloquium class—a one-credit course specifically designated as an "open space" for dialogue between theory and practice on environmental issues—to the STARS project. Eighteen students signed up for the course from across the disciplines at Earlham and included sophomores, juniors, and seniors. We used two texts: Paul Hawken's *Blessed Unrest* and Rappaport & Creighton's *Degrees That Matter*. Students were divided into work teams to begin researching the various elements of campus activity related to sustainability, in order to input data into the STARS online inventory. Class time sometimes alternated between "theory" oriented topics (drawing from Hawken's discussions of environmental movements) and "applied" topics (dealing with logistical questions about the STARS process or various other technical matters of sustainability tracking). Outside of class, students were tasked with various research assignments, submitting written reports and reflections on a bi-weekly basis.

Often, a rather natural and powerful blending of theory and practice occurred in class. During one memorable session, students on the Greenhouse Gas Inventory Team were discussing their findings and were questioned on their calculations by other members of the class. A rather heated discussion ensued about issues of validity with estimation, the differences between precision and accuracy, and the importance of numeric literacy for those interested in environmental causes and issues. In another class, there appeared to be a fair amount of confusion among students about who was in charge of what area at the College. After putting up an organizational flow chart of the college administrative leadership on the screen, students talked through the pros and cons of hierarchical versus more horizontal forms of administrative leadership and debated what types of organizational structures were more effective in advancing a culture of sustainability on campus.

Throughout the semester, students learned more about how their college actually works and gained a much deeper empathy for the complexity of administration and governance. They also gained specific and practical skills related to completing sustainability inventories, including mastery of fairly complex Excel spreadsheets and how to organize large data sets. The texts gave them a theoretical anchor to their applied work, and we often saw examples of theory playing out before our eyes during the research. There were also other, surprising outcomes from my perspective as an instructor. I had little idea how naïve many students were in relation to the basics of "work etiquette." Several weeks in, I had to back-up and give a series of lessons on how to talk with an administrator, key tips on effective email communication, and what to do when the first answer is "no" when requesting information from an office assistant. I suspect (and hope) these skills will last with these students far beyond their time at Earlham.

Of course, as with the energy dashboard project, learning laboratories such as these come with significant limitations. Not all students carried their "burdens" well. After the course, we had to go back and double check the data collected by students and some of it was sub-par or widely inaccurate. Because students were the ones out and about doing the research and asking for data, college personnel would sometimes brush them off, and it would take phone calls from my office to motivate them to be more responsive to student requests for information. Like the energy dashboard project, using students and a class setting to complete this work slowed our progress significantly, and we missed some data points that we might have found with a more concentrated and systematic approach. As an instructor, I also found this type of teaching to be incredibly challenging. There was no chance I could be an expert in all the areas covered during this semester. I often felt like a fish out of water as I relied on my students to teach me the technical specifics of "scope 2 emissions" or what a "positive investment screen" entailed. Sometimes I simply felt overwhelmed trying to manage five separate work teams at the same time. However, I am convinced that having students intimately involved—as "crew"—in this learning laboratory amplified the learning experience for all involved. And crucially, because the STARS work is an ongoing process, opportunities will exist to engage more students in future Colloquium classes with sustainability-related research. Thus, the learning environment itself is "sustainable." In fact, we will be using this basic model in the fall of 2013 as we work to create the College's first Climate Action Plan. Let the burdens continue for our crew.

Vignette #3

Researching The Native: The Ethics of Community-Based Project Work

In the Spring of 2012, the Environmental Studies Senior Seminar class at Earlham completed a sustainability map of the Richmond community using a Google-map based software interface called "GreenMap." The work was a component of the course called the Integrated Research Project (IRP). From the syllabus, "The purpose of the IRP is for students to initiate, in a collaborative setting, a project that draws together field-based, experiential research with coursework from various Environmental Studies classes and additional scholarly research." One of the central requirements of the IRP, from the standpoint of the faculty in the Environmental Studies program at Earlham, is that it asks students to do research outside of campus and in the community. Once removed from the comforting confines of the campus computer lab, students must wrestle with many of the ethical and practical issues of community-based work and research—central themes in just about any type of environmental work.

Learning laboratories do not solely exist as on-campus projects. Once the general pedagogical framework of a learning laboratory is understood, laboratory ideas can emerge from a surprising variety of locations and sources—many of which extend beyond the boundaries of the campus itself. Indeed, one of the most promising applications of the learning laboratory approach is its ability to bridge so-called "town-gown" relationships and present students with more of a place-based awareness and understanding of the communities that encompass their particular campus. As David Gruenwald notes,

> The point of becoming more conscious of places in education is to extend our notions of pedagogy and accountability outward toward places. Thus extended, pedagogy becomes more relevant to the lived experience of students and teachers, and accountability is re-conceptualized so that places matter to educators, students, and citizens in tangible ways. (646)

In this particular case, the students decided to complete their IRP by developing an online sustainability map of Richmond, Indiana—the town where Earlham is located. Early on in the semester, these seniors rehashed many of the debates they had learned and engaged with in terms of operationally defining sustainability throughout their four years of coursework in Environmental Studies. The difference here, of course, was that they had to actually *decide* on some form of definition and *act* on it, rather than simply fall back to a too-easy critique on the nature of the term. This proved difficult, but nowhere near the difficulty they encountered in thinking through the purposes of the project itself: who the research was for and to what ends. As part of the course, we read several provocative articles on the ethics of community mapping, including Brenda Parker's "Constructing Community Through Maps? Power and Praxis in Community Mapping," where she notes that "intentional exclusion, limited resources, and lack of critical reflection can impede map projects from attaining input from diverse groups, and questions remain about who constitutes 'community'" (475). We also read and discussed Linda Tuhi-Wai Smith's challenging essay "On Tricky Ground: Researching the Native in the Age of Uncertainty," about community research methodology.

These articles and discussions helped students think critically and skeptically regarding their project's goal to "help" Richmond with their sustainability map. Difficult questions emerged about why we felt empowered to map "Others" and about who would get left out by our definition of sustainability. Some students wondered if we had any right to complete the map in the first place, given that they felt like visitors to Richmond rather than locals. Others wondered about class issues and how an online map such as this would actually serve social justice-related sustainability aims, when it was unlikely to be used or seen as valuable by working class and poor communities in town. Countering this ethical paralysis was very challenging.

However, as students began to talk with community members and hear their excitement about what a project like this could do for the city, some (but not all) of their concerns were allayed. Nevertheless, a constant tension throughout the project between students in the seminar was the theme of social justice and the ethical question of what it really meant to "do good work" in the community related to sustainability. As a colleague of mine (Joanna Swanger, personal communication) noted about the term "learning laboratory" itself:

Furthermore, part of the local community's suspicion toward Earlham stems from the view that (much akin to the point raised above vis-à-vis Study Abroad programs) we are here to learn *about* Richmond and *use* it as our "laboratory." The current emphasis upon experiential learning need not be compromised by a revision of the view of "using" Richmond. Instead, it is crucial to take a step further and recognize the self-sufficiency and the production of knowledge that happens in this region, without any intervention at all from Earlham. The residents of Richmond, in fact, have a wealth of knowledge about how to survive in the face of economic challenge, and Earlham and Richmond should look to each other as "teachers"—indeed, as collaborators.

As my colleague articulates, placing the notion of a "laboratory" alongside community action research presents some problematic frames of meaning. What kind of action is trivial? What is meaningful? What is empowering? What is hegemonic?

These questions reveal one of the real limitations and challenges of community-based learning laboratories: positionality and power. Certainly, viewing the community in a deficit orientation with the college or university as the benevolent and all-knowing savior smacks of the worst kinds of neo-colonial mind-sets. Yet, this need not lead to ethical paralysis and the cessation of any attempt at college-community research. Perhaps "laboratory" is the wrong term. But, the point is to emphasize the opportunities for students to test out their ideas in partnership with others. This form of pedagogical activity should not preclude ethical queries. In fact, they can and should be central. It is one of the principle reasons the Environmental Studies Senior Seminar course requires the Integrated Research Project be community-based in the first place.

In the end, the larger point of community-based learning laboratories is to re-engage students and faculty with what Gruenwald calls "the pedagogical power of places." As he states, "Once one begins to appreciate the pedagogical power of places, it is difficult to accept institutional discourses, structures, pedagogies, and curriculums that neglect them" (641). For too long, many college campuses have existed as "Universities of Nowhere." It is as if the learning that occurs on campus could happen anywhere—completely removed and de-contextualized from its social, cultural, and geographical context. The so-called "town-gown" conflicts seen in many college towns are merely symptomatic of much deeper historical structures in the Academy which often serve to isolate knowledge domains and promote disassociated learning. As the seismic forces shift the ground underneath the 21st century college and university campus, faculty and administrators would do well to find stability through branching out to the larger community to forge real, collaborative partnerships. Community-based learning laboratories are one potentially powerful way to build those bridges.

Conclusion

The learning laboratory approach yields a number of provocative questions for faculty, students, and university administrators moving forward. For administrators, how do our institutions of higher learning move beyond slick marketing campaigns and "greenwashing" to substantive educational responses in relation to sustainability?

For faculty, what are the pedagogical implications of extending the classroom beyond the traditional four walls and out into multiple (and public) places and spaces? For students, what might the differences be between learning "about" sustainability and learning "through" it? Questions such as these return us to a fundamental query: what is college for? The learning laboratory opens up space to consider new possibilities in answering this question—possibilities at the intersecting spaces between problems and projects, colleges and communities, co-learners and collaborators, and knowledge and responsibility.

As the pressure increases on colleges and universities to demonstrate strong and effective learning outcomes for students, disciplines in the humanities and social sciences can often struggle to prove the value of the educational experience and preparation they offer. Students (and their parents) are looking for a curriculum that is more relevant, outcome-oriented, and practical. Yet, this is not simply a market-driven value. These attributes are also strongly supported by the new science of learning. Learning environments that are active, complex, multi-sensory, reflective, and community-oriented support deeper and more long-term understanding and retention of information (Bransford). The increase in the use of learning laboratories, service learning, place-based instruction, and other forms of experiential education points to new pedagogical possibilities in higher education. At a time when the fixed-seat, large lecture hall serves as the very symbol of outmoded "instructional delivery," experiential learning represents a pedagogical approach that cannot be outsourced to the Internet. Learning laboratories, both on and off-campus, with their problem-based, active, collaborative, and practical orientation, offer one model of how to successfully navigate the uneven terrain of higher education in the 21st century.

Notes

1. As a further testament to this new era, Stanford's Sebastian Thrun made headlines in the fall of 2011 when his online Artificial Intelligence course enrolled over 160,000 students. According to the *New York Times* ("Harvard and MIT Team Up To Offer On-Line Classes," May 2, 2012), Thrun's new venture, Udacity, has enrolled 200,000 students into six courses thus far.

2. It is certainly the case that many of these approaches are not necessarily new—any student of early twentieth century progressive education will recognize elements of the experiential pedagogy. Many K-12 schools, such as Expeditionary Learning and Place-Based Learning schools, are incorporating these pedagogical principles. Yet, I would contend that these sorts of progressive educational approaches have been slower to gain a foothold in higher education. And, this is perhaps most true within the traditional social sciences and humanities. The natural sciences and the fine arts have always seemed to have a more experiential streak written into their pedagogical DNA.

3. These three examples are not meant to imply that Earlham is doing something other colleges and universities are not. I am aware of many institutions that have similar learning laboratories focused on sustainability education. The vignettes from Earlham

are included simply because I am intimately familiar with them and they seem to encompass the larger pedagogical issues around the use of learning laboratories in higher education.

Works Cited

Arum, Richard, and Josipa Roksa. *Academically Adrift: Limited Learning on College Campuses*. Chicago, IL: University of Chicago Press, 2011. Print.

Bok, Derek. *Our Underachieving Colleges: A Candid Look at How Much Student Learn and Why They Should Be Learning More*. Princeton, NJ: Princeton University Press, 2006. Print.

Bransford, John, Ann Brown, and Rodney Cocking, eds. *How People Learn: Brain, Mind, Experience, and School*. Washington, DC: National Academy Press, 2000. Print.

Darling-Hammond, Linda. *The Flat World and Education: How America's Commitment to Equity Will Determine Our Future*. New York, NY: Teachers College Press, 2010.

Delbanco, Andrew. *College: What It Was, Is, and Should Be*. Princeton, NJ: Princeton University Press, 2012. Print.

Dewey, John. *Experience and Education*. New York, NY: Collier Macmillan, 1938. Print.

Ferrall, Victor. *Liberal Arts On The Brink*. Cambridge, MA: Harvard University Press, 2011. Print.

Friedman, Thomas. *The World Is Flat*. New York, NY: Farrar, Straus, and Giroux, 2005. Print.

Gruenewald, David A. "Foundations of Place: A Multidisciplinary Framework for Place-Conscious Education." *American Educational Research Journal* 40.3 (2003): 619-654. Print.

Hawken, Paul. *Blessed Unrest: How the Largest Movement in the World Came into Being and Why No One Saw It Coming*. New York, NY: Viking, 2007. Print.

Miner, Joshua, and Joseph Boldt. *Outward Bound USA: Crew Not Passengers*. Seattle, WA: Mountaineers Books, 2002. Print.

Orr, David. *The Nature Of Design: Ecology, Culture, and Human Intention*. New York, NY: Oxford University Press, 2002. Print.

Parker, Brenda. "Constructing Community Through Maps? Power and Praxis in Community Mapping." *The Professional Geographer* 58.4 (2006): 470-484. Print.

Rappaport Ann, and Sarah Creighton. *Degrees That Matter: Climate Change and the University*. Cambridge, MA: MIT Press, 2007.

Smith, Linda T. "On Tricky Ground: Researching the Native in the Age of Uncertainty," *Sage Handbook of Qualitative Research*. Eds. Norman Denzin and Yvonna Lincoln. Thousand Oaks, CA: Sage Publications, 2005. 85-103.

Exploring Sustainability through On-Campus Consulting

Lisa K. Barlow

Abstract: This essay addresses the pragmatic side of sustainability: how do we move toward a more sustainable way of being in the world, focusing on change in an institutional setting? Students learn valuable lessons by being agents of change. The service learning consulting model used for a course at the University of Colorado at Boulder gives students the opportunity to expand efforts beyond individuals actively involved in attempting to live a more sustainable lifestyle to those who are not actively involved. While researching and developing strategies for change, students learn the importance of addressing human behavior in tandem with the use of materials or infrastructure.

Lisa K. Barlow, Ph.D., is a Senior Instructor in the Baker Residential Academic Program for the Natural Sciences and the Environment and in the Environmental Studies Program at the University of Colorado at Boulder. She became interested in the dynamics between human choices and climate/environmental vulnerability while working as a physical scientist on climate variability over the last 1000 years from the Greenland Ice Sheet Project 2(GISP 2) ice core record. Dr. Barlow's research is currently focused on individual and community-based logistical and behavioral change for advancing toward a more sustainable future. In addition to teaching Sustainable Solutions Consulting, she also teaches courses on climate change, physical geology, and the personal path toward sustainability. She has presented numerous talks at the Association for the Advancement of Sustainability in Higher Education (AASHE).

Introduction

Colleges and universities can be viewed as entities with operational, fiscal, personnel, and clientele considerations that are similar to municipalities, large businesses, or government organizations. Therefore, they serve as an excellent classroom for teaching the pragmatic side of sustainability: how do we move toward a more sustainable way of being in the world? A critical opportunity here is to expand efforts beyond individuals actively involved in attempting to live a more sustainable lifestyle to those who are not actively involved. Sustainable Solutions Consulting (ENVS 3001) at the University of Colorado at Boulder is one example of a service-learning course that provides students the opportunity for real-world problem solving and experiential learning. This class gives students skills and perspective to be agents of change by helping the University move toward its stated goals.

The consulting format of this service-learning course is similar to on-campus service-learning courses taught at other institutions: campus Operations units, tasked with carrying out the University's official plan for a more sustainable future, propose specific projects to the Instructor who acts as Project Manager. The scope of the project is defined, deliverable outcomes are agreed upon, and the students and their Instructor/Project Manager have a semester to research, survey, analyze, and present recommendations for change. Students come to the class aware of the three-legged stool of sustainability: environment, social equity, and economics, and we take a very short amount of time to discuss the meaning of "sustainability." The focus of the course is not on coming to a deeper understanding of the definition; it is about coming to a deeper understanding of what it takes for an institution to make progress toward a more sustainable future. An institution is a human construct; students learn through their own experience the importance of addressing human behavior when researching and developing strategies for change.

The call for essays for this compendium implies that we are still trying to figure out how to fit sustainability into our traditional disciplinary divisions. This also implies that ideas we share are generated from our own unique perspectives. My perspective is that the challenges we face over this century are so daunting that sustainability should not be presented as an "add-on" to conventional courses when problem solving for a more sustainable future is the focus of the course

Sustainable Solutions Consulting has been a service learning course for eleven years. The last nine years of project reports are at: http://envs.colorado.edu/undergrad_program/C106/ENVS-3001/. One key learning opportunity for students is that the great bulk of effort in our transition to greater sustainability will be working with established entities. It is easier to get closer to sustainability goals when building from nothing than when transitioning an established entity. Students tend to forget about existing infrastructure, whether it be in human organizations or in built infrastructure. For example, students tend to focus on newly constructed, net zero emissions buildings as solutions and overlook the vast, existing inventory of academic buildings, administrative buildings, residence halls, and off-campus apartments. The projects we take on in this class are a part of the transition of existing entities, and as such are complex. The following section is a discussion of my sense of key learning opportunities for students that come from the on-campus consulting experience.

Recognize that a sustainable solution is a moving target

Sustainability in action is intelligent adaptation to current or predicted pressures. Whether the topic is climate change, ocean resources, financial resources, inequity, or myriad other dynamic systems, humanity is facing moving targets. Therefore, one of the first lessons for students in ENVS 3001 is that their task as consultants is to move the University further in a direction *toward* sustainability, not to deliver an "end-game" solution. This is most easily conveyed to students through discussion on technological advances, how fast some of those advances have occurred, and how fast they have changed societies. For example, most students can grasp this concept from their own experience of the evolution of cell phone technology during their lifetimes. This personal experience with rapid advances in cell phone technology teaches students that strategic technological solutions they offer to their clients are based on current options that could change.

In addition, through a semester of problem solving for the client, missteps will be taken, lessons will be learned and adjustments made. It is critical that students understand that the process of movement toward sustainability will have both advances and setbacks, especially because our educational system puts so much emphasis on correct answers as final answers. It has been my observation that upper division undergraduates are not accustomed to having little to show for effort invested. This tends to challenge a student's self-perception of high achievement and leads to frustration. In ENVS 3001, students learn that "dead-ends" that they have put time and effort into researching are not wasted time, but learning experiences that strengthen the expertise they are building on a subject. This understanding is commonly gained through an honors thesis experience. The majority of students in the class have not chosen to pursue honors in their discipline, as they are more focused on entering the workforce than graduate school.

View the project from a systems perspective

The University of Colorado community, including myself and the vast majority of my students, are members of a highly industrialized and highly consumptive United States society. We did not reach our current level of unsustainability overnight, but over time that stretches back beyond our personal lifetimes. The unsustainable aspects of our current lifestyle and social norms are built on layer upon intertwined layer of industrial, chemical, and technological progress. Moving to a more sustainable way of living involves exploring as many ramifications of a specific technological or cultural change as possible in order to improve the potential for success of the change. This exploration benefits from a systems perspective. There are many opportunities to introduce change into a system, and at many levels or subsystems within the system. The smallest change requires a diligent assessment of the interconnectedness of that which has been identified for change. A systems perspective helps to conceptually organize the current situation and to identify components that are critical for success.

For example, the 2011 class was tasked with helping University of Colorado staff and faculty shift from personal desk-side printers to networked, multifunction copy/print/scan/fax devices that are designed to replace large volume departmental copy machines. The system involved for this project is the Boulder campus and its current pool of desk-side devices with printers at different stages of their lifetimes. A printer inhabiting a desk-side location could be a large, single-sided printer, manufactured before energy efficiency standards; a small, new, double-sided, energy efficient print/copy/scan device, or some version with functionality and age lying between these two ends of the printer spectrum. Paper, ink/toner, and electricity are inputs to the Boulder campus printer system, while paper and empty ink and toner cartridges are outputs. Within the campus system, printers function to assist humans in different ways; for example, paper documentation of contracts, student class schedules, master prints of exams, or drafts of research papers. The way that an individual printer is used influences the potential for its elimination, as does the proximity of the networked replacement. Issues affecting human willingness to change, such as proximity, time, privacy, and networked machine maintenance also influence the success of the proposed change. Hence, the systems perspective includes attention to human behavior of those currently using desk-side printers.

With a lens of sustainability, other components of the system feeding into printers are also investigated, such as paper sourcing, ink production, and printer life cycles, with emphasis on manufacturer ethics and especially pre- and post-consumer working conditions. This research resulted in suggestions for changes in university purchasing guidelines, capture of lost revenue, and greater communication with non-administrative, on-campus venues. In many projects as large and far-reaching as the printer project, identifying important components of the system is an evolutionary process: initial components are identified, research begins, and new, important components of the system are discovered and added. For example, interview questions on printing habits revealed that many networked printers and multifunction devices with double-sided printing capability were printing single-sided pages because computer default settings had not been switched. This single change can lower paper consumption for the campus.

Anchor strategies for change on human behavior

Conscious efforts to move away from unsustainable activities are, in many cases, efforts that hinge on the willingness to accept change while change is still a choice. Thus, the sustainable systems approach must add the component of human motivation when exploring avenues for successful change. I have found the work of McKenzie-Mohr's Community-Based Social Marketing (CBSM) approach to be very useful in orienting students to this component. A major lesson from the CBSM approach is the identification of external and internal barriers to behavioral change. Students are tasked with determining feasibility of multiple strategies for change by first considering internal and external barriers.

External barriers are physical inhibitors to successful adoption of a new behavior, such as lack of infrastructure or limited resources (McKenzie-Mohr 9). Some external barriers may be currently insurmountable; for example, it would be difficult to require elimination of high volume, desk-side printers for offices in a small annex building that could not justify the expense of its own, new, on-site multifunction device. Other external barriers may be modified for easier adoption, such as placing a new multifunction device for a large, open office floor-plan in a more centralized location than the old copy machine.

Internal barriers are personal to an individual, such as perceptions, priorities, or confusion about how to carry out a new behavior (McKenzie-Mohr, 9). Ideas for internal barriers may come from literature or from familiarity with the behavior, but these ideas must be tested with the target group of the project. After gathering information from informal interviews and observation, the students often develop surveys, with voluntary anonymous participation, for identifying the most common internal barriers that inhibit adoption of a new behavior. Through researching internal barriers, students develop skills in non-judgmental observation and assessment, as they learn tools from McKenzie-Mohr such as social norming and commitment. Identifying external and internal barriers to change helps students to clarify their approach, customize their strategies, and recognize that one-size-fits-all solutions are not optimal.

The following are examples of the application of external and internal barriers from the printer project. An office unit of approximately 24 staff is housed on a single floor, consolidated in one large area, and isolated from public passing (walking) traffic. The existing copy machine is a few steps away, with no need to cross through public traffic. In this situation, shifting print output to the familiar location of the old copy machine presents a low external barrier, as the physical path is within current behavior. For some staff, the idea of getting up from their cubicle periodically to retrieve prints was perceived as a health benefit. This is the optimal situation for lowering internal barriers, as the individual perceives that a benefit of the new behavior outweighs perceived barriers.

For individuals with high volume printing as a condition of their job, the perception of losing their desk-side printer and of additional time and energy wasted in retrieving prints means that internal barriers outweigh perceived benefits. The strategy for the latter staff would be education about the new feature's option to hold jobs before printing, in addition to developing strategies for reducing the need for paper prints. Additionally, in this office example, the receptionist is expected to print documents for students and is also expected to remain at his desk as the welcoming face of the office. For the receptionist, eliminating his desk-side printer would compromise his job requirements. His situation reinforces the need to investigate feasibility of printer elimination at the level of the individual user.

For large, multistory, academic departments with traditionally isolated teaching offices that border public hallways full of students, barriers to voluntary adoption are much higher. The Department of Anthropology at the University of Colorado volunteered to participate in the class study and presents an example of such a scenario. The department is housed in an historic four-story building with administrative offices and departmental copiers on the third floor and the majority of professorial offices on the first, second, and fourth floors. Isolated professorial offices open into main hallways that are filled with students, especially during passing periods. The client basis for cost savings for all departments is a one-to-one replacement of departmental copiers with multifunction devices and, secondarily, cost savings on reduced desk-side printer purchases and ink and paper savings from double-sided prints.

Consider the situation of a professor with an office on the first floor, toward the outer edge of the building (the administrative office is in the center of the third floor). Currently, with a desk-side printer, a professor can quickly access drafts of research papers, hard copies of data, material for lectures, and master copies of exams, and assignments can be quickly printed and proofed before going to the third floor copier. Consider the shift from these familiar behaviors to a necessity of exiting one's office to a sometimes crowded and noisy hallway, down the hallway, up the (crowded and noisy) stairs, into and through the administrative office suite to the copy room, where you may have to wait in line to release your print job, then retrace your steps back to your office, for every paper print you want to make. In this scenario, the likelihood of greater benefits for the individual faculty member affected by elimination of desk-side printers is very low. It would be difficult for administrators to justify the time lost by faculty in retrieving prints. Furthermore, as the class conducted desk-side printer surveys in various departments, it was clear from casual conversations with some faculty and research staff that eliminated desk-side printers would be replaced at personal expense.

An alternative strategy for this departmental situation could be to increase the number of rental contracts for the new multifunction devices, so that one device could reside on each floor. This option would at least triple the monthly rental cost and, as the students discovered in interviews, would raise logistical questions about simple maintenance and responsibility for such maintenance. In the current situation, problems with department-owned copiers and multifunction devices, such as fixing paper jams, loading staples, or changing toner, are quickly identified and attended to by department office staff, as the machines are within the administrative office suite. The placement of large machines on other floors of the building met with a strongly negative reaction from the understaffed office administrators, as they would be expected to oversee problems with the new machines in locations that are out of sight. The combination of higher expenses and understaffing made this strategy unlikely to succeed.

A third strategy could be to modify project goals for these types of situations to include paper and ink reductions while leaving desk-side printers in place or, if possible, consolidate smaller clusters of printers into networked printers. Time constraints dictated that only a few academic departments were included in the printer project; however, from the students' familiarity with the buildings and logistics of many departments, it is evident that customization will be necessary in most circumstances.

What students learn from working with external and internal barriers is that all strategies for change must incorporate the perspective and needs of people who will be affected by the change. The worst-case scenario for an implemented change would be that it is completely circumvented, as it appears would be the case if personal printers were eliminated for all faculty and staff, regardless of their logistical setting or printing needs. As interviews revealed, there would be a certain population who would purchase their own printers. Although privately purchased printers would be off University records, few institutions appreciate negative publicity stemming from a claim of progress toward sustainability that does not fit the ground truth of their campus.

Include the clients' world view of the project—
but their world view may need expanding

People come to conclusions about the correct path for change from their personal experience. Students learn the importance of understanding the client's experience of the target behavior because situations arise where broadening the client's worldview may be beneficial. For example, the client for the multifunction device/printer project favored elimination of desk-side printers and held a strong bias that underlying resistance would be linked to a sense of entitlement more than any actual necessity. The client's expectations for successful printer elimination were based on his experience of a large, single-floor staff office suite, isolated from hallway traffic, in a department that did not interact with students. The ENVS 3001 consulting team needed to educate the client on significant barriers faced by individuals in other office situations, such as the aforementioned receptionist and Anthropology Department faculty members. In this way, students learn that their consulting role may include representing the voice of the target population to the client, so that the client's expectations of a successful outcome can be revised.

This brings up a second critical point about communication with the client. Informal progress reports during the semester keep the client informed of the evolution of the student consultants' thinking about workable solutions. This also helps the students, because they can gauge the "buy-in" of the client to proposed strategies. As Project Manager, it is always my preference that, at the final oral presentation, the students are presenting strategies that have already been embraced by their client.

Weave monetary considerations into strategies

Capitalism still rules as the dominant form of practicality: if a proposed strategy costs too much, it will not be adopted. "Externalities" are important to account for and present as we reinforce the need to consider downstream and upstream consequences of our choices; however, the bottom line remains out-of-pocket expense.

Students learn to sell their suggestions for change with the language of costs and benefits, with a combination of well-researched data and infectious enthusiasm. For example, the printer project included researching and ranking ethics and sustainability claims of printer manufacturers, along with new purchasing guidelines and proposals for specific, competitively priced, double-sided printers. This research was not originally requested by the client, but was proposed by the students and incorporated as it became evident that specific situations prohibited the elimination of desk-side printers.

One advantage of consulting for an educational institution is the value placed on the reputation of the school for its sustainability efforts. The Sustainability Tracking and Recording System (STARS), sponsored by the Association for the Advancement of Sustainability in Higher Education (AASHE), helped raise administrative interest in sustainability as a recruiting tool. Students can capitalize on this interest to help sell strategies that are financially marginal.

Separate proposed strategies into short-term and long-term changes

It is part of human nature to be interested in immediate action that can produce immediate change. Students learn to organize and present actions that can be done in a now-to-six-months' time frame first in order to keep the interest of the client focused, and to build momentum for buy-in of longer term strategies. It is my experience that students appreciate the opportunity to suggest changes that can occur in the near future. The most positive outcomes for students are to see a proposed strategy has been implemented; or, even better, to be hired by Operations to continue work on the project after the class has ended. Longer-term strategies (two to five years out) give students an opportunity to propose where they would like the University to go in the future if, for instance, funding can be secured or technology becomes available and affordable.

Sustainability is a moving target, revisited

Requiring that student strategies for change be grounded in fiscal realities puts my consulting course squarely in Bill McDonough's categories of being "less bad," and being eco-efficient instead of eco-effective (McDonough and Braungart). The course falls short of its title. We are nipping at the fringes and maybe buying time. However, we all teach students with the expectation that they will take what we offer and advance it beyond our current knowledge. Technological advances will alter future options for better balance with our planet, but we humans need practice in voluntary behavioral change; we need practice in listening to the voices of individuals who will be affected by changes that we and our students help to craft; we need practice in recognizing opportunities for change; and we need practice in resilience. As other authors have stated in this volume, sustainability is a practice that we move towards and, hopefully, get better at with time.

Works Cited

McDonough, William, and Michael Braungart. *Cradle to Cradle: Remaking the Way We Make Things.* New York, NY: North Point Press, 2002. Print

McKenzie-Mohr, Doug. *Fostering Sustainable Behavior: An Introduction to Community–Based Social Marketing.* Third Edition. Gabriola Island, BC: New Society Publishers, 2011. Print

SEEDing the Pedagogical Landscape: a Design-based Approach to Sustainability Education

Dina El-Mogazi, Bucknell University

Abstract: At Bucknell University, Sustainable Energy and Ecological Design (or SEED) projects are being used to create a pedagogical landscape focused on sustainability education. These student-designed demonstration-scale models of sustainable practices are linked to course work in "Introduction to Ecological Design." Ecological design is an area of study which integrates knowledge across multiple disciplines, including humanities, social sciences, and natural sciences. Through this process, students experience connections and disconnections with the natural world, and thus opportunities to incorporate an ethic of environmental sustainability. Most often, design is studied through exclusive programs oriented toward specific professions, but the common element of design process can be taught successfully within a liberal arts curriculum. This essay reflects on twelve years of teaching ecological design in a liberal arts institution, with a special focus on connections to campus sustainability programming.

Dina El-Mogazi has served as Director of the Bucknell University Environmental Center's Campus Greening Initiative (CGI) since 2008, and has taught Ecological Design as an adjunct professor in Bucknell's Environmental Studies Program since 2000. As CGI Director, she serves as the primary facilitator and advocate for sustainable environmental practices, environmental literacy, and ecologically sound campus design and planning at Bucknell. Dina holds a Master's Degree in Landscape Architecture from the University of Georgia and a Bachelor of Science Degree in Chemistry from Louisiana State University. Prior to joining the Bucknell community, she held professional positions in the fields of environmental biology and environmental justice.

Embarking on a new course: *Introduction to Ecological Design*

This essay chronicles the evolving "symbiotic" partnership between campus sustainability programming at Bucknell University and coursework in ENST 230: Introduction to Ecological Design. Introduced in the spring semester of 2000 as a social sciences elective in the University's environmental studies program, this course allowed students to approach environmental issues from a new perspective. At that time, most of the courses in the program approached study of the environment from the disciplinary perspectives of policy or science, with some courses also taking the perspectives of literature, history, philosophy, and religion.

At the same time, the field of ecology was beginning to create a major impact on the design professions of architecture, landscape architecture, urban design, and industrial design but, since these fields were not commonly accessible to undergraduates at a liberal arts college like Bucknell, students were often left unaware of the impact of design professions on local and global environmental sustainability. When taken as a whole, this impact is highly significant—design decisions affect a whole host of environmental consequences, including natural resource depletion, energy use, and air, water, and soil pollution. Equally significant is the fact that design decisions influence the human experience of the environment, affecting such intangibles as "sense of place" and awareness of the connections between humans and the natural world.

Simultaneously, at Bucknell and many other universities, interest in campus sustainability was building momentum. Although environmental values had impacted campus life since before the first Earth Day in 1970, the campus sustainability movement was a different animal, directed inwardly at campus operations and practices, rather than outwardly at national politics and environmental disasters. As this movement took root at Bucknell, a fertile opportunity arose in which students could now apply environmental values to their own temporary home: the university campus.

In the spring of 2000, ENST 230 became a natural fit for the exploration of projects aimed at improving the environmental sustainability at Bucknell. This fit was particularly good because one of the overarching principles of ecological design is to allow design solutions to emerge from the specific and unique qualities of the local environment. This principle has long been espoused by visionaries in the field, including McHarg, Van der Ryn, and others. Course learning objectives, listed below, illustrate how this principle is incorporated into the overall philosophy of the course:

ENST 230 Course Objectives:

- To understand how human design at different scales (including architecture, landscape architecture, urban design, and regional planning) shapes the environment and influences quality of life.
- To understand the functional relationship between the built environment (buildings, communities, and cities) and the natural environment (earth, water, air, energy, and living things).

- To understand how to obtain information on local environmental conditions, and apply this information to design problems.
- To develop basic graphic communication and map interpretation skills necessary to communicate design ideas.
- To learn to apply all of the above knowledge and skills in a real design project of local significance.
- To reflect upon the design process through in-class discussion and a formal presentation of design proposals.

In the early years of ENST 230, student projects, although focused on the campus theoretically, were largely disconnected from actual campus transformation. When it came time to propose final design projects, students envisioned modular residences in the shape of geodesic domes, proposed waste-treatment wetlands for the center of the academic quad, or suggested that Jefferson's Monticello be re-imagined on the banks of the Susquehanna. Although fanciful and creative, these kinds of design proposals were very unlikely to take root in the actual campus soil. The campus sustainability movement at Bucknell would need to evolve into a real initiative with specific goals before this would happen.

The Campus Greening Initiative

The development of the campus sustainability movement at Bucknell is closely tied to the growth of the Bucknell University Environmental Center (BUEC). Conceived in 2004 as an academic center for interdisciplinary research and teaching on local, regional, and global environmental issues, the BUEC set in motion a Campus Greening Initiative (CGI) as one of its first endeavors. Capitalizing on faculty, staff, and student interest, the Environmental Center became the coordinating force behind "walking the walk," where institutional values of environmental sustainability were concerned. The fact that this effort was housed in the academic side of the University, rather than in the operational side (where these efforts reside in most educational institutions), strongly influenced the character of the initiative, as can be seen in the strategic goals quoted from the CGI's strategic plan below:

Bucknell's Campus Greening Initiative has two overarching goals which go hand-in-hand:

1. To model environmentally sustainable practices within the University, so as to promote a culture of environmental awareness and minimize the adverse ecological impact of University operations.
2. To provide Bucknell students with meaningful and consequential learning experiences in environmental sustainability, the philosophy concerned with preserving quality of life and the natural environment for future generations."

As a fledgling initiative with a lofty agenda, the CGI had to work toward these goals with one dedicated staff member and a diminutive annual operating budget. This set of circumstances led to the obvious question: where to begin?

First things first: A Comprehensive Environmental Assessment of Bucknell University

The CGI began in earnest in fall 2007 with its first major undertaking, a comprehensive environmental assessment of the University. This groundbreaking investigation was conducted through the collaborative voluntary efforts of over seventy students, faculty, staff, and community members who researched and compiled information on the environmental impact of a broad range of policies and practices in the areas of administration, education, energy, water, waste, hazardous materials, dining, purchasing, built environment, and landscape. Surveys developed by the CGI director were distributed to teams of volunteers, who then had approximately two semesters to research and answer an extensive list of questions in each of the above areas. Two honors theses and several student research internships were also associated with the assessment. The resulting report, consisting of over two hundred pages of data and recommendations, was made public on the CGI website in May of 2009 (El-Mogazi) and was presented at the 2009 conference of the Association for the Advancement of Sustainability in Higher Education (AASHE).

The environmental assessment provided the first real opportunity for students in ENST 230 to connect with the Campus Greening Initiative. In spring of 2008 each ENST 230 student completed a life cycle analysis on common products and materials used on campus, and several of these were incorporated into the final assessment report. This emphasis on the life cycles of common objects and materials represented a new development in the "analysis" portion of the ENST 230 course content. Students were required to brainstorm, diagram, and research all phases of the life cycle of their assigned product or material (including resource extraction, production, manufacturing, consumption, and post-consumption impacts), and to make use of technical documents such as the Environmental Protection Agency's Sector Notebooks. Objects of investigation included Bucknell's standard printer paper, sweatshirts sold at the campus store, several types of meat served in the cafeteria, and disposable utensils and to-go containers used in the take-out dining venues.

Students attacked these assignments with a sense of curiosity and enthusiasm that had been lacking in the previous years of ENST 230 coursework. Their familiar and immediate connection to the objects of interest allowed them to identify more directly with the environmental impacts of their everyday choices than the initial analytical assignments, which had been based on exercises such as slope determinations and storm water runoff calculations. The life cycle research also provided students with important insights into the origins and fate of materials used in the design of the built environment, and exposed them to alternative product design strategies, such as those espoused by William McDonough and Michael Braungart in *Cradle to Cradle*. As a result of this experience, from this point forward, the ENST 230 course material was revised to include life cycle analysis of common objects as a major course component.

The emerging SEED project concept

The experience gained through the environmental assessment project proved that students in ENST 230 could contribute meaningfully and significantly to the Campus Greening Initiative. But significant challenges in moving the University forward in the direction of environmental sustainability still loomed. For one, the environmental assessment had revealed so many areas of concern, and produced so many recommendations, that it was difficult to know where to begin in tackling them all. The lack of staff and resources for accomplishing institutional transformation remained an issue.

Like many colleges and universities, Bucknell formed a sustainability committee, the Campus Greening Council, to discuss prioritization of projects and recommend policy changes to management. Bucknell's president also signed the American College and University Presidents Climate Commitment (ACUPCC), setting in motion a chain of obligations for documenting and reducing the University's greenhouse gas emissions. The Environmental Center worked with the Curriculum Committee to implement an environmental course requirement, capitalizing on a rare opportunity to revise the core curriculum of the College of Arts and Sciences. Bucknell Facilities continued to implement changes in operations where feasible and economically viable; for instance, replacing fixtures as renovation schedules allowed. All of these were positive steps in the right direction, but the Campus Greening Initiative, as an essentially academic endeavor, still needed to come up with a strategic way of balancing the goals of research, teaching, and operational change on a small annual budget, and this need brought forth the idea of SEED Projects.

Sustainable Energy and Ecological Design or "SEED" Projects were adopted as a central strategy of the Campus Greening Initiative in 2010. These educational-scale demonstration projects encompass multiple aspects of green technology, living systems, and sustainable culture, and serve several functions within the CGI such as:

- providing students with experiential learning opportunities in sustainability;
- providing faculty with research and teaching opportunities in sustainability;
- serving as prototypes for larger-scale sustainable design projects on campus;
- and providing the region with hands-on models of sustainable systems, which can be observed and replicated at the residential and community scales.

The triangular diagram below (see figure 1) illustrates how the Campus Greening Initiative attempts to balance the activities of research, education, and operations toward a more sustainable campus. In this diagram, SEED projects fall squarely in the middle, tying together the three activities. Because of this, they are an economical use of time and resources, contributing to all the goals of the Campus Greening Initiative simultaneously. Furthermore, what's most attractive about the SEED project concept from the programming point of view is that SEED projects have the potential to grow and reproduce as they "catch on" in the university culture.

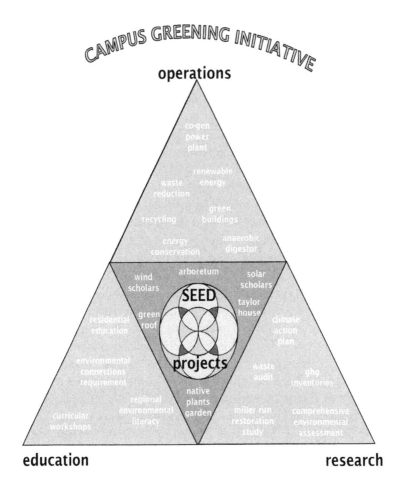

CAMPUS GREENING INITIATIVE

operations

co-gen power plant

renewable energy
waste reduction

green buildings
recycling

energy conservation
anaerobic digestor

wind scholars
arboretum
solar scholars

SEED

taylor house

residential education
green roof
climate action plan

environmental connections requirement

projects

waste audit
ghg inventories

native plants garden

regional environmental literacy

curricular workshops

miller run restoration study
comprehensive environmental assessment

education

research

Bucknell University Environmental Center

Figure 1 Model of Bucknell University Campus Greening Initiative and SEED projects.

In order to work effectively, the SEED Projects each require two basic phases of development: 1) an implementation phase involving an initial investment in research, design, materials, and construction; and 2) an ongoing stewardship phase, involving at least one student, one faculty member, and one staff member to ensure the continued maintenance, monitoring, and study of the system in question.

Table 1 below outlines Bucknell's existing and potential SEED projects, their current status, and stewardship needs. SEED projects are particularly well suited to ENST 230 final projects, which are intended to integrate and synthesize multiple aspects of the course material into a real design proposal of local significance. Several of the projects listed in the table were conceived in this manner. Others began for different reasons and were adopted by the CGI to fit the SEED project model.

Table 1. Existing and Potential SEED Projects as of Fall 2012

Project Name	Status	Description	Stewardship Needs
Solar Scholars	Existing since 2006	Photovoltaic solar arrays at two campus locations, one solar hot water installation, data collection and web-based display system	1-2 faculty, 2 students, 2 staff engineers
Native Plants Garden	Existing since 2006; ongoing	Demonstration garden containing over 50 species of native plants. Ongoing improvements include educational signage and stormwater management features.	1 faculty, 1 student, 1 staff gardener
Bucknell Arboretum	Existing since 2010	Interactive walking trail and database of existing campus trees	2 faculty, 1-2 students, 1 staff arborist, 1 staff web consultant
Wind Scholars	Under development as of summer of 2009	Demonstration scale wind turbine to be designed and constructed on campus	1 faculty, 2 students, 1 staff, 1 outside consultant
Green Roof(s)	Existing since 2010, second roof constructed in 2011	Modular and integrated green roofs constructed at Dana Engineering Bldg.	2 faculty, 1 student, 1 staff grounds supervisor
Green-theme Student Residences	Existing with ongoing program development	Experiential residences for approximately 20 students; includes Taylor House co-op, Solar Modular residence	1-2 faculty, 2 students, 1 staff in residential education
BUEC Rain Garden	Under development	Experimental garden for storm water capture, associated with the BUEC building and grounds	1 faculty, 1 student, 1 staff gardener
Bucknell Landing	Potential	Native riparian buffer plantings with educational signage, at campus access to river	1 faculty, 1 student, 1 staff grounds supervisor
Solar Brigade	Potential	Solar installation at a Bucknell-affiliated health clinic in Nueva Vida, Nicaragua	2-3 faculty, several students, one staff administrator

Most importantly, SEED projects allow students to follow through and implement their design ideas. Perhaps the most successful example of a Bucknell SEED project to date is the demonstration green roof installed on the Dana Engineering Building. Conceived in 2009 as a final project by an ENST 230 student, this modular green roof is now fully instrumented for collection of soil moisture, temperature, and precipitation data, and became the topic of two summer research internships and an honors thesis. This seed project can be said to have "reproduced" or "spread" as it provided a level of comfort and familiarity with green roof technology that paved the way for a second green roof to be constructed on the same building, and a third, much larger green roof to be designed for the University's newest academic building now under construction.

Another very successful seed project emerged from the landscape assessment team of the Comprehensive Environmental Assessment project. Faculty leaders of that team were asked to undertake a biodiversity inventory of the campus as part of their survey. Deciding to focus on trees, these two faculty members involved student interns in mapping, dating, and inventorying all of the mature trees on the campus grounds, at which point it became clear that the University had a sufficiently diverse and well-established tree population to constitute an arboretum. The Bucknell Arboretum has now evolved into an interactive online GIS database and a self-guided tree walk complete with visible labels and accompanying documentation. The Arboretum continues to be the subject of summer research internships by students in the biology and geography programs.

Funding for SEED projects has come from a variety of sources, including outside foundation grants, the Provost's office, the College of Engineering, and individual donors. One particularly vital source of funding for SEED projects at Bucknell has been the McKenna Summer Research Internship Program, which sponsors several environmentally-themed internships each year by providing student interns with a stipend and a small budget for materials. ENST 230 final projects, which are now completed in the fall semester, are tailored toward easy conversion into McKenna internship proposals for the following summer. Depending on student availability, an ENST 230 final project might be developed into a summer internship by its original author, or the project proposal might be handed off to a different student for further development into a summer internship, independent study, or honors thesis.

Connecting the dots: creating a pedagogical campus landscape

If the seeds of campus sustainability are nurtured and allowed to spread, the ultimate result is the creation of a pedagogical campus landscape, a rich environment *in which* and *from which* the entire campus community is able to learn. SEED projects provide an initial step in this direction, but other efforts are involved as well. With the vision of a pedagogical campus landscape in mind, the following goals comprise an overall strategy for the continuation of the Campus Greening Initiative as an integral part of BUEC programming and university sustainability. These have now been incorporated into the CGI's strategic plan:

1. *Continue seeding environmental sustainability campus-wide:* The basic guiding principle of the CGI is to seed environmental sustainability throughout relevant operational and programmatic units of the University in a systemic and self-sustaining manner. This means that the CGI plants and nurtures the seeds initially, while the ultimate responsibility for maintaining the projects lies with the operational and/or programmatic units themselves. Prioritization of projects is based on a number of fluctuating factors including current faculty and student interest, educational potential, availability of resources, and contribution to the overall environmental sustainability of the University.

2. *Provide guidance and support to large-scale collaborative sustainability projects:* As campus-wide interest in sustainability continues to grow, the CGI must play an integral role in guiding, supporting, and facilitating larger scale collaborative and interdisciplinary projects. At Bucknell, these have included restoration of the campus stream, green building design and construction, and residential sustainability education programming.

3. *Advance campus-wide sustainability assessment and communications:* A challenging component of advancing the CGI is keeping the campus community informed and educated on the many projects, programs, and activities that the initiative undertakes. A CGI website has been in existence since the initiative began, but achievements of the initiative have grown to the extent that a broader communications strategy is necessary to advance the "green" reputation of the University to a higher level. A general strategy of the CGI in the years to come is to create a productive partnership with Bucknell Communications to work toward this goal. Additionally, further documentation in the form of an updated environmental assessment is needed. A preliminary step in this direction will involve completing the Sustainability Tracking and Rating System (STARS) survey administered by AASHE as a follow-up to the original assessment completed in 2009.

4. *Create a pedagogical campus landscape:* The ultimate strategic goal of the CGI in the years to come is to create a campus landscape that teaches environmental sustainability by example. All of the above strategic goals feed into an ultimate vision of a campus that speaks to its students, faculty, staff, and community about the University's commitment to environmental stewardship. Equally as important is that this goal be achieved in the spirit of learning, experimentation, and academic excellence. A pedagogical campus landscape would integrate SEED projects, campus planning, sustainability communications, and curriculum in a way that would communicate an obvious emphasis on values of environmental sustainability to all those who experience Bucknell University.

Concluding thoughts: reflections on the challenges of transforming the campus landscape

As efforts toward creating a pedagogical landscape ensue at Bucknell, several dynamics are in play. Among a select group of faculty, students, and staff who have become champions of sustainability, there is great enthusiasm to advance the prospect of a "living learning laboratory," in which the entire campus makes a transition to learning by example, experience, and doing. The goal of a pedagogical landscape fits squarely into this effort, and SEED projects provide successful examples on which to build future momentum. At the same time, there are distinct attitudinal barriers that will need to be addressed and overcome before this seemingly noble effort takes root in the larger campus culture.

As noted over a decade ago by Leith Sharp, pioneer in Harvard University's sustainability programs, the barriers to creating a sustainable campus are often a result of a historical disconnection between the operational side of the university (administrative and support staff) and the academic side of the university (faculty and students). Although the two complement each other, they seldom collaborate. For instance, the operational side of the university works on a distinctly different calendar than the academic side, adhering to different work schedules and different deadlines than the academic side. The operational side of the university is concerned with order, efficiency, aesthetic appeal, and profitability, while the academic side is concerned with learning objectives, original publications, and the pursuit of open-ended questions. Historically, there has been a distinct division between these two university sectors, with the operational side supporting the academic side, but not intermingling with it. A pedagogical landscape, or living learning laboratory, turns this historic division on its head by requiring the two sides of the university to work in synchronicity to achieve common goals. SEED projects have become the test bed for these collaborations at Bucknell, and several have proven their viability. The next step, and larger challenge, is for champions of sustainability to persist in bridging the gap between operations and academics, so as to establish an institutional environment in which these types of projects can grow, replicate, flourish, and eventually become the rule of campus culture rather than the exception.

Works Cited

El-Mogazi, Dina, ed. *A Comprehensive Environmental Assessment of Bucknell University.* Bucknell University, 2009. Web.

McDonough, William, and Michael Braungart. *Cradle to CradleRemaking the Way We Make Things.* New York, NY: North Point Press, 2002. Print.

McHarg, Ian L. *Design with Nature.* Garden City, NY: Natural History Press, 1969. Print.

Sector Notebooks. Environmental Protection Agency. Web.

Sharp, Leith. "Green Campuses: The Road from Little Victories to Systemic Transformation." *International Journal of Sustainability in Higher Education* 3.2 (2002): 128-145. Print.

Van der Ryn, Sim, and Stuart Cowan. *Ecological Design.* 10th Anniversary Edition. Washington, DC: Island Press, 2006. Print.

Reflections from a Classroom that Uses the Campus as a Sustainability Teaching Tool

Suzanne Savanick Hansen, Macalester College

Abstract: Using the buildings and grounds of a college campus as a sustainability educational tool can improve pedagogy and connect students to useful, real-world projects. This essay reviews the successes and challenges of using the campus as a teaching tool at Carleton College and Macalester College. The benefits of campus projects include: a) connecting students with the opportunity to apply theoretical frameworks to practical problems and b) developing meaningful recommendations with imperfect information. Challenges include selecting practical topics and needing extra support when students interview staff and vendors. If done well, student papers can be useful in both moving the campus towards sustainability and improving sustainability pedagogy.

Suzanne Savanick Hansen is the Sustainability Manager at Macalester College. Previous publications on campus sustainability include "Case Study for Evaluating Campus Sustainability: Nitrogen Balance for the University of Minnesota," published in *Urban Ecosystems*; "Using the Campus Nitrogen Budget to Teach about the Nitrogen Cycle" in the *Journal of Geoscience Education*; and "Using a Class to Conduct a Carbon Inventory" in the *International Journal of Sustainability in Higher Education*. She also developed a website module for geoscience faculty looking to use the campus as a teaching tool, "Campus-Based Learning" for the Science Education Resource Center. She earned her Ph.D. in conservation biology from the University of Minnesota, a master's degree in environmental management from Duke University, and a bachelor's degree in geology from Carleton College.

I first heard about using the campus as a teaching tool when I was a graduate student attending a conference where David Orr from Oberlin College spoke about campus sustainability. His idea of using the buildings and grounds of a campus as a tool for teaching resonated with me. Traditionally, campuses are locations for classes, but the buildings and grounds are a mere backdrop. Nevertheless, college buildings and grounds are hidden teaching tools, inadvertently teaching that conservation of campus electricity, water, and heat are not important (Orr, "Architecture as Pedagogy," "Architecture as Pedagogy II," and *The Nature of Design: Ecology, Culture, and Human Intention*). However, faculty have an opportunity to use buildings and grounds as sustainability teaching tools.

In my experience, using the campus as a teaching tool offers the opportunity for students to engage with real-world projects in a local setting. These projects have provided me with pedagogical and practical benefits, but these projects also come with challenges. In what follows, I offer a reflection of my teaching experiences and describe opportunities for faculty teaching humanities and social science classes to connect with campus sustainability projects. In addition, I share sustainability resources I typically promote to faculty at Macalester College.

My experience

Macalester College signed the American College and University Presidents' Climate Commitment (ACUPCC) in 2007 and my position was created in 2008, in part to shepherd the process of upholding this commitment. The ACUPCC requires each school to annually track greenhouse gas emissions, create a plan to reduce greenhouse gas emissions, and include climate neutrality and sustainability as part of the educational experiences for all students ("American College & University Presidents' Climate Commitment"). As part of my job, I promote the use of campus as a teaching tool for faculty and also teach (or co-teach) classes for the Environmental Studies department.

My experience using the campus as a teaching tool predates the ACUPCC and the corresponding increase in sustainability officer positions. As a graduate student at the University of Minnesota, I coordinated the Sustainable Campus Initiative; my job was to facilitate the use of campus buildings and grounds as a sustainability teaching tool. I worked with faculty and students to develop an environmental assessment of the University and restore a campus wetland. Over the following ten years, I taught three classes at Carleton College and four classes at Macalester College. In both settings, class projects were campus-based and sustainability-focused (Table 1).

At Carleton College, I also worked for the Science Education Resource Center, where I developed pedagogical websites, including "Campus-based Learning," which describes step-by-step how to use the campus as a sustainability teaching tool. Intended for geoscience faculty, the material can be adapted to other fields (Savanick). I have also recently advised students' independent study projects on campus energy use, waste reduction, and food.

Table 1: Classes Using the Campus as a Teaching Tool

Year	Class	School	Class Project	Campus Field Trip Locations
2002	Environment and Technology Studies Junior Colloquium	Carleton College	Practical campus greening projects in small groups	No formal field trips
2005	Environment and Technology Studies Junior Colloquium	Carleton College	Drafted potential environmental policy for the college	Steam plant Campus food service
2006	Environment and Technology Studies Junior Colloquium	Carleton College	Developed college sustainability assessment	Steam plant Campus food service
2008	Environmental Studies Senior Seminar	Macalester College	Greenhouse gas emissions inventory for ACUPCC	Steam plant Campus food service Mechanical room of science building
2009	Environmental Studies Senior Seminar	Macalester College	Developed recommendations for college Climate Action Plan	Steam plant Campus food service
2010	Environmental Studies Senior Seminar	Macalester College	Researched topics related to campus Zero Waste goal in small groups	E-waste recycler Landfill Campus food service Waste sort

Benefits of using the campus as a teaching tool

Using the campus as a teaching tool has benefitted my classes by allowing students to apply theoretical frameworks to practical sustainability problems. In addition, field trips on the campus allow students to understand the campus in a hands-on way and to develop change-agent skills that will be useful in later careers. The approach is also practical.

Real world projects

In my experience, students find the idea of working on a real-world project engaging. A survey of Carleton College students indicated those who took a course with a significant hands-on component found that, even five years later, it had a huge impact on both their academic and personal development (Savanick, Strong, and Manning). In 2008, during the first senior seminar I co-taught at Macalester College, a course survey reported that students were highly motivated by a useful and tangible accomplishment that also provided an opportunity to gain useful skills (Wells, Savanick, and Manning). Class evaluations of subsequent classes showed the same trend; students wanted classwork to be useful and liked applying theoretical frameworks to practical projects.

These real projects also gave students experience with "messy" data and forced them to make decisions based on imperfect information. Handling "less-than-perfect" data was one of the largest challenges for a class that calculated the college's greenhouse gas emissions for every year from 1988 to 2007 (Wells, Savanick, and Manning). These students learned to state their assumptions and craft recommendations, despite the challenges with data sets. All of the students will use this skill sometime later in their careers.

These "real world" projects had potential for implementation on campus. The most powerful projects were those which students could get established immediately. For example, the students at Carleton College who proposed and succeeded in getting a place in the library to recycle ink jet cartridges were more satisfied with their project than students who surveyed storm water projects on campus, but didn't implement anything on the grounds. In addition, one of the most excited groups in the Macalester College 2010 senior seminar successfully worked with a community group to obtain compost bins for students living off campus. Another Macalester College student analyzed energy data from the college EcoHouse and found a spike of energy use in the summer, when no one lived in the building. He discovered an old dehumidifier in the basement that had been running nonstop for months. Due to this observation, a new energy star dehumidifier with a humidistat was purchased for the house (Francis). The student was thus sufficiently inspired to use campus energy data in his capstone research.

Field trips

After I co-organized a faculty development seminar on sustainability at St. Olaf College for Carleton and St. Olaf faculty, and took faculty on campus field trips, I included similar campus field trips in my classes. The field trips followed the resource flows of energy or food across the campus. For instance, in the dining hall, we started at the loading dock, looked at food storage and discussed sources of food eaten in the dining hall, checked out the prep kitchen and service counters, and, finally, took a peek at the dish room, food waste, recycling, and trash. Following a resource flow across the campus gave the field trip a structure and gave the participants a deeper understanding of the network of people and natural resources needed to provide food that is eaten in the college dining hall. All the campus field trips produced reactions such as, "I never thought about how the food was prepared here" and "Wow! That's a lot of food waste!"

The field trips affected me, too. When I first led a class through the steam plant at Carleton College, I felt as if I had slid down Alice in Wonderland's hole and found myself in a different universe. I studied at Carleton for four years and worked on staff for two years, but had never given any thought to the smoke stack behind the old brick building. I had never once wondered how the buildings were heated and/ or how three huge boilers burn natural gas and fuel oil to keep the campus buildings warm enough to survive without our winter coats and jackets in the frigid Minnesota winter! My students seemed as shocked as I was to see the brightly colored pipes that keep us warm, and look at the blue flames in the small peephole in front of the boiler. Seeing the steam plant showed me (and my students) what infrastructure is needed for my own comfort. My understanding of the College, and our society more broadly, changed that day. I noticed how connected all of us are, but how few of us really notice the connections. All of us unconsciously depend on a web of natural and social resources that allows us to spend time indoors (writing essays, for instance) during winter instead of freezing. The fuels used to create electricity and indoor heat all create greenhouse gas emissions, but few of us see the process.

Change agent skills

Campuses also offer a unique opportunity for students to practice their change agent skills. I often tell students on our sustainability tours to "never underestimate the potential for a student project on a campus, particularly if the project saves money and the environment." At Macalester, students were deeply involved with nearly all of our major sustainability efforts. Our wind turbine, green roofs, prairie, rain garden, and urban chickens all started from student projects. Students advocated for the signing of the Talloires Declaration, ACUPCC, Commitment to Sustainable Practices of Higher Education Institutions on the Occasion of the United Nations Conference on Sustainable Development, and the Real Food Challenge. Some of these student projects started as or spawned academic papers or projects. For example, one of our raingardens was a class project, and a green roof was used as a guide for an academic research project. The standard sustainability tour document that is widely used in my office was an expansion of a class project ("Macalester Sustainability Tour"). At Carleton College, a class originally researched the potential for wind energy in the surrounding farmland. The project eventually became the first large scale wind turbine at a college in the United States (Savanick, Strong, and Manning).

Using the campus as a teaching tool offers a way for more faculty and staff to guide student energy and enthusiasm toward useful projects that are beyond the scope or ability of the staff. Students can write proposals, gain project support, find funding, and even implement sustainability projects. The college gets better student projects and the students get real-world experience that could be replicated outside the college. All of our students will need to think critically and creatively to solve our current and upcoming world problems. If they can learn some of these skills as part of their academic experiences, they will be better suited for future challenges.

Practical Benefits

Using the campus as a teaching tool offers pedagogical benefits, but this approach is also practical. Every campus has buildings, and these buildings need to be heated or cooled. Energy and water use is often relatively easy to obtain from utility bills. Campus facilities staff can serve as class speakers. Campus field trips can also be completed in a regular class period and thus not require extra time or expense for transportation.

Challenges

Although using the campus as teaching tool offers clear benefits, the approach also includes challenges. I find that practical topic selection remains the biggest challenge, followed by group dynamics, non-traditional research needs, and the need for more project management support.

Topic Selection

The topic selected for a large research project is crucially important. A poor or impractical topic will inevitably lead to frustration and a less than useful final project. Projects are one of two types: "large, comprehensive projects" or small, "themed" projects. The large, comprehensive projects have one overarching project and all small groups contribute a section of a large document. The large, comprehensive approach tends to be used when a large project needs to be done and all aspects need to be covered and one document is produced, i.e. a greenhouse gas emissions inventory or a sustainability assessment of a college (Wells, Savanick, and Manning; Savanick, "Environmental Assessment Course"). These projects tend to be more useful from a staff point of view, but have less flexibility for students to research their own special interests.

The smaller, "themed" projects have independent groups working on the same issue, but do not need to be incorporated in the same document. Students research projects under an overall theme, such as campus sustainability or campus waste, and present their findings. The students have more choice over their topic and this type of class tends to diminish some of the student frustration with topic selection. However, themed projects tend to be less useful to the college staff, as students may be very interested in projects that are not high priorities for the college.

In the required classes I taught, a small group of students inevitably did not like the overall topic. I found this reaction most often in large, comprehensive projects where all topics needed to be covered and someone ended up with their second or third choice. For example, in one class a baseline sustainability assessment needed to have all of its subtopics covered. For some of the science-focused students, collecting data on living wages and health benefits seemed odd, as they did not fully understand that sustainability includes environmental, social, and economic aspects. After several discussions with the students involved, they came away with a more comprehensive view of sustainability. In subsequent classes, I added more framing in the beginning of the class to make these connections more obvious. To blunt some criticism of the topic, the Environmental Studies department at Macalester College polls the junior class on possible senior seminar topics.

In addition, I have often found that some students get an idea of what they want their outcome to be at the outset of the project, prior to discussing their idea with staff members. This is frustrating for everyone involved. When their project(s) turned out to be impractical, the students were disappointed and their project(s) ended up less useful for staff. Requiring a "needs assessment" meeting with key staff early in the project curtails this problem. Another approach is to pre-select topics for students. A colleague at the University of Michigan, who teaches a class similar to mine, uses this approach with his students; in his classes, a group can research another topic, but need to develop an extensive proposal (Shriberg). I am considering this approach for my next class.

In addition, if student campus projects are poorly archived, then students can repeat the same project several times. Carleton College had a series of very similar composting projects because the students didn't know that a previous class had researched the same questions. This also happens when there is one "hot topic" for the students that everyone wants to research. At Macalester College, my "Cities, Sustainability, and the Campus" class had two groups working on different aspects of composting that continually needed to make sure that they were not asking the same staff people the same questions twice.

Groups

Group projects allow students to dig deeply into topics, collaborate with each other, and lower the amount of time needed for faculty to grade and manage the topics. However, group projects can be a logistical, communications, and grading challenge. At Carleton and Macalester, all of the students live on or near campus, so group projects that require time outside of class are possible, but students' schedules tend to conflict. I found that allowing some in-class time is necessary to organize these projects and meet with me.

I had a surprisingly low number of serious group issues, but some group experiences ended up not as positive as was hoped for. One of my students at Macalester suggested a group contract used by a colleague and I adapted it for my next class. The document is available through the Macalester College Sustainability Office. Clear expectations laid out in the contract helped students talk about expectations of each other and what process to follow if a group member does not fulfill their role.

The largest challenge I found was appropriately grading group work. To get a sense of individual input on the group project, I use a peer survey to have the students evaluate each other. The survey is available in "Campus Based Learning" (Savanick). The students' insights on their peers appeared nearly always honest and realistic, and the different group members seemed to write the same things. I learned more about the internal dynamics and individual efforts than I would have otherwise.

Non-traditional research

Students often find projects that are investigative in nature to be quite challenging, as they tend to be uncomfortable with open-ended questions without a set answer. The types of research required of campus sustainability projects is nearly all non-traditional research. This type of project requires students to meet with staff people and talk on the phone to vendors. My students are often booked so solid during the day that finding a time to meet with a staff person during business hours can be a challenge. In addition, I have found that students will often give up after a single attempted email. They often do not realize that staff people are not on student schedules and a staff person is not likely to answer an email late on a Friday night or first thing on Monday morning.

I make sure to mention that students need to give themselves ample time for this type of non-traditional research. I also try to warn staff ahead of time, if possible. Prior to the senior seminar that would draft the first college greenhouse gas emissions inventory, my co-instructor and I met with the Director of Facilities Services. We developed a consistent point of contact for students looking for data. We also tried to anticipate what data would be needed. This helped maintain a good working relationship with the Facilities Services staff and kept frustration down for everyone involved (Wells, Savanick, and Manning).

Deadlines

Despite what I thought were an appropriate number of deadlines, I repeatedly found that students need more "scaffolding" and intermediate deadlines than I anticipated. I firmly believe that students need to develop their own project management schedules, but most do not have the tools to do that, and deadlines in the syllabus are often not sufficient. In my last class, I had students develop a project management schedule, adapted from a corporate trainer colleague, available from: http://www.macalester. edu/sustainability/currriculumresources/incorpsustain.html   (MacalesterCollege

Sustainability Office). Since then, my independent study students also used this tool to help organize their time. The structure seems to help students who have not yet organized a very large project.

In one of the classes, I brought in some outside reviewers from the community who critiqued the students' work at the mid-term point. This outside review increased the importance of the project, helped the students focus the rest of their projects, and aided in keeping the students accountable.

Recommendations

I find that students are often intimidated by the idea of making recommendations. Most students do not write strong enough recommendations and do not back up their ideas sufficiently. Often they do not believe they have enough background to make recommendations and doubt that anyone will listen to their advice, even when the project is framed as offering recommendations to decision-makers. In fact, at the end of their research, the students are the resident experts on their topics and, if the topic interests staff with authority, there is a possibility of implementation.

Having a clear audience for their report helps lessen hesitancy and lack of confidence. Where possible, I tried to get the students to present directly to the Sustainability Advisory Committee or any staff who can implement their recommendations. At Carleton and Macalester Colleges, I invited the college presidents and other senior staff to meet with the classes and talk about why sustainability is important to the college. This helps students frame their recommendations and has the added bonus of increasing importance of class work in the eyes of the students.

Opportunities for Social Science and Humanities Classes

Often campus sustainability issues get stereotyped as "science" issues, but sustainability by definition includes social and economic issues, as well as environmental issues. Social science and humanities frequently offer better tools for handling social change and communication issues than does traditional science—though these tools are underutilized in campus sustainability. The often overlooked educational requirements of the ACUPCC lend themselves particularly well to communication and behavior change projects for social science and humanities classes. In fact, behavior change, social justice, and policy are particularly fruitful topics for the social sciences and humanities to address.

Changing human behavior requires more than statistics, and the humanities have a special role in communicating ideas that cannot be expressed by charts or statistics. At Macalester College, for example, a student in a humanities class created a "Trash Tree," made out of recyclable materials incorrectly thrown in the trash. This tree is still used five years later as a visual representation of how to recycle. In addition, students in the library created a tower of paper representing the amount of paper used in the library computer lab. The image of the towering stack is more influential than merely presenting the number of sheets of paper printed in the library.

Social sciences also offer tools for campus sustainability projects. The Psychology for Sustainable Behavior Class at Macalester College has used campus projects as class projects for a number of years. Students, for example, developed a pilot project for composting on campus and researched how well individuals followed the directions on the bins. Their research is currently used to inform the new composting program on campus. Another group surveyed students about "Clean Plate Days" in the dining hall and recommended changes to the program based on student feedback.

In addition, social justice is one of the three pillars of sustainability, but one that has less common understanding. Social science and humanities faculty have numerous opportunities to lead in this area. One of the current leaders in this area is Pomona College in Claremont, California; it has been successful in explicitly linking environmental justice and sustainability in its Sustainability Action Plan, by calling out environmental justice as a key issue (President's Advisory Committee on Sustainability and Pomona College Sustainability Integration Office). Many projects also have an opportunity for changing campus policy. This is an area ripe with leadership opportunities. Policy changes can use well-developed arguments and presentations from students. Many of our campus sustainability projects (ex: wind turbine, green roofs, and rain garden) started as student initiatives. Changing campus policy is a good example where students learn the important change agent skills discussed earlier.

Support for Faculty

To support teaching of climate and sustainability issues in classes, I consolidated website resources available for faculty on the Macalester Sustainability website, available at http://www.macalester.edu/sustainability/currriculumresources/incorpsustain.html (Macalester College Sustainability Office). Included on the website is a link to "Campus-Based Learning," a website module in the Science Education Resource Center that describes, step-by-step, how to use the campus as a teaching tool (Savanick, "Campus-Based Learning"). In addition, the website includes resources such as the Piedmont Project, a faculty development seminar from Emory University that has been replicated in many locations. At the time of this writing, projects or syllabi were listed from seventy humanities classes and twenty-eight social science courses (http://anthropology.emory.edu/piedmontproject/). The website also includes the Disciplinary Associations Network for Sustainability, with resources by discipline related to sustainability education, as well as links to Minnesota-specific sustainability data.

The Association for the Advancement for Sustainability in Higher Education (AASHE) also has a section on their website for education and research resources that includes a listing of courses focusing on campus sustainability, sustainability-related course syllabi, and general information (Association for the Advancement of Sustainability in Higher Education). These resources are available for anyone at AASSHE member schools.

Another recent resource for faculty on campuses looking to connect construction with education is the United States Green Building Council's Center for Green Schools resources for a higher education, available at http://centerforgreenschools.org/green-campus.aspx. If your school is building a Leadership in Energy and Environmental Design (LEED) building, this curriculum can assist in setting up educational activities ("Center for Green Schools").

One resource of particular use to social science and humanities faculty is Jim Farrell's book, *The Nature of College*. The book is based on the experiences of his Campus Ecology class at St. Olaf College. The book highlights campus culture as a subset of American culture, and the hidden ways that college culture affects environmental, social and economic sustainability.

Conclusion

Using the campus as a teaching tool can improve pedagogy without adding a budget or time for off-campus field trips. I have found that students engage with real-world projects and campus field trips. This type of class is not without challenges, but pedagogical and sustainability benefits outweigh them.

Social sciences and humanities have ample opportunities to connect with campus sustainability projects. Tools from social sciences and humanities may be better suited for behavior change initiatives than those in traditional science courses. If done well, sustainability class projects can move the campus towards sustainability and connect local issues with global sustainability challenges.

Using the campus as a teaching tool is part of a liberal education, the kind of education we need if our society is to make the changes needed for a sustainable future. This kind of education cannot be a pet project of one faculty member or one sustainability staff person. We don't need more well-educated people who earn higher salaries and create more environmental impacts. We need people who can create a sustainable future. To meet that need, let us start using the creative talents of our students to create a more sustainable campus, one that can serve as a model for a more sustainable world.

Works Cited

"American College & University Presidents' Climate Commitment." Web.

Association for the Advancement of Sustainability in Higher Education. "Resources on Sustainability Curriculum." Web.

"Center for Green Schools." The Center for Green Schools. Web.

Farrell, James. *The Nature of College*. Minneapolis, MN: Milkweed Editions, 2010. Web.

Francis, Ben. *Energy Efficiency: Energy Use of the Eco House*. Macalester College Independent Study Project, 2011.

Macalester College Sustainability Office. "Curriculum Resources Incorporating Sustainability." 2012. Web.

"Macalester Sustainability Tour." Macalester University. Web.

Orr, David. "Architecture as Pedagogy." *Conservation Biology* 7.2 (1993): 226–228. Print.

---. "Architecture as Pedagogy II." *Conservation Biology* 11.3 (1997): 597–600. Print.

---. *The Nature of Design: Ecology, Culture, and Human Intention.* New York, NY: Oxford University Press, 2002. Web.

President's Advisory Committee on Sustainability and Pomona College Sustainability Integration Office. *Pomona College Sustainability Action Plan.* 2011. Print.

Savanick, Suzanne. "Campus-Based Learning." *Campus-Based Learning.* 2007. Web.

---. "Environmental Assessment Course." *Environmental Assessment Course.* 2001. Web.

Savanick, Suzanne, Richard Strong, and Christie Manning. "Explicitly Linking Pedagogy and Facilities to Campus Sustainability: Lessons from Carleton College and the University of Minnesota." *Environmental Education Research* 14.6 (2008): 667–679. Print.

Shriberg, Mike. "Graham Institute: U-M Campus Course." Web.

Wells, Christopher W., Suzanne Savanick, and Christie Manning. "Using a Class to Conduct a Carbon Inventory: A Case Study with Practical Results at Macalester College." *International Journal of Sustainability in Higher Education* 10.3 (2009): 228–238. Web.

Appendix A

COURSE SCHEDULE: PART ONE

WEEK ONE
January 17   Introductions to each other and to the course
January 19   Historical Perspectives on Sustainability
                                Readings: Merchant, "Mining the Earth's Womb."

WEEK TWO
January 24   Geographical Perspectives on Sustainability
                                Readings: Mather and Sdasyuk, *Global Change:*
                                Geographical Perspectives, Ch. 2
January 26   Non-Sustainable Practices and Collapse: Three
                                Ancient Examples

WEEK THREE
January 31   Terrestrial Ecosystems: The Basis for Environmental
                                Productivity
                                Readings: *Global Change, Ch. 2*
February 2   Population Trends—Globalization – Sustainability
                                Readings: Population Reference Bureau Report

WEEK FOUR
February 7   Abrupt Climate Change (*reaction paper due in class)
                                Readings: Galgano, F. A., 2011. *An Environmental*
                                Security Analysis of Abrupt Climate Change Scenarios.
                                International Handbook of Military Geography, Vol.
                                2. Proceedings of the 8th International Conference on
                                Military Geosciences, Vienna, Austria, 15 – 19 June 2009:
                                196 – 208.
February 9   Sustainability, Agriculture, and Ethics (Mark Graham)

WEEK FIVE
February 14   Sustainability and Cities (Ellen Stroud, Bryn Mawr College)
February 16   Sustainability and Engineering I (Andrea Welker)

WEEK SIX
February 21   Sustainability and Engineering II (Andrea Welker)
                                Readings: Heinberg and Lerch, *The Post-Carbon Reader-*
                                Part Ten
February 23   Sustainability, Religion, and Justice

WEEK SEVEN
February 28   Local sustainability case study 1: Chester, PA
March 1   Mid-term Essays due in class

WEEK EIGHT
SPRING BREAK: Rest, Relax, Recuperate, Take a long walk in the woods

COURSE SCHEDULE: PART TWO

WEEK NINE
March 13   Library Information Session: Falvey Ground Floor
March 15   Local sustainability case study 2– Green Building
                                     Tour, Newtown Sq., PA

WEEK TEN
March 20   Sustainability and the Law
                                     Readings: *Post-Carbon Reader*-Part Two
March 22   Global sustainability case study I -- Brazil

WEEK ELEVEN
March 27   Sustainability and Health (Ruth McDermott Levy)
                                     Readings: *Post-Carbon Reader* -Part Thirteen
March 29   Sustainability and Energy (Krakowka)
                                     Readings: *Post-Carbon Reader*-Part Eight

WEEK TWELVE
April 3   Global sustainability case study II – China
                                     (*reaction paper due in class)
                                   Readings: Economy, *The River Runs Black, Ch. 1*
April 5   Easter Break

WEEK THIRTEEN
April 10   Economics of sustainability I: Green Business ethics
                                 (Jonathan Doh)
                                 Readings: tba
April 12   GIS Lab Session

WEEK FOURTEEN
April 17   Economics of sustainability III: Green Science for better
                                 living   (Ross Lee)
April 19   No Class: Attend Earth Day Keynote Lecture and events

WEEK FIFTEEN
April 24   Research consultations
April 26   Research presentations

WEEK SIXTEEN
May 1   No Class
May 3   Research Presentations continued
                                 ***All papers due in class

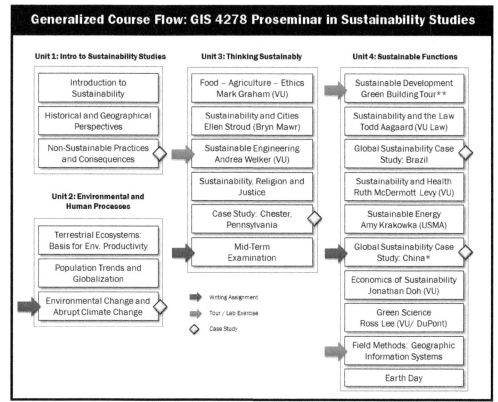

Figure 1. GIS 4278 Course Flow.

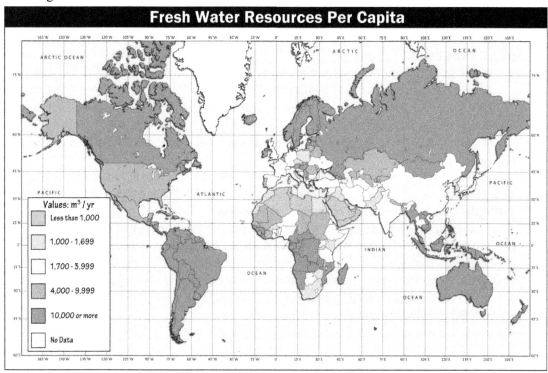

Figure 2. Water scarcity and stress. After Gleick (1993). Cartography by the authors

GIS 4278: Introduction to Sustainability Studies Spring 2012
Dr. Frank Galgano/Dr. Paul Rosier
Research Paper Guidelines
What: Research Paper
Why: To give you an opportunity to explore a topic of your choice. Plus, it will sharpen your research skills, which will come in handy in other courses and in real life.
When due: Not for awhile but soon enough (May 3)
How: Choose a topic to explore, develop a bibliography with the help of the reference librarian in Falvey (jutta.seibert@villanova.edu), look at a variety of sources including newspaper articles (the *New York Times* is available online), scholarly articles, books, and primary documents if available (be sure to utilize Jutta's course page: http://library.villanova.edu/research/course-guides/pro-seminar-in-sustainability-studies/). Use of the web is not prohibited but use the web judiciously and not exclusively. <u>At the most</u>, web sources should constitute 25% of your sources; your bibliography should include roughly 10-12 different sources.
How Long?   13-15 pages (15 pages max)
Possible topics:
Biographical essay of environmentalists
Sustainability social movements
Geographically specific case studies, i.e. China, India, Brazil, etc.
Urban sustainability issues/case studies
Political issues i.e. International Environmental forums such as Kyoto, Rio de Janeiro
Climate justice issues
These are suggested topics but by no means the only ones. We encourage each of you to determine your particular interest and to develop an appropriate research focus.

GIS 4278: Proseminar in Sustainability Studies
REACTION PAPER 1 (5 pts)
>   Gagosian, R. B. 2003. Abrupt Climate Change: Should We Be Worried? World Economic Forum, Davos, Switzerland, 27 January 2003
>   Galgano, F. A., 2011. *An Environmental Security Analysis of Abrupt Climate Change Scenarios*. In, <u>International Handbook of Military</u> Geography, Vol. 2, (eds.), Häusler, R., and Mang, R., Vienna, Austria: AV+Astoria Druckentrum GmbH, pp. 196 – 209.

Assignment:
According to the Gagosian paper, the U.S. National Academy of Sciences indicated, "available evidence suggests that abrupt climate changes are not only possible but likely in the future, potentially with large impacts on ecosystems and societies."
>   1) Digest this quote and provide a critical analysis based on your reading of the two papers provided for this lesson. As part of your analysis, discuss the evidence that support the abrupt climate change scenario, and how this scenario differs from the accepted and publicized models for climate change (i.e., gradual global warming over the next nine decades).
>   2) Given the evidence in these papers, how might an abrupt climate change affect regional and global sustainability?

Administrative Requirements: not more than 3-4 pages; due in class 21 February, 2012

REACTION PAPER 2 (5 pts.)

Sources to be used:

1)Death of Huai River (book chapter)

2)China: Viewing Cable (U.S. State Dept. cable)

3)China's Future is Drying Up (newspaper article)

4) 1 OTHER ARTICLE/ESSAY of your choice (indicate the source and where you found it)

Assignment:

Employing course themes and concepts (including recent ones of law and health), assess China's environmental challenges and crises and discuss their implications for Chinese and global sustainability, using the assigned readings and 1 additional source that you locate, which should offer insight into these challenges and crises and implications.

Administrative Requirements: not more than 3-4 pages; due in class 2 April, 2012

Appendix B

Course Syllabus, 2012

Fall 2012

SOCI 304/ENST 302: Environmental Issues—Rice into the Future

Instructors: Professors Elizabeth Long and Richard Johnson

Course Overview

Inspired by the campus greening movement, this class allows students to engage in environmental issues and possible solutions in a tangible way at Rice.

Learning Outcomes

Students will be introduced to the concept of sustainability and to a general framework for understanding the impact of humans on the environment. They will also be introduced to the environmental movement at large, and more specifically to the campus environmental movement. Students will learn how to plan, implement, and assess the effectiveness of environmental change via a group project using the Rice campus as their laboratory. Through a series of readings, students will be exposed to selected broad environmental topics, and as part of their group project will be challenged to pursue a narrower set of subject-specific readings and research and to demonstrate their understanding of the subject material.

This course should not be confused with a comprehensive introduction to environmental studies or environmental sciences.

Overview of Assignments

Almost all of the graded work in the class is connected to the group project experience. Each project group will submit:

- a detailed project plan in late September describing the goals, timeline, and environmental justification for the project;
- a topical research paper in October thematically related to the final project with extensive benchmarking of other universities, accompanied by a graded in-class presentation.
- a final report due on the last day of classes, accompanied by a graded in-class presentation.

Students will be required to evaluate their team members' performance and their own performance on the project both midway through the course and after completion of the final project. While the evaluations themselves are not graded, they are used to calculate the individual performance grade of each team member. Therefore, failure to submit evaluations (or submission of unhelpful evaluations) will result in a penalty on the final course grade. We will also require students to post brief responses and reactions to certain assigned course materials via the course blog. We reserve the right to administer pop quizzes to further assess student understanding of course readings and lectures. There is no final exam.

Grading

Each assignment will be reviewed by both instructors as well as the teaching assistant. This helps to ensure that students receive consistent and balanced grading. However, this approach adds time to the grading process. We request and appreciate your patience regarding turn-around time for grading.

Project Plan:	5 points
Green Campus Research Report:	20 points
Green Campus Research Report Presentation:	5 points
Project Final Report:	30 points
Project Final Presentation:	10 points
Project Individual Performance:	25 points
Blog responses to readings:	5 points
Total points:	100

Attendance is mandatory. If you anticipate missing a class, please send advance notice to both instructors as well as to the teaching assistant. We reserve the right to adjust your grade based on attendance and class participation. In particular, we reserve the right to adjust your grade if you are found to be using your laptop or other electronic devices to engage in web-surfing, texting, social networking, etc. that is unrelated to the class. We also reserve the right to change the weighting of how grades are calculated, as well as the number of assignments. This is a dynamic and flexible syllabus, subject to change.

Please be advised that this class relies heavily upon your ability to work on a project team. As such, we grade your individual performance based in part on evaluations provided by your peers. Further, please note that your performance may impact the grades of others. If you intend to take this class using a pass/fail option, please think carefully and selflessly about your obligations to your classmates. We have high expectations for your level of commitment to this class and are not unwilling to fail a student who does not deserve to pass.

Any student with a documented disability needing academic adjustments or accommodations is requested to contact the instructors during the first two weeks of class. All discussions will remain confidential. Students with disabilities should also contact Disability Support Services in the Ley Student Center.

Course Texts

Required texts:
- Guha, Ramachandra. *Environmentalism: A Global History*. New York: Longman, 2000.
- Pollan, Michael. *The Omnivore's Dilemma: A Natural History of Four Meals*. New York: Penguin Press, 2006.

Most of the course readings will be made available via OWL-Space. However, the Ramachandra Guha and Michael Pollan readings will not be placed online.

Contacts

Elizabeth Long, elong@rice.edu, x3483
Richard Johnson, rrj@rice.edu, x5003
Andrea Galindo, teaching assistant cses@rice.edu, x5736

Schedule

Week 1 – Introduction

Tuesday, August 21ˢᵗ: Course Introduction

Students will learn about the course, and will participate in a group exercise to assess perceived environmental strengths, weaknesses, and attitudes at Rice.

Thursday, August 23ʳᵈ: What is Sustainability?

Prof. Johnson will provide an overview of the concept of sustainability and a general framework for understanding the impact of humans on the environment.

Required reading:
- Brown, Lester R. "On the Edge." In *World on the Edge: How to Prevent Environmental and Economic Collapse*, 3-18. New York: W.W. Norton & Company, 2011. http://www.earth-policy.org/images/uploads/book_files/wotebook.pdf
- McDonough, William and Michael Braungart. "A Word of Abundance." *Interfaces* 30:3 (2000): 55-65.
- Global Footprint Network. "Footprint Basics – Overview." Last modified April 22, 2011. http://www.footprintnetwork.org/en/index.php/GFN/page/footprint_basics_ overview/

Required viewing:
- Dr. Albert A. Bartlett. "Arithmetic, Population, and Energy." View all 8 parts of his lecture at http://www.youtube.com/view_play_list?p=6A1FD147A45EF50D
  - Blog Response, due at noon on 8/23:
    - How would Dr. Bartlett respond to McDonough/Braungart, and vice versa?

Required Exercise:
- Go to http://www.footprintnetwork.org/en/index.php/GFN/page/calculators/ and calculate your ecological footprint using the footprint calculator. Record how many global acres of the Earth's productive area are necessary to support your lifestyle, and how many Planet Earths we would need if everyone lived and consumed like you. Be prepared to share these numbers in class.

Week 2 – Setting the Context

Tuesday, August 28ᵗʰ: The Environmental Movement

Prof. Long will introduce the concept of a social movement and ways of thinking about different social movements. She will then outline the history of the environmental movement.

Required reading:
- Goodwin, Jeff and James M. Jasper. "Editors' Introduction." In *The Social Movements Reader: Cases and Concepts*, 3-7. Lanham, MD: Rowman & Littlefield, 2004.
- Hawken, Paul. "The Beginning," "Blessed Unrest," and "Restoration." In *Blessed Unrest*, 1-8, 9-26, 166-190. New York: Viking, 2007.
- Guha, Ramachandra. "Part II: Environmentalism's Second Wave." In *Environmentalism: A Global History*, 63-145. New York: Longman, 2000.

- Johnson, Richard R. and Andrea Larson. "An Overview of the Historical Context for Sustainable Business in the United States, 1960-2000." Charlottesville, VA: University of Virginia Darden School Foundation, 1999.

Blog Response, due at noon on 8/28:
- Please provide your feedback on today's set of readings.

Required Exercise:
- Introductory Memo: Please draft a 1-page memo telling us
    - who you are (including year/major),
    - where you are from,
    - what your interests are,
    - why you are taking this class,
    - what sort of background you have with environmental activities (if any),
    - what is your favorite outdoor place/natural site,
    - and what you hope to get out of this class.

Please submit the memo via OWL-Space by the beginning of class. This is just for informational purposes, and will not be graded (although failure to submit an introduction will be noted as part of your class participation).

Thursday, August 30th: The Campus Sustainability Movement

Continuing the theme of the environmental movement, Prof. Johnson will discuss the rise of the modern campus environmental movement, including at Rice. In preparation for the topical research paper, Prof. Long will then outline techniques for interviewing environmental leaders and change agents on other university campuses.

Required reading:
- Johnson, Richard R. "Connecting Campus Sustainability with the Classroom." In *Greening of the Campus VII Conference Proceedings*, ed. Robert J. Koester, 251-255. Ball State University, 2007.
- Orr, David. "What is Education for?" *In Context* #27 (Winter 1991): 52-55. http://www.context.org/ICLIB/IC27/Orr.htm

Blog Response, due by noon on 8/30:
- What is your reaction to Dr. Orr's essay?

Required assignment:
- Go to www.aashe.org and using your Rice University email address, please create an account.
- Then, go to http://www.aashe.org/connect/enewsletters/bulletin and enter your email address in the box labeled "Subscribe to Bulletin." This will put you on the mailing list to receive the free weekly AASHE new bulletin, which reports highlights of campus sustainability projects all across the US.

Optional Resource:
- Consider "liking" the Sustainability at Rice University Facebook page.

Week 3 – Selecting Your Issue

Tuesday, September 4th: Discuss / brainstorm project ideas

We will bring the focus of the class specifically to Rice today and begin a process of brainstorming ideas for group projects.

Required reading:
- Review the Project Ideas document in the resources section of OWL-Space to jump-start the discussion about possible project topics.
- Go to the archives of the AASHE Bulletin and skim the four most recent editions. http://www.aashe.org/resources/aashe-bulletin-archives#bulletin

Blog Response, due by noon on 9/4:
- Share your thoughts based on skimming the four most recent editions of the AASHE bulletin. Your comments can be wide-ranging or narrowly focused.

Required assignment:
- Think about project topics of interest to you (e.g. food, recycling), and browse the AASHE Bulletin archives to see what others are doing to improve their performance in that area.

Thursday, September 6th: Discuss and reduce project list, apply for project.

Whereas Tuesday was all about putting ideas on the board, today will be a day of focusing those ideas and eliminating some topics. By the end of class, we intend to have five general project ideas for class projects. We will then provide you with a voting sheet, which must be turned-in by Friday at noon so that we can assign you to a project team.

Week 4 – Launching Your Project, Learning about Rice

Tuesday, September 11th: Projects assigned, meet with groups.

Today you will receive your group project assignments and hold your first meeting with your team members. You will also receive your green campus research report topic. We will spend some time in class discussing this assignment, which will be due on Friday, October 19th.

Required reading:
- Weklar, Diane. "Becoming a Change Agent." 2004. Last accessed June 16, 2011. http://www.dfw-asee.org/archive/0409meet.ppt
- Anderson, Carol E. and D. Min. "Practices of Effective Teams." Unpublished. Developed for and shared by Mike Shriberg, University of Michigan.

Thursday, September 13th: Green Cleaning—Eusebio Franco, Facilities Engineering and Planning

Today's class will feature a guest lecture from Eusebio Franco, Director of Custodial and Grounds, and several members of his team. Mr. Franco oversees campus grounds-keeping, the cleaning in all academic and administrative buildings, and the handling of solid waste and recycling. If you are working on a project that is connected to any of these topics, this is an excellent opportunity to interact with a key stakeholder.

Required reading:
- Ashkin, Stephen and David Holly. "Why is Green Cleaning Important?" In *Green Cleaning for Dummies: ISSA Special Edition*, 21-30. Hoboken, NJ: Wiley Publishing, 2007.

- Miller, G. Tyler, Jr. "Solid and Hazardous Waste." In *Living in the Environment*, 519-545. 15th ed. Canada: Thomson, 2007.

Blog Response, due at noon on 9/13:
- Please provide your feedback on today's set of readings.

Week 5 – Launching Your Project, Learning about Rice, Part 2

Tuesday, September 18th: Greening the Residential Colleges—Mark Ditman, Housing and Dining

Today's class will feature a guest lecture from Mark Ditman, Associate Vice President for Housing and Dining. Mr. Ditman oversees the residential colleges and serveries, as well as food service in the RMC. If you are working on a project that is connected with the colleges, this is an excellent opportunity to interact with a key stakeholder.

Required assignment:
- Complete the self-guided campus sustainability walking tour.

Thursday, September 20th: Group Consultations

We will meet directly with each project team for about 15 minutes. For the remainder of that time, you should work with your team. If you need to leave class as a group to meet with someone related to your project, you may do so with prior approval.

Week 6 – Contextualizing Your Project, Part 1

Tuesday, September 25th: Student-led discussion / group work session

How does your project fit within the broader environmental context? What global, national, or regional environmental issues will your project at Rice help to address? Today we will begin a series of student-led discussions with readings selected by each project team. Following the discussion you will work with your project team, and with prior approval you may leave class as a group to meet with someone related to your project. We encourage you to use this time to work on your Project Plan, which is due on 9/28.

Required reading:
- Group 1 selection

Blog Response, due at noon on 9/25:
- Please provide your feedback on today's reading to help Group 1 prepare for their discussion.

Thursday, September 27th: Student-led discussion / group work session

Today we will continue with student-led discussions. Then we will provide additional class time for teams to work on their Project Plan.

Required reading:
- Group 2 selection

Blog Response, due at noon on 9/27:

- Please provide your feedback on today's reading to help Group 2 prepare for their discussion.

Assignment due:
- Project Plan due by 5PM on Friday, September 28th – submit via OWL-Space

Week 7 – Contextualizing Your Project, Part 2

Tuesday, October 2nd: Student-led discussions

We will devote the entire class today to student-led discussions of assigned readings that contextualize the projects.

Required reading:
- Group 3 selection
- Group 4 selection
- Group 5 selection

Blog Response, due at noon on 10/2:
- Please provide your feedback on today's readings to help Groups 3-5 prepare for their discussions.

Thursday, October 4th: Group Consultations

We will meet directly with each project team for about 15 minutes to return and discuss the Project Plan. For the remainder of the time, you should work with your team. If you need to leave class as a group to meet with someone related to your project, you may do so with prior approval.

Week 8 – Presenting Lessons from Other Universities, Part 1

Tuesday, October 9th: Green Campus Presentations

An important part of implementing change is examining what others have done and learning from their successes and failures. The green campus research presentations will help us to understand how other universities are tackling the issues that you are addressing with your project. The order of the presentations will be determined in part to provide a thematic flow. Presentation guidelines are posted on OWL-Space. Please stay within your time limit.

Thursday, October 11th: Centennial Celebration Days (No Scheduled Classes)

Heads-up! You have a lot of reading due later this month, including over 200 pages from *The Omnivore's Dilemma.* Plan your time wisely, and consider getting a head-start.

Week 9 – Presenting Lessons from Other Universities, Part 2

Tuesday, October 16th: Group Consultations

We will meet directly with each project team for about 15 minutes. For the remainder of the time, you should work with your team. If you need to leave class as a group to meet with someone related to your project, you may do so with prior approval. Professor Johnson will not be in attendance for today's class.

Thursday, October 18th: Green Campus Presentations

Today is the last day of the green campus presentations. By the end of class, we should have a composite view of how universities are working to improve their environmental performance in our five project areas. Broader themes and lessons are likely to emerge that cut across the five areas.

Friday, October 19th: Green Campus Research Papers Due by 5PM

Week 10 – Focus on the Campus Landscape

Tuesday, October 23rd: The Ecology of Place

This week we focus on the campus landscape and explore the sense of connection that humans feel for nature and how this shapes our sense of place. Today's class will feature an in-class viewing of the documentary "The Nature of Cities" featuring Prof. Timothy Beatley of the University of Virginia.

Required reading:
- Gullone, Eleonora. "The Biophilia Hypothesis and Life in the 21st Century: Increasing Mental Health or Increasing Pathology?" Journal of Happiness Studies 1.3 (2000): 293-322.
- Leopold, Aldo. "The Land Ethic." From *A Sand County Almanac*. New York: Oxford University Press, 1948.
- Wilson, E.O. Interviewed by Peter Tyson. "A Conversation with E. O. Wilson." April 1, 2008. http://www.pbs.org/wgbh/nova/nature/conversation-eo-wilson. html

Required viewing:
- Go to http://fon-gis.rice.edu/ricetrees/ and explore the campus tree map. Use the map to identify trees that are of interest to you.
- Richard Louv, "Videos about *Last Child in the Woods*," http://richardlouv.com/ books/last-child/videos/

Blog Response, due at noon on 10/23:
- Please provide your feedback on today's set of readings.

Required Assignment:
- Prior to class, take a self-guided walking tour of highlights of the Lynn R. Lowery Arboretum, which encompasses the entire Rice campus. Tour maps will be provided in advance.
- Come to class prepared to talk about your ideal place of peace, tranquility, creativity, comfort, security, etc. during your childhood and here at Rice.

Optional Resource:
- Consider "liking" the Lynn R. Lowery Arboretum at Rice University Facebook page.

Thursday, October 25th: The Flora and Fauna of Rice University

Today Dr. Scott Solomon of the Department of Ecology and Evolutionary Biology will lead the class in an exploration of the flora and fauna of the Rice University campus.

Required viewing:
- Go to YouTube and search for "Rice University is named a Tree Campus USA" and view the video uploaded on February 22, 2012. Following is the url: http://www.youtube.com/watch?v=2nLOs6Ql0U8&feature=plcp
- Go to YouTube and search for "Birding at Rice University" and view the video uploaded on December 1, 2011. Following is the url: http://www.youtube.com/watch?v=FaAw5r4BRCc&feature=plcp
- Go to YouTube and search for "Centennial Series: The man who left his green thumbprint on the Rice campus" and view the video uploaded on June 22, 2012. Following is the url: http://www.youtube.com/watch?v=FdKhFYFEOF8&feature=plcp

Required Assignments:
- Submit the mid-term self and team-member evaluation form via OWL-Space.

Week 11 – Focus on Food

Tuesday, October 30th: The Omnivore's Dilemma

We will use today's class to discuss our complicated relationship with food. Following class, we encourage you to visit the Rice University Farmers' Market, which operates in the South Stadium Lot on Tuesdays from 3:30 – 7:00 PM.

Required reading:
- Pollan, Michael. *The Omnivore's Dilemma: A Natural History of Four Meals*. New York: Penguin Press, 2006. Pages 1-119, 123-133, 185-273.

Required viewing:
- Food, Inc. http://www.youtube.com/watch?v=OEu27wZZtHI

Blog Response, due at noon on 10/30:
- Please provide your feedback on both *The Omnivore's Dilemma* and Food, Inc. Both are provocative and polarizing—let us know what you really think! Feel free to include personal experiences and observations if you'd like.

Thursday, November 1st: Food Panel

Today's class will feature a panel of four guests who participate in Rice's food system: Cathy Sullivan of Sullivan's Happy Heart Family Farm, Rice University Farmers' Market manager CJ Claverie, Chef Cari Clark of Baker College, and Rice University dining director David McDonald.

Required reading:
- Johnson, Richard R. "Lessons from Hosting a Farmers' Market at Rice University." In *Greening of the Campus VIII Conference Proceedings*, ed. Robert J. Koester. Ball State University, 2009.
- Visit http://farmersmarket.rice.edu/

Required viewing:
- Go to YouTube and search for "Rice University Farmers Market" and view the video uploaded on July 14, 2011. Following is the url: http://www.youtube.com/watch?v=qSfCnSl7djA&feature=player_embedded

Required Assignments:
- Come to class prepared to ask at least one question of our panelists.
- Prior to class, do one of the following:
  - Visit the Rice Coffeehouse and ask about the organic, fair-trade certified coffee that they serve.
  - Eat lunch or dinner at the Baker College Kitchen and ask for local or organic food options.
  - Visit Salento in the Brochstein Pavilion, order their peanut butter, jelly, and brie sandwich, and ask the cashier where they buy the jelly for their sandwich.
  - Go off-campus and have a meal at Ruggles Green at 2311 West Alabama, Local Foods at 2424 Dunstan in the Rice Village, or Haven: A Seasonal Kitchen (warning: a bit pricey!) at 2502 Algerian Way near the intersection of Kirby and US 59.

Blog Response, due at noon on 11/1:
- Briefly share your experiences from the required assignment.

Week 12—Focus on Your Projects

Tuesday, November 6th: Group Consultations

With deadlines rapidly approaching for the submittal of your first draft, we will use today's class to meet with each project team to get a status report and to answer questions. Come prepared to use this meeting time effectively. For the remainder of the time, you should work with your team. If you need to leave class as a group to meet with someone related to your project, you may do so with prior approval.

Thursday, November 8th: Project group status presentation to class

What have the other groups been up to? Today we will ask each group to informally spend 5-10 minutes updating the class on the scope and status of their project.

Week 13—Tying it all Together: The Campus, The Class, The Projects

Tuesday, November 13th: Project Team Work Session

With a deadline approaching to submit the first draft of your final report, we are giving you time in class to work with your team on your report. This is not a time for meetings outside of class, but rather to work specifically on the report. The first drafts are due in class on Thursday, November 15th.

Thursday, November 15th: Ideas for Rice, Ideas for the Course

As we approach the end of the semester, we ask for your input on how to make Rice a more sustainable campus, and how to improve the quality of the class.

Assignment due:
- The first draft of your team's final report is due in class. They will be returned with comments on Tuesday. We will meet with each team on Tuesday to discuss the comments.

Week 14 – Preparing Your Final Report

Tuesday, November 20th: Group Consultations

Today we will meet at a pre-scheduled time with each group. We will return the first draft of your final report with comments.

Thursday, November 22nd: Thanksgiving—NO CLASS

Week 15 – Presenting Your Work

Tuesday, November 27th: Final Presentations

Today is the first day of final presentations of group projects. Guidelines for final presentations are posted in the resources section of OWL-Space. The day and order of final presentations will be announced prior to Thanksgiving.

Thursday, November 29th: Final Presentations
Today is the last day of final presentations, and the last day of class. Guidelines for final presentations are posted in the resources section of OWL-Space. Following the last presentation, we will discuss your responsibilities regarding self- and team-member evaluations, and also devote a few minutes for final comments regarding the class. Your final project papers are due at the close of business tomorrow.

Friday, November 30th: End of semester—Final Reports Due by 5PM
Wednesday, December 12th: End of finals—Self and Team Member Evaluations Due by NOON

Appendix C

Professor Wendy Petersen

HIST 315 - Western Civilization and Sustainability: Beginnings to 1600
Spring 2013

"Higher education has tended to fashion itself into an industry beholden to other industries . . . and is thereby complicit in larger societal and global problems. In Thomas Berry's words, we have fostered 'a mode of consciousness that has established a radical discontinuity between the human and nonhuman.' . . . and we take pride in equipping our students to do well-paying work in an unsustainable economy – the rough equivalent of preparing them for duty on the *Titanic*." -- David Orr, "Can Educational Institutions Learn?" *Sustainability on Campus: Stories and Strategies for Change*

"Human beings, it appears, do indeed belong to the universe and share its unstable, evolving character. . . [W]hat happens among human beings and what happens among the stars looks to be part of a grand, evolving story featuring spontaneous emergence of complexity that generates new sorts of behavior at every level of organization from the minutest quarks and leptons to the galaxies, from long carbon chains to living organisms and the biosphere, and from the biosphere to the symbolic universe of meaning within which human beings live and labor, singly and in concert, trying always to get more of what we want and need from the world around us." –William McNeill, "History and the Scientific Worldview"

"'Who am I? 'Where do I belong? 'What is the totality of which I am a part?' . . . Knowledge systems, like maps, are a complex blend of realism, flexibility, usefulness, and inspiration. They must offer a description of reality that conforms in some degree to commonsense experience. But that description must also be useful. It must help solve the problems that need to be solved by each community, whether these be spiritual, psychological, political, or mechanical . . . .In their day, creation myths offered workable maps of reality, and that is why they were believed. They made sense of what people knew." – David Christian, *Maps of Time, An Introduction to Big History*

"Have you ever wondered how we will be remembered a thousand years from now, when we are as remote as Charlemagne?" E.O. Wilson, *The Future of Life*

How did our civilization get to be so unsustainable? What can we learn from our past? What would it mean to possess historical consciousness in an age of climate change? What would a historical narrative framed by the desire for sustainability look like? This course is designed to begin to ask, and answer, these questions. Although many indicators point to the last 200 years as most significant, in fact the trends that mark our current crises have deep roots in the pre-modern past. In addition, our understanding of the problems and formulations of solutions today often suffer from historical amnesia, overlook past insights, and ignore our rich cultural heritage. A critical examination of the history of pre-modern period offers the opportunity for a unique understanding, observations, perspective, and wisdom regarding the issues of sustainability.

Course description: This course is an upper division course cross listed in the History and Earth and Environmental Science Departments designed to explore the interactions between humans and the natural world in the European West prior to 1600 and to examine the historical roots of sustainability. The course begins with a critical assessment of the term "sustainability" and then focuses on a series of key moments in the history of the West prior to 1600: the transition to agriculture; the thought and practices of classical Athens; the spread of Christianity and the development of science and technology in the Middle Ages; and the era of contact between European and other civilizations in the age of global commerce and colonization in the fifteenth century. For each of these periods we will read environmental, eco- and traditional histories and analyze primary texts that speak to the human-nature relationship. Along the way we will attend to the 'big' questions of historical analysis: Where do historical narratives begin and end, and why? What are the assumptions about the nature of what it means to be human, or what "nature" is? How *ought* the history of the West be told? Is it ultimately a narrative of decline, progress, or devastation -- or something else altogether? The goals of the course are to develop a more complex understanding of sustainability, to understand how our current context has deep roots in the past, to engage pre-modern ideas on what it means to be human, and to analyze how values shape the structure and content of historical narratives.

Learning Outcomes

Thinking Historically: This course is part of Willamette's General Education Program designed to meet the requirement for the "Thinking Historically" Mode of Inquiry. What does that mean? It means you will learn to think with more depth, complexity, and specificity about the past, how we make meaning from it, and why it matters today. It means that after taking this course you should have significantly developed your understanding of how human consciousness, action and agency are historically embedded, how continuity and change are related in human experience, and how study of the past helps to make sense of the present and anticipate the future. Specifically, this course will develop your ability to:
1. Identify significant historical questions, and articulate them with sophistication.
2. Appreciate that a variety of historical interpretations of the same event are possible and become familiar with a wider range of theoretical or interpretative frameworks for working with historical material.
3. Demonstrate a strong grasp of primary and secondary literature on the subject you are studying.
4. Understand how to read and use a variety of sources from the past.

This course is also designed as part of Willamette's sustainability education program, and as such it should contribute significantly to your understanding of the complex set of issues implied by this term. Specifically, this course will develop your ability to:
1. Synthesize multiple approaches to sustainability challenges informed by a historical perspective.
2. Understand the relationship between ecological and social systems, including the role of feedbacks, systemic limits, and interdependence.
2. Gain a historical perspective on how human systems can and do threaten ecological systems, and how natural systems shape human civilization.
3. Evaluate and synthesize competing definitions of sustainability and create critically reflective responses to proposals for sustainable futures.
4. Think with more complexity about human culture and values with respect to issues of sustainability.

Requirements
Class attendance, careful preparation of the assigned readings, class participation: 40%
Writing – see assignments below: 60%

Required Texts:

Author	Title	ISBN	Ed.	Publisher
Plato	Plato: Symposium and Phaedrus	0486277984		Dover Thrift Edition
Thucydides, trans. Woodruff	On Justice, Power, and Human Nature	0872201686		Hackett
Ponting, Clive	A New Green History of the World	014303892	Rev. Ed	Penguin
Williams, Michael	Deforesting the Earth	0226899470	abridged	U of Chicago
More, Thomas	Utopia	0140449108		Penguin Paperback
Bonaveture	Soul's Journey Into Good	0872202003		Hackett

Schedule
Unit I: Interrogating "Sustainability"
1/15 (T) Course Introduction
> "Running the Numbers: An American Self-Portrait," artist Chris Jordan, Seattle http://www.chrisjordan.com
> "The World Without Us," http://www.worldwithoutus.com
> Jared Diamond, "What's Your Consumption Factor?" Op Ed, *NY Times*, Jan. 2, 2008
> Mark Lynas, "Humanity's All-Time Greatest Challenge," *Adbusters*

1/17 (TH) Looking over the abyss
> Lester Brown, Preface and Chapter 1 (to pg. 17 only), "On the Edge," *World On the Edge*
> James Gustav Speth, Introduction (including graphs, to p. 13 only), *The Bridge at the End of the World: Capitalism, the Environment, and Crossing from Crisis to Sustainability*
> For reflection: Joanna Macy, "The Greatest Danger: *Apatheia*, the deadening of mind and heart," *Coming Back to Life*

Reading synthesis assignment - Bring to class a 1-2 pp., single-spaced synthesis of the readings in which you: 1) synthesize the facts or ideas you found the most significant, compelling, or troubling, and 2) articulate where you stand personally in relationship to the ideas and information in today's reading.

1/22 (T) Derek Jensen, "Upping the Stakes," *Orion*, Nov/Dec 2012
> Bill McKibbon, "Small Change," *Orion*, Nov/Dec 2012
> Trebbe Johnson, "Gaze Even Here," *Orion*, Nov/Dec 2012
> David James Duncan, "Being Cool in the Face of Global Warming," *Moral Ground*, 434-439.

Reading response assignment - bring to class: 1-2 pp. single-spaced personal reflection on the readings. It should be clear from your reflection that you have read and engaged all the material for today, although you may focus the bulk of your response on 1-2 readings.

1/24 (TH) Sustainability - Interrogating the Term

        J.R. McNeill, "Prologue: Peculiarities of a Prodigal Century," *Something New Under the Sun: An Environmental History of the Twentieth Century World*

        Carl Mitcham, "The Concept of Sustainable Development: Its Origins and Ambivalence" *Technology in Society*

1/29 (T) Sustainability– Interrogating the Term, II

        Costanza, Prugh, Daly, "Preface" and Chapter 1, "Introduction," T*he Local Politics of Global Sustainability*

        David Orr, "The Four Challenges of Sustainability" *Conservation Biology*

        Sheila Watt-Cloutier, "The Inuit Right to Culture Based on Ice and Snow," *Moral Ground*, 25-29

        Daniel Quinn, "The Danger of Human Exceptionalism," *Moral Ground*, 9-14

1/31 (TH) <u>**Seminar Paper #1**</u> - 2-3 pp. single-spaced. As richly, fully, and succinctly as you can, and drawing on our readings thus far in the course, write your own definition of what we ought to mean by "sustainability." What are the central ideas, questions, critiques, and history you want to have in mind when you use the term? What shouldn't we sustain? What is worth sustaining?

Unit 2: In the Beginning

2/5 (T) Where to begin the story? Three options – what would you choose?

        1. Standard Western Civilization textbook: *The West: Encounters and Transformations*, Levack, Muir, Veldman, and Maas, "The Birth of Civilization," pp. 11-18

        2. Eco-history: Clive Ponting, *A Green History of the World*. Skim through chapter 1, "The Lessons of Easter Island," and chapter 2, "The Foundations of History." Read carefully chapter 3, "Ninety-nine percent of Human History"

        3. Brian Swimme and Thomas Berry, Prologue, *The Universe Story*

2/7 (TH) Transition to Agriculture

        E.O. Wilson, "The Fate of Creation is the Fate of Humanity," *Moral Ground*, 21-24

        Jack Harlan, "Views on Agricultural Origins," *Crops and Man*, 2nd edition, 31-48.

        Diamond, *Guns, Germs, and Steel*, chapter 6, "To Farm or Not to Farm"

2/12 (T) Transition to Agriculture, cont.

        Michael Williams, *Deforesting the Earth*, preface, chapter 1 - 3

<u>Reading synthesis assignment</u> due in class: 1-2 pp. synthesis of the readings in this unit. How would you construct a narrative of the beginnings of human civilization up through the transition to agriculture, given what you now know about where we stand today? What about the transition to agriculture seems important for others to know given the issues of sustainability?

Unit 3: The Classical World

2/14 (TH) Michael Williams, *Deforesting the Earth*, chapter 4, "The Classical World" (73-100)

        Wendell Berry, "Faustian Economics: Hell Hath No Limits"

2/19 (T) Thucydides (460-395 BC), *On Justice, Power and Human Nature*, "Introduction" (pp. ix-xxiii - skim); Chapter 1, "Early History and Method" (pp. 11-13), and chapter 2, "Origins of the War" (pp. 15-37)

2/21 (TH) Thucydides, Chapter 3, "Pericles and the Plague," and "The Melian Dialogue," (pp. 102-109)

2/26 (T) Plato (428-348 BC), *Phaedrus*

2/28 (TH) *Phaedrus*, continued

3/5 (T) Plotinus, *The Enneads*, excerpts

3/7 (TH) Alan Weisman, "Obligation to Posterity?" *Moral Ground*, 32-37
        Derrick Jensen, "You Choose," *Moral Ground*, 60-64
        Terry Tempest Williams, "Climate Change: What is Required of Us?" *Moral Ground*, 429-433

<u>Seminar paper #2 due in class</u>: 3 pp. single-spaced. What from the history of the classical period and the primary texts we have read for this unit seems crucial to understanding our current crisis? What would you want others to know today about human nature and the roots of Western culture from the history and texts of this period?

Unit 4: The Medieval Period
3/12 (T) Michael Williams, *Deforesting the Earth*, chapter 5, "The Medieval World" (pp. 102-142) WISE
        Ponting, *Green History*, chapter 6, "The Long Struggle"

3/14 (TH) Lynn White, "The Historical Roots of Our Ecological Crisis"
        B. Minteer, R. Manning, "Appraisal of the Critique of Anthropocentrism and Three Lesser Known Themes in Lynn White's 'The Historical Roots of our Ecological Crisis'"

3/19 (T) Nikola Patzel, "European Religious Cultivation of the Soil," and "The Soil Scientist's Hidden Beloved" (WISE)

3/21 (TH) St. Francis (1181-1226), "Canticle of the Sun" (WISE)
        Thomas Celano, *First and Second Lives of St. Francis*, http://www.fordham.edu/halsall/source/stfran-lives.html
        Lisa J. Kiser, "The Garden of St. Francis: Plants, Landscape, and Economy in Thirteenth-Century Italy," from *Environmental History*

        - Spring Break -

4/2 (T) Bonaventure, *The Soul's Journey Into God*

4/4 (TH) Bonaventure, *The Soul's Journey Into God*, cont.

Unit 5: The Age of Discovery
4/9 (T) Michael Williams, *Deforesting the Earth*, chapter 6, "Driving Forces and Cultural Climates, 1500-1750" and chapter 7, "Clearing in Europe, 1500-1700"; chapter 8, "The

Wider World, 1500-1700": Team presentations.

4/11 (TH) John F. Richard, *The Unending Frontier: An Environmental History of the Early Modern Period*, 1-57, 309-333

4/16 (T) Thomas More (1478-1535), *Utopia*

4/18 (TH) More, *Utopia*, cont.

4/23 (T) More, *Utopia*, concluded.

4/23 or 4/24: **Evening film showing of Cloud Atlas**

4/25 (TH) Discussion of Cloud Atlas

4/30 (T) Final day of class
> Charles Mann, "State of the Species," *Orion*, Nov/Dec 2012
> Paul Hawken, "Commencement Address," University of Portland
> Dave Foreman, "Wild Things for Their Own Sake," *Moral Ground*, 100-102

Reading synthesis assignment due in class: 1-2 pp. What points would you make based on your work in this class if you were to have a conversation with Charles Mann and Dave Foreman?

Take home final due at the time of the final for this class: Tuesday, May 7, 11:00 a.m.

Take Home Final - HIST 315, Western Civilization and Sustainability: Beginnings to 1600
Professor Wendy Petersen Boring

Short Answer – 2 questions, 40 points total

I. Medieval Unit – choose 1 (20 points)
A. Thomas of Celano's *Lives of St. Francis*, Francis's "Canticle of the Creatures," and St. Bonaventure's *Journey of the Soul Into God* provide powerful critiques of the dominant trends in medieval society. What were they critiquing, and why? What alternative visions of a meaningful human life do they offer? What from these writings is worth appropriating into your own historical awareness?

B. In "The Roots of our Ecological Crisis," Lynn White argues that in order to understand why European society gravitated towards technology, conquest, and domination of nature in the early modern period, we must turn to the Middle Ages, in particular the influence of Christianity, the developments in technology, and the rise of western science. Assess White's article in light of the evidence we examined in the readings for the medieval period. Do you agree with White? What about the medieval period is significant for environmental history and sustainability?

II. Early Modern Unit – choose 1 (20 points)
A. Michael Williams and John Roberts describe trends that while present in earlier societies reach new levels of intensity and new forms of organization in the early modern period. They also describe "whole new worlds" of discovery, invention, and exploitation. What do you see as historically significant in the early modern period? How do Francis Bacon's *Novum Organum* and Thomas More's *Utopia* create a "new world" that simultaneously

serves as a critique of their own world -- and ours?

B. Write your own utopia (or dystopia) with the themes of this course and Thomas More's *Utopia* in mind. Is "sustainability" ultimately a utopian idea? What do you mean by utopia?

Comprehensive Essay – 2 questions, 60 points total (30 points each)
Choose two:

A. Paul Hawken began his commencement address at the University of Portland in 2009 by saying: "Class of 2009: you are going to have to figure out what it means to be a human being on Earth at a time when every living system is declining, and the rate of decline is accelerating. . . .Basically, civilization needs a new operating system, you are the programmers, and we need it within a few decades, ("The Most Amazing Challenge," *Moral Ground*, 464). What have you figured out about what it means to be a human being on this Earth at this time? Reflect on our texts for this class. Draw on your own experience, thoughts, intuition, and wonderings. Weave them together to write a mini-manifesto -- a personal ethic of sustainability.

B. Why study history in the face of climate change, resource scarcity, population growth, biodiversity loss, and global inequity? Why study history before 1800? What have you learned as a result of this class about the history of the pre-modern period that is significant for sustainability issues today?

C. Write an essay in response to Charles Mann's "State of the Species" (*Orion*, Nov/Dec 2012, WISE), Paul Kingsnorth's "Dark Ecology" (*Orion*, Jan/Feb 2013, WISE), Wendell Berry's "The Total Economy" (*What Matters*, WISE), or another text from our readings (which you clear in advance with me), in which you engage our readings for the course to articulate your own view on the themes the essay treats.

CPSIA information can be obtained
at www.ICGtesting.com
Printed in the USA
LVOW02s1329110516

487760LV00015B/230/P